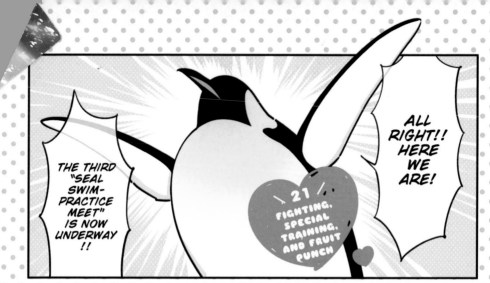

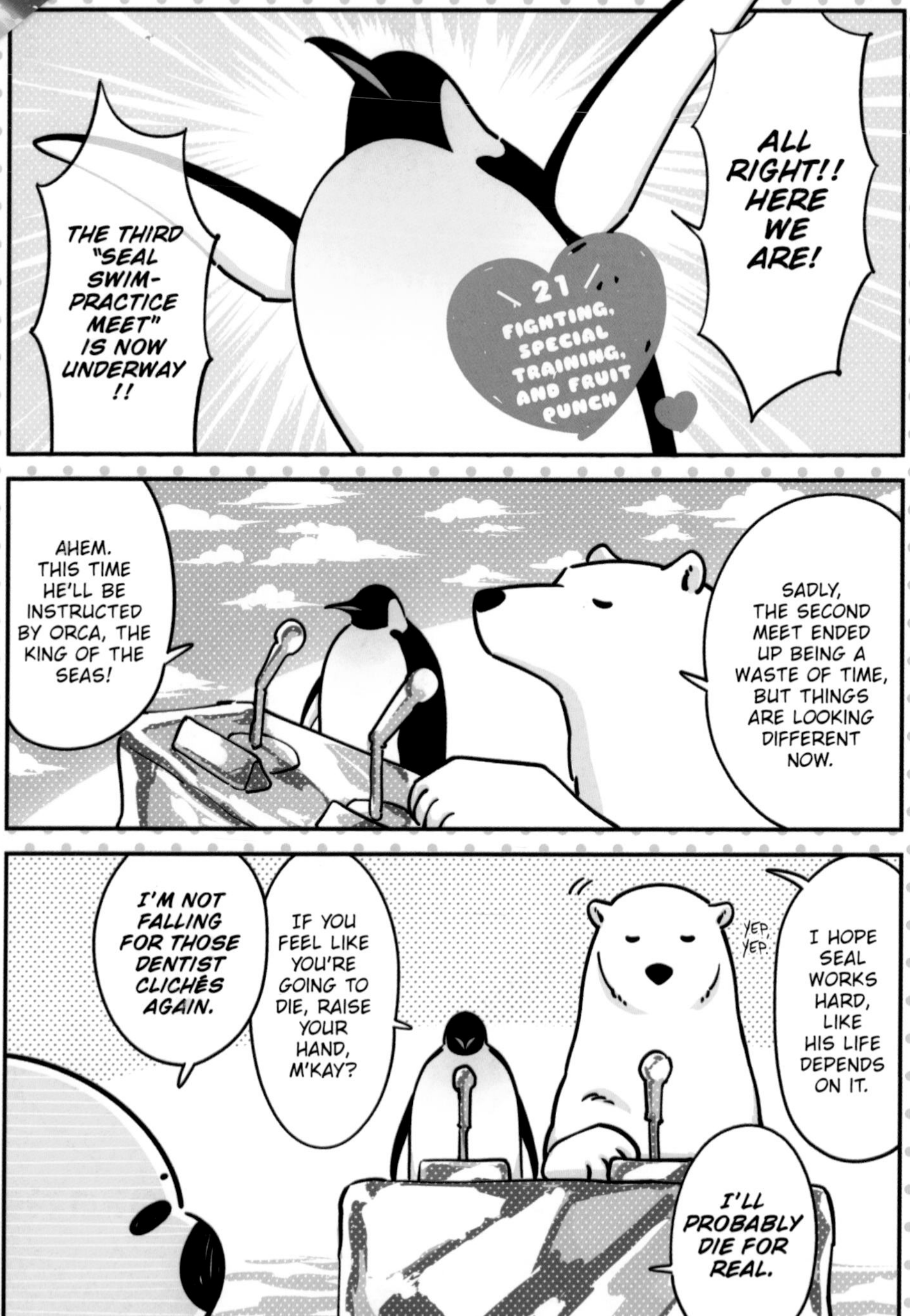
ALL RIGHT!! HERE WE ARE!
21
FIGHTING, SPECIAL TRAINING, AND FRUIT PUNCH
THE THIRD "SEAL SWIM-PRACTICE MEET" IS NOW UNDERWAY!!
SADLY, THE SECOND MEET ENDED UP BEING A WASTE OF TIME, BUT THINGS ARE LOOKING DIFFERENT NOW.
AHEM. THIS TIME HE'LL BE INSTRUCTED BY ORCA, THE KING OF THE SEAS!
I HOPE SEAL WORKS HARD, LIKE HIS LIFE DEPENDS ON IT.
YEP, YEP.
I'LL PROBABLY DIE FOR REAL.
IF YOU FEEL LIKE YOU'RE GOING TO DIE, RAISE YOUR HAND, M'KAY?
I'M NOT FALLING FOR THOSE DENTIST CLICHÉS AGAIN.

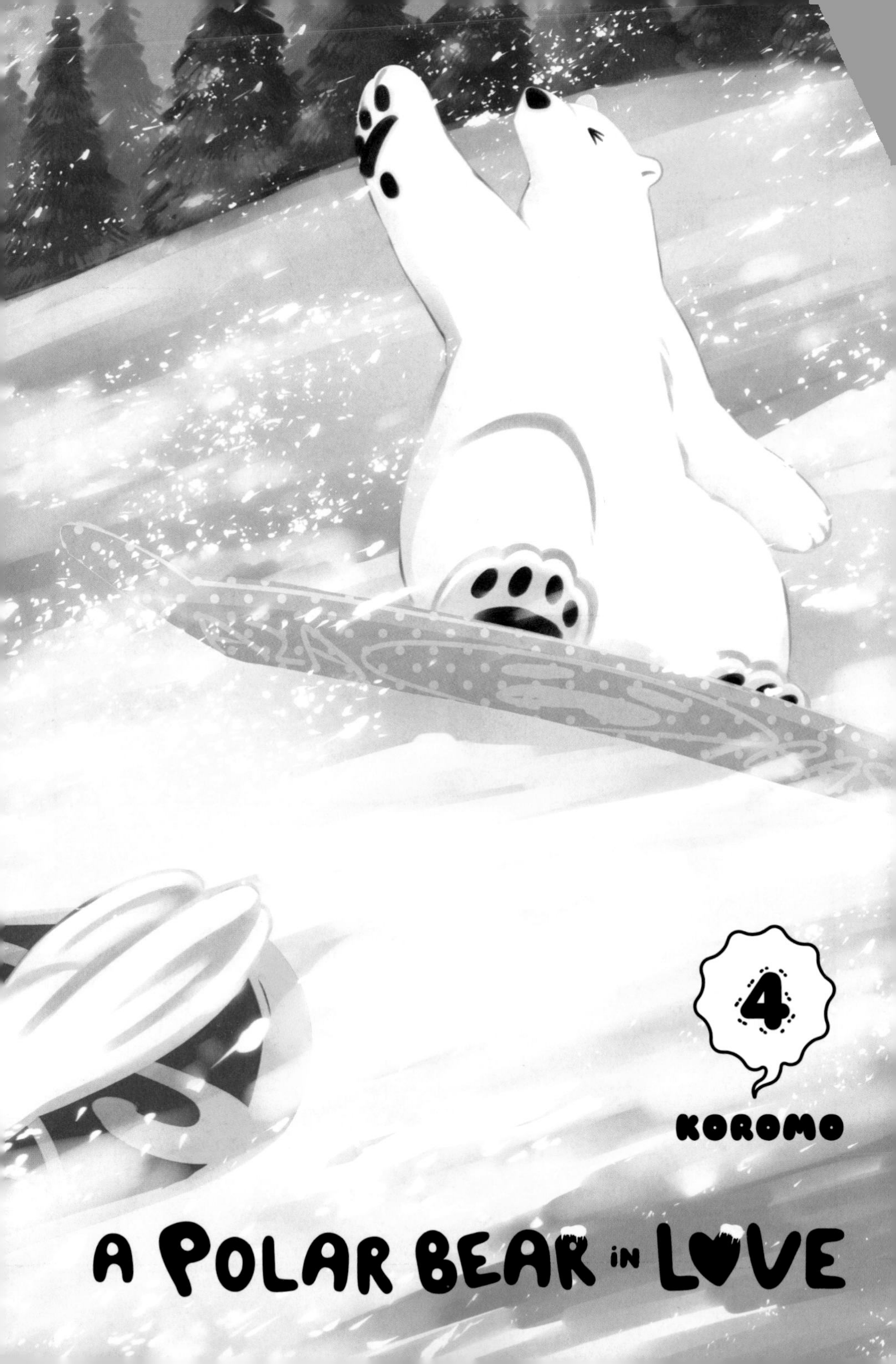
4
KOROMO
A POLAR BEAR in LOVE

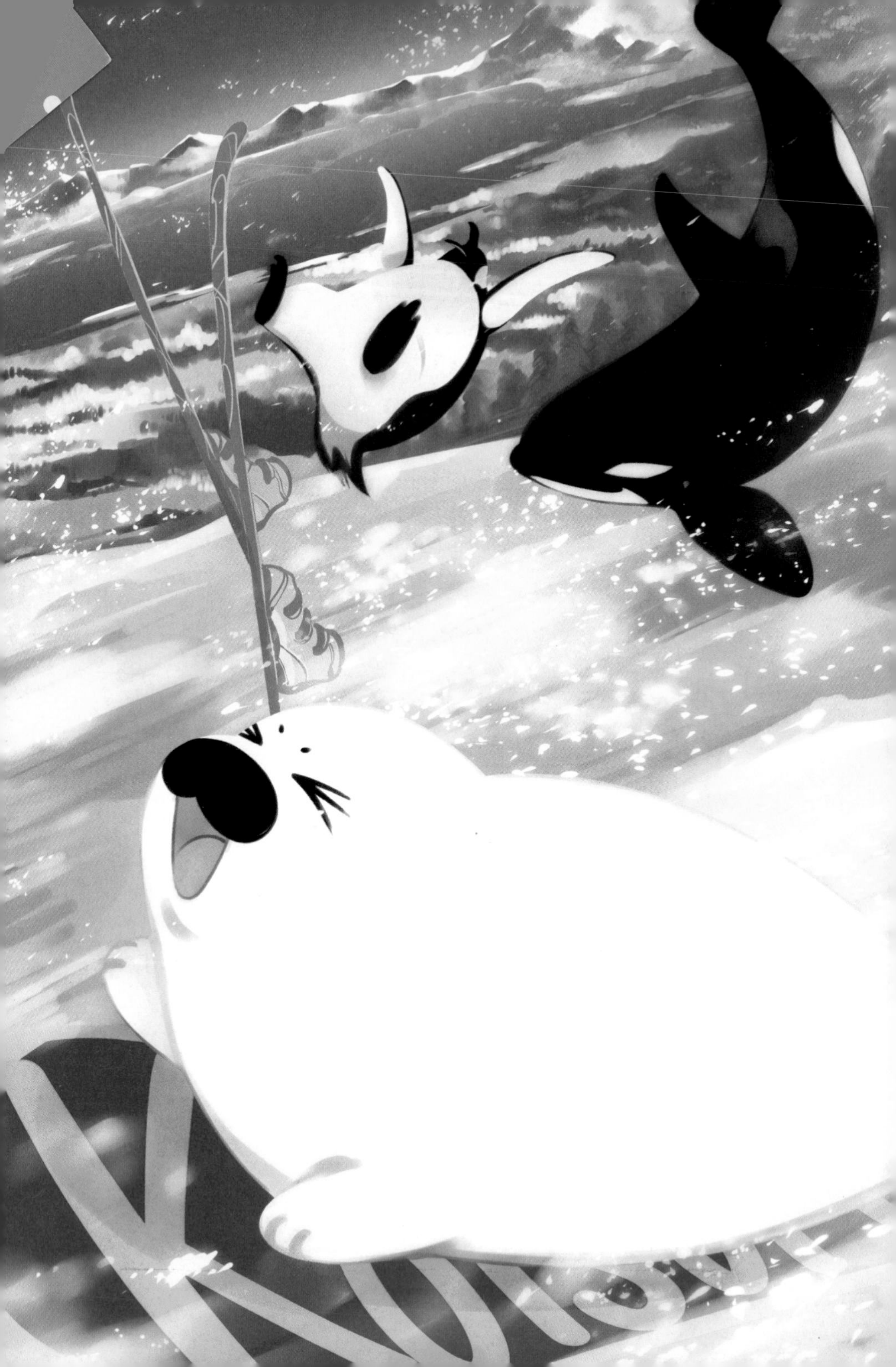

c o n t e n t s

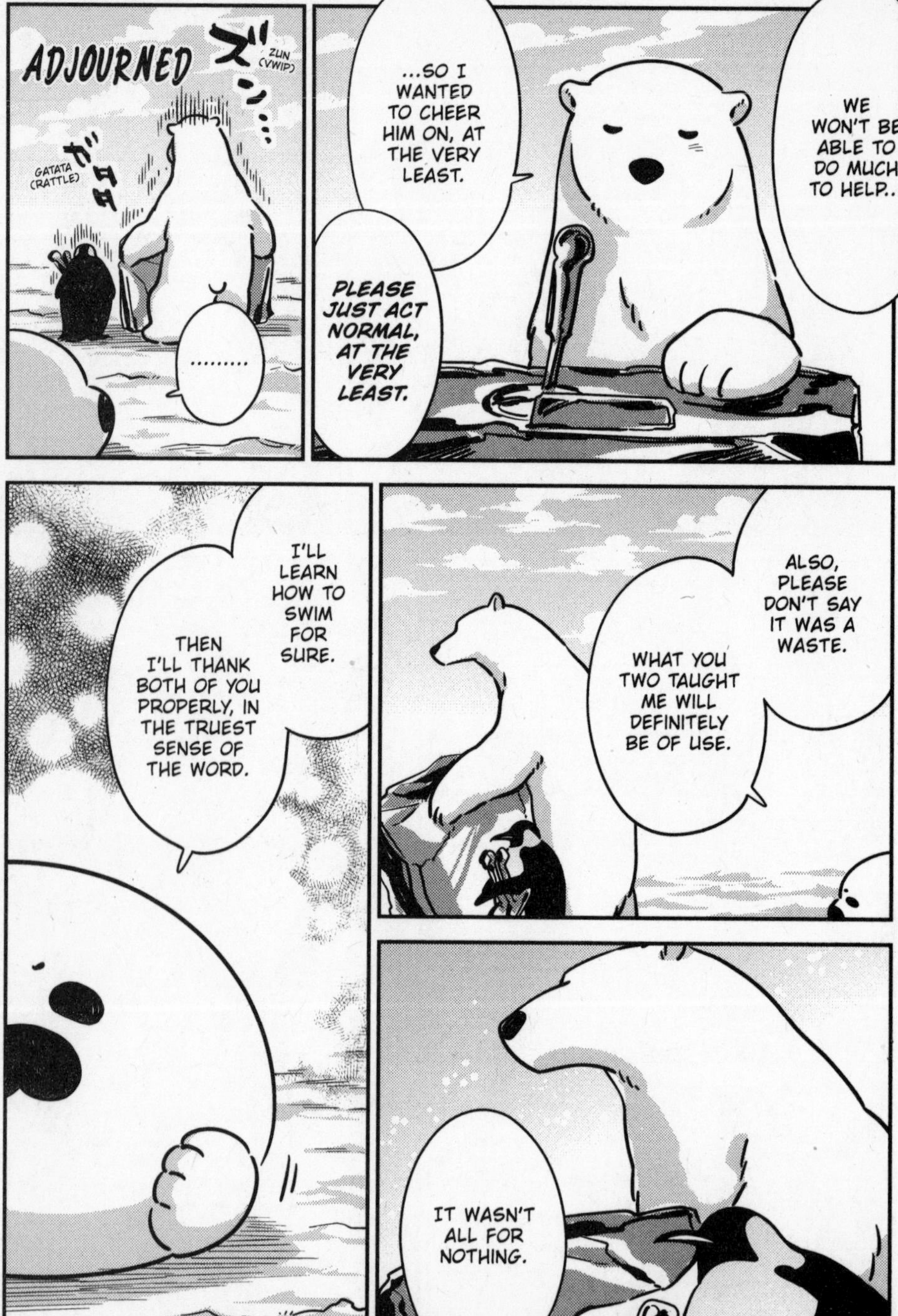
WE WON'T BE ABLE TO DO MUCH TO HELP...
...SO I WANTED TO CHEER HIM ON, AT THE VERY LEAST.
PLEASE JUST ACT NORMAL, AT THE VERY LEAST.
ZUN (VWIP)
ADJOURNED
GATATA (RATTLE)
....
ALSO, PLEASE DON'T SAY IT WAS A WASTE.
WHAT YOU TWO TAUGHT ME WILL DEFINITELY BE OF USE.
IT WASN'T ALL FOR NOTHING.
I'LL LEARN HOW TO SWIM FOR SURE.
THEN I'LL THANK BOTH OF YOU PROPERLY, IN THE TRUEST SENSE OF THE WORD.

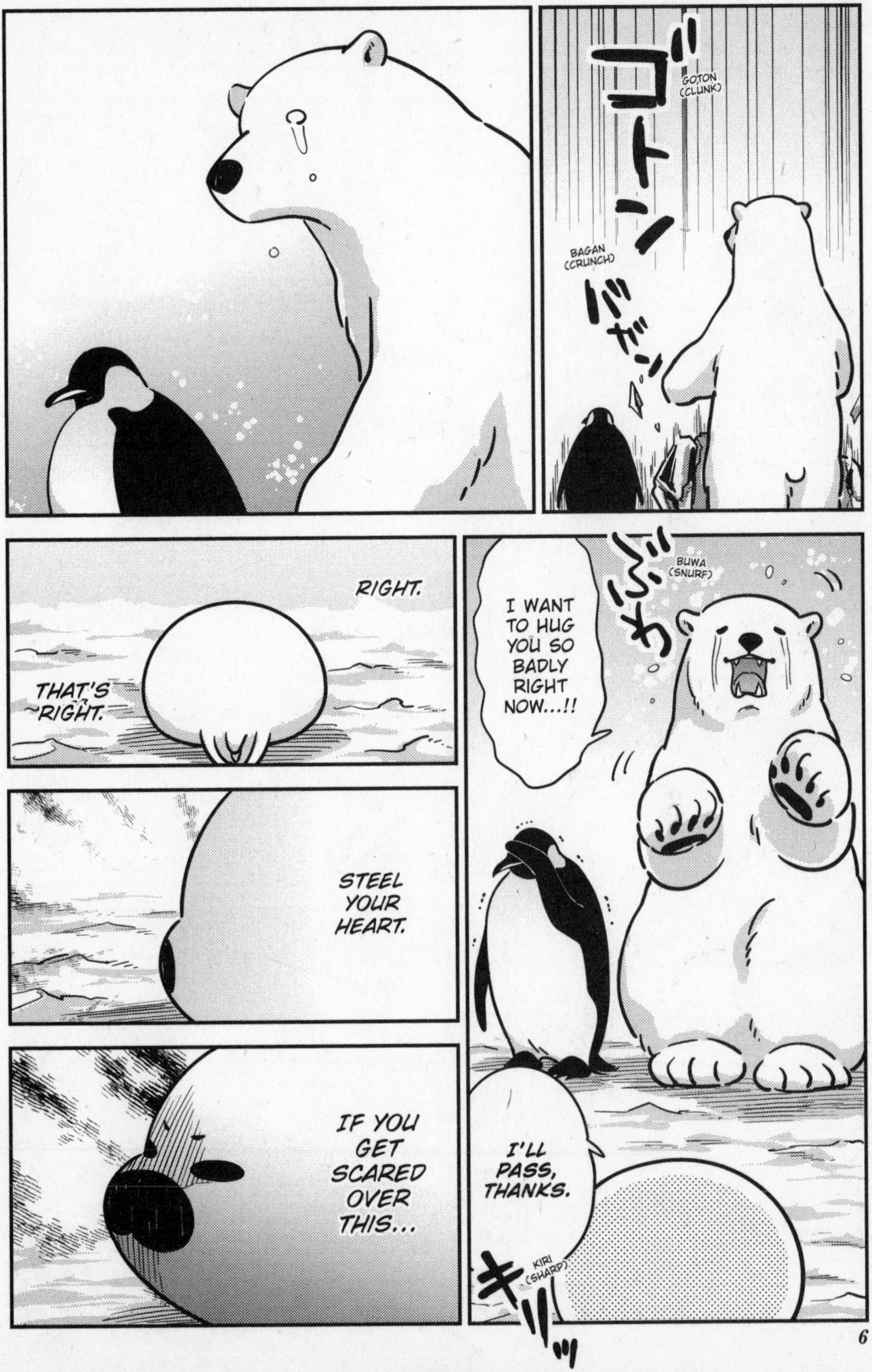
GOTON (CLUNK)
BAGAN (CRUNCH)
BUWA (SNURF)
I WANT TO HUG YOU SO BADLY RIGHT NOW...!!
I'LL PASS, THANKS.
KIRI (SHARP)
RIGHT.
THAT'S RIGHT.
STEEL YOUR HEART.
IF YOU GET SCARED OVER THIS...

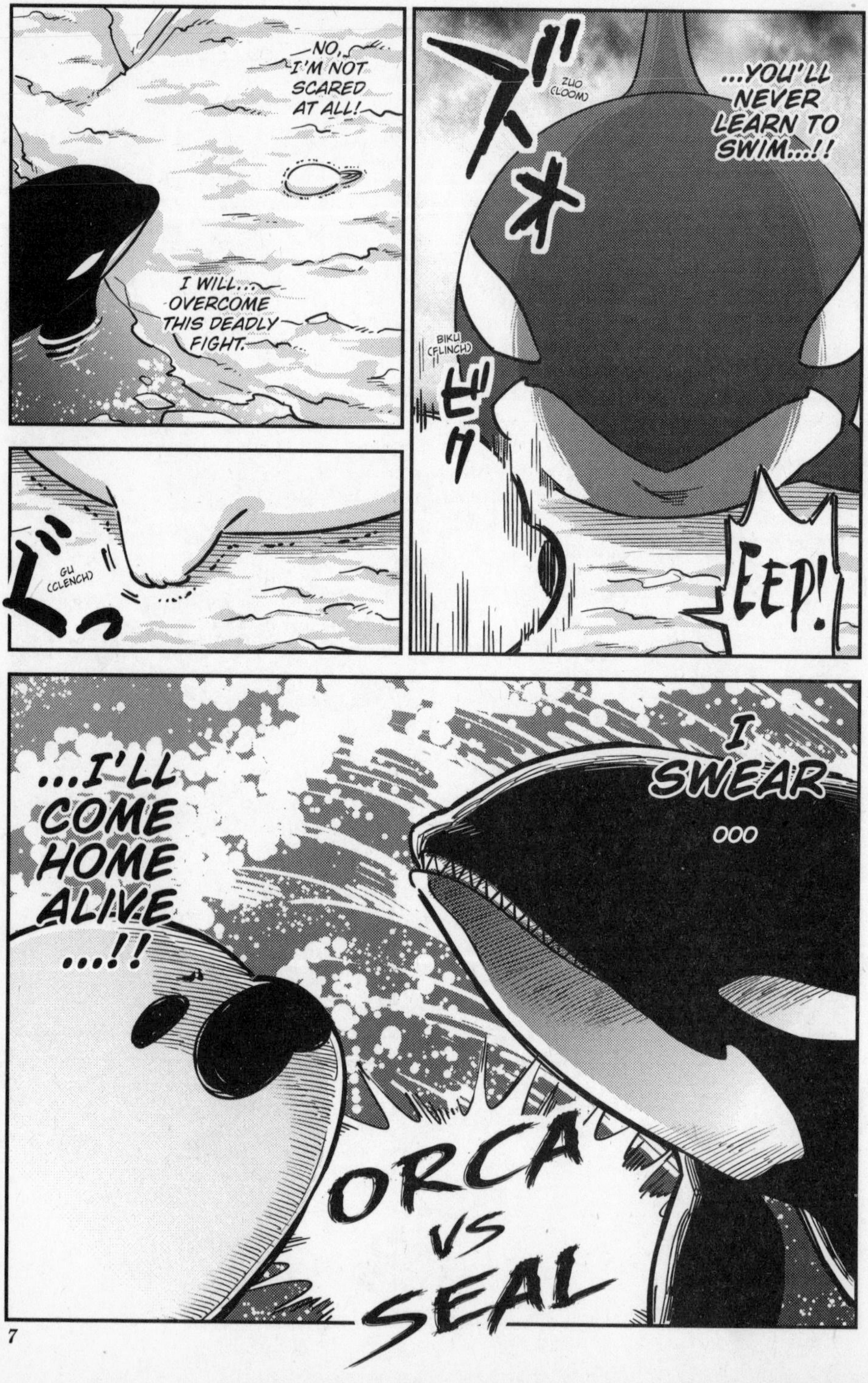
ZUO (LOOM)
...YOU'LL NEVER LEARN TO SWIM...!!
BIKU (FLINCH)
EEP!
—NO, I'M NOT SCARED AT ALL!
I WILL... OVERCOME THIS DEADLY FIGHT.
GU (CLENCH)
I SWEAR...
...I'LL COME HOME ALIVE...!!
ORCA VS SEAL

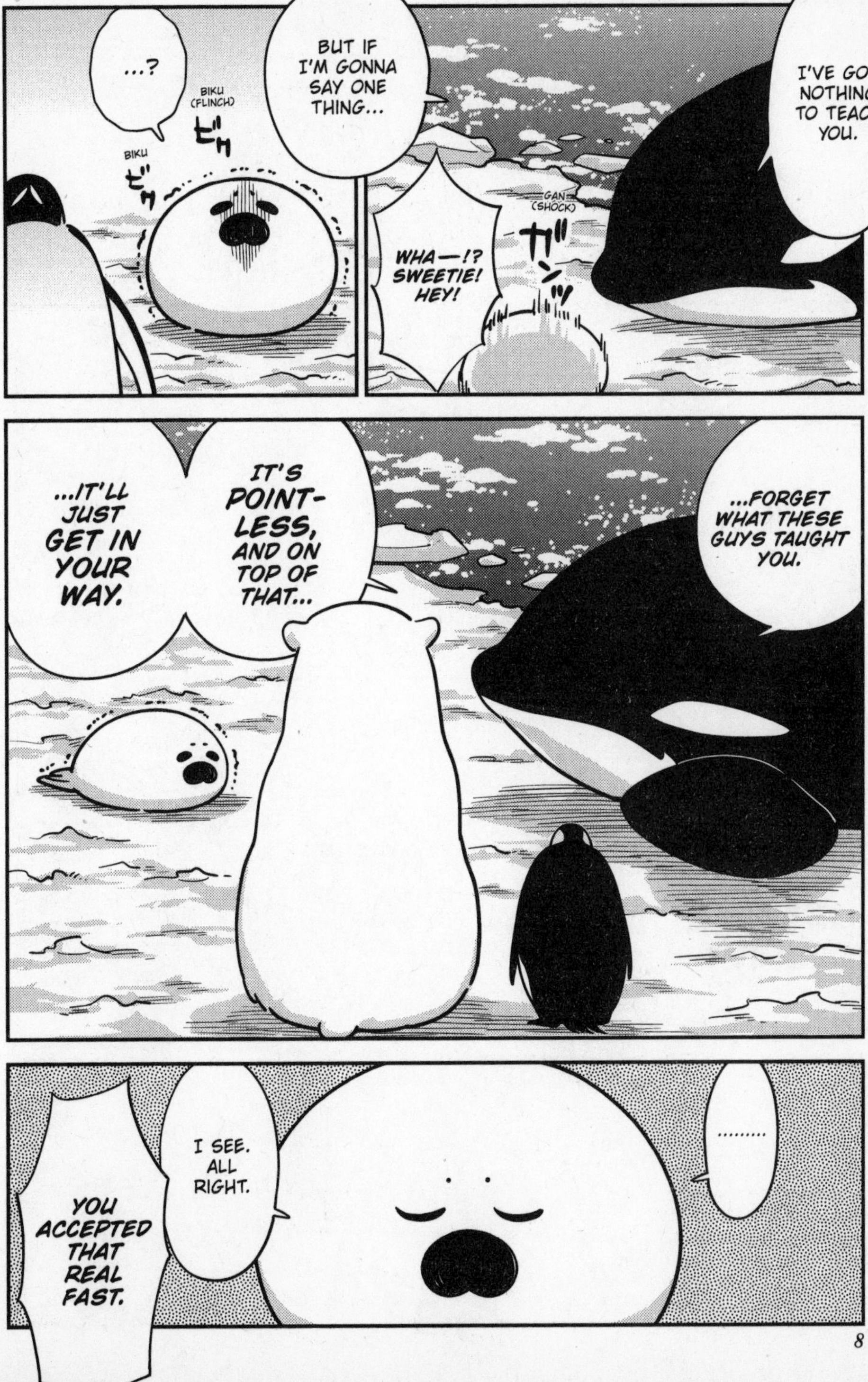
I'VE GOT NOTHING TO TEACH YOU.
GAN (SHOCK)
WHA—!? SWEETIE! HEY!
BUT IF I'M GONNA SAY ONE THING...
BIKU (FLINCH)
BIKU
...?
...FORGET WHAT THESE GUYS TAUGHT YOU.
IT'S POINT-LESS, AND ON TOP OF THAT...
...IT'LL JUST GET IN YOUR WAY.
....
I SEE. ALL RIGHT.
YOU ACCEPTED THAT REAL FAST.

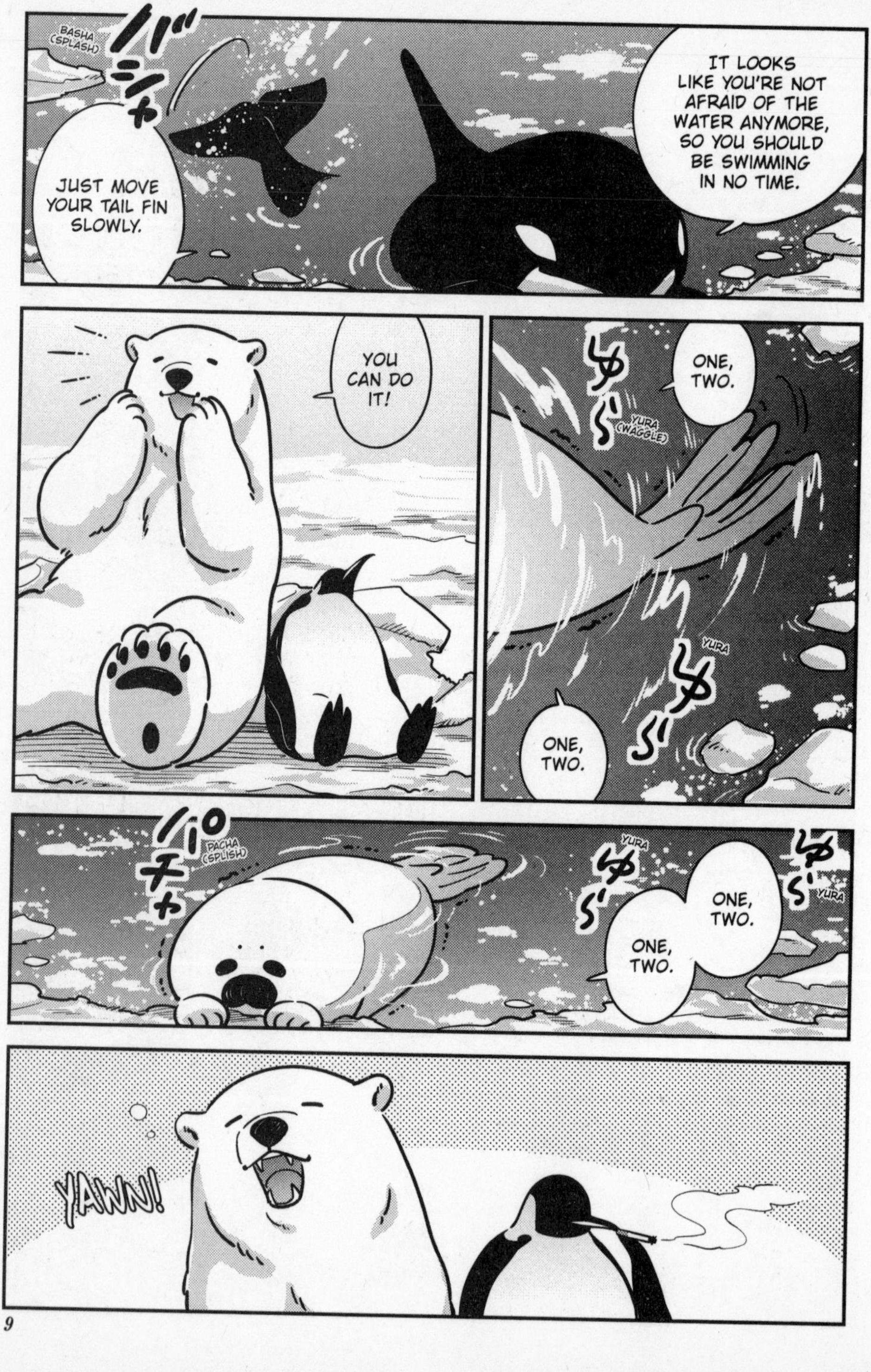
IT LOOKS LIKE YOU'RE NOT AFRAID OF THE WATER ANYMORE, SO YOU SHOULD BE SWIMMING IN NO TIME.
BASHA (SPLASH)
JUST MOVE YOUR TAIL FIN SLOWLY.
ONE, TWO.
YURA (WAGGLE)
YURA
ONE, TWO.
YOU CAN DO IT!
YURA
ONE, TWO.
YURA
ONE, TWO.
PACHA (SPLISH)
YAWN!

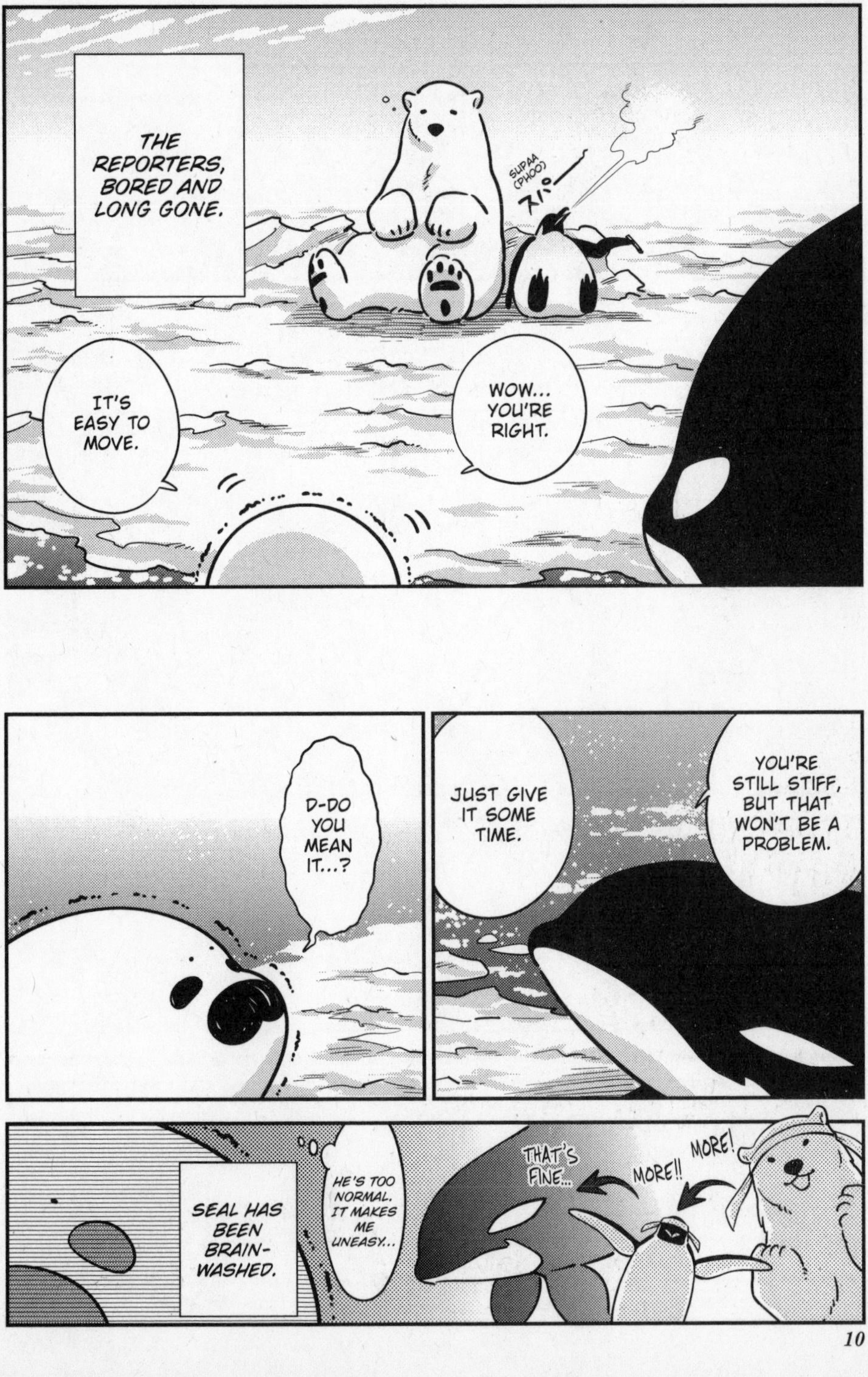
THE REPORTERS, BORED AND LONG GONE.
SUPAA (PHOO)
スパー
WOW... YOU'RE RIGHT.
IT'S EASY TO MOVE.
YOU'RE STILL STIFF, BUT THAT WON'T BE A PROBLEM.
JUST GIVE IT SOME TIME.
D-DO YOU MEAN IT...?
MORE!
MORE!!
THAT'S FINE...
HE'S TOO NORMAL. IT MAKES ME UNEASY...
SEAL HAS BEEN BRAIN-WASHED.

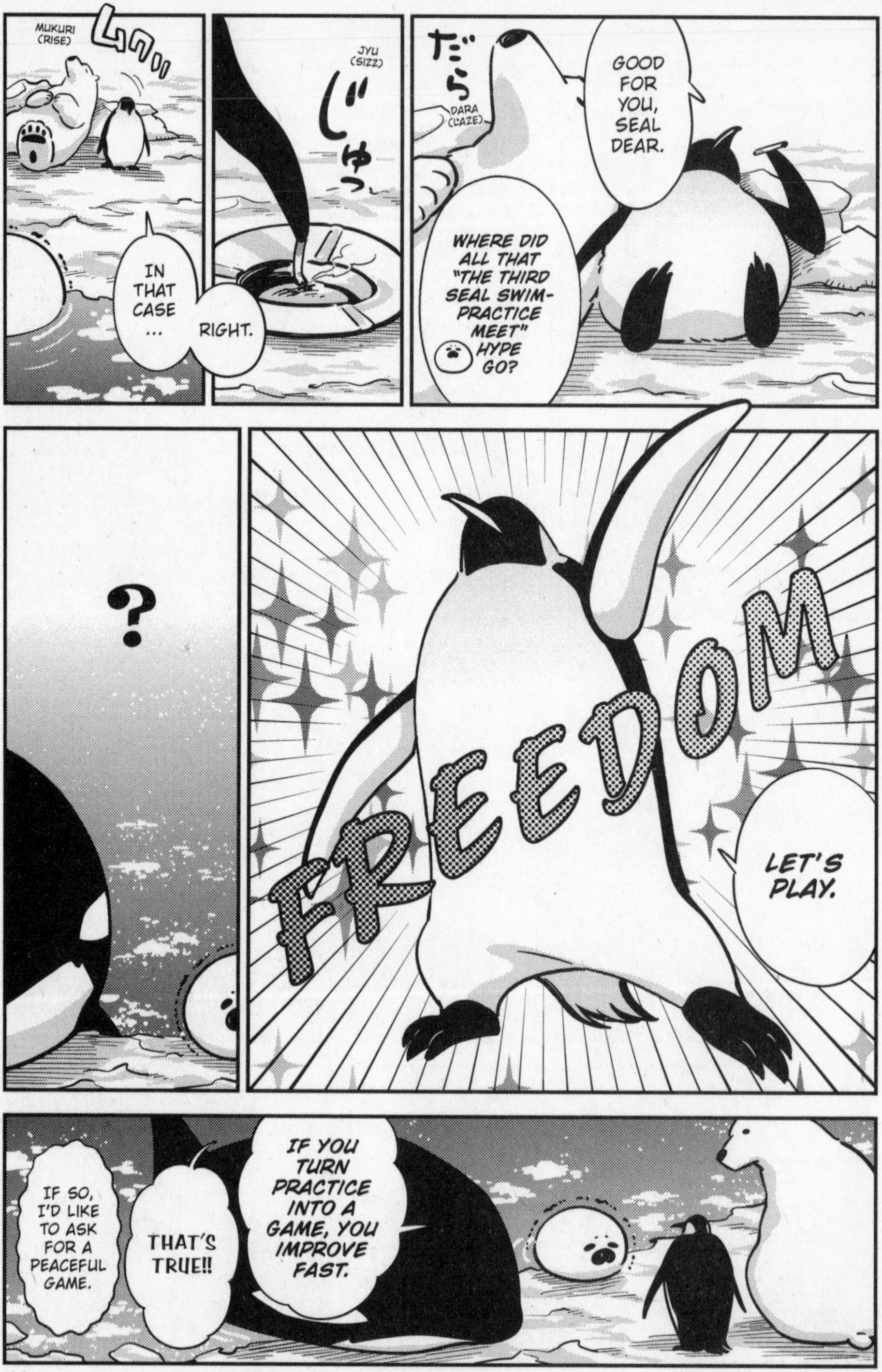
だら
DARA (LAZE)
GOOD FOR YOU, SEAL DEAR.
WHERE DID ALL THAT "THE THIRD SEAL SWIM-PRACTICE MEET" HYPE GO?
JYU (SIZZ)
じゅっ
RIGHT.
MUKURI (RISE)
ムクッ
IN THAT CASE ...
FREEDOM
LET'S PLAY.
?
IF YOU TURN PRACTICE INTO A GAME, YOU IMPROVE FAST.
THAT'S TRUE!!
IF SO, I'D LIKE TO ASK FOR A PEACEFUL GAME.

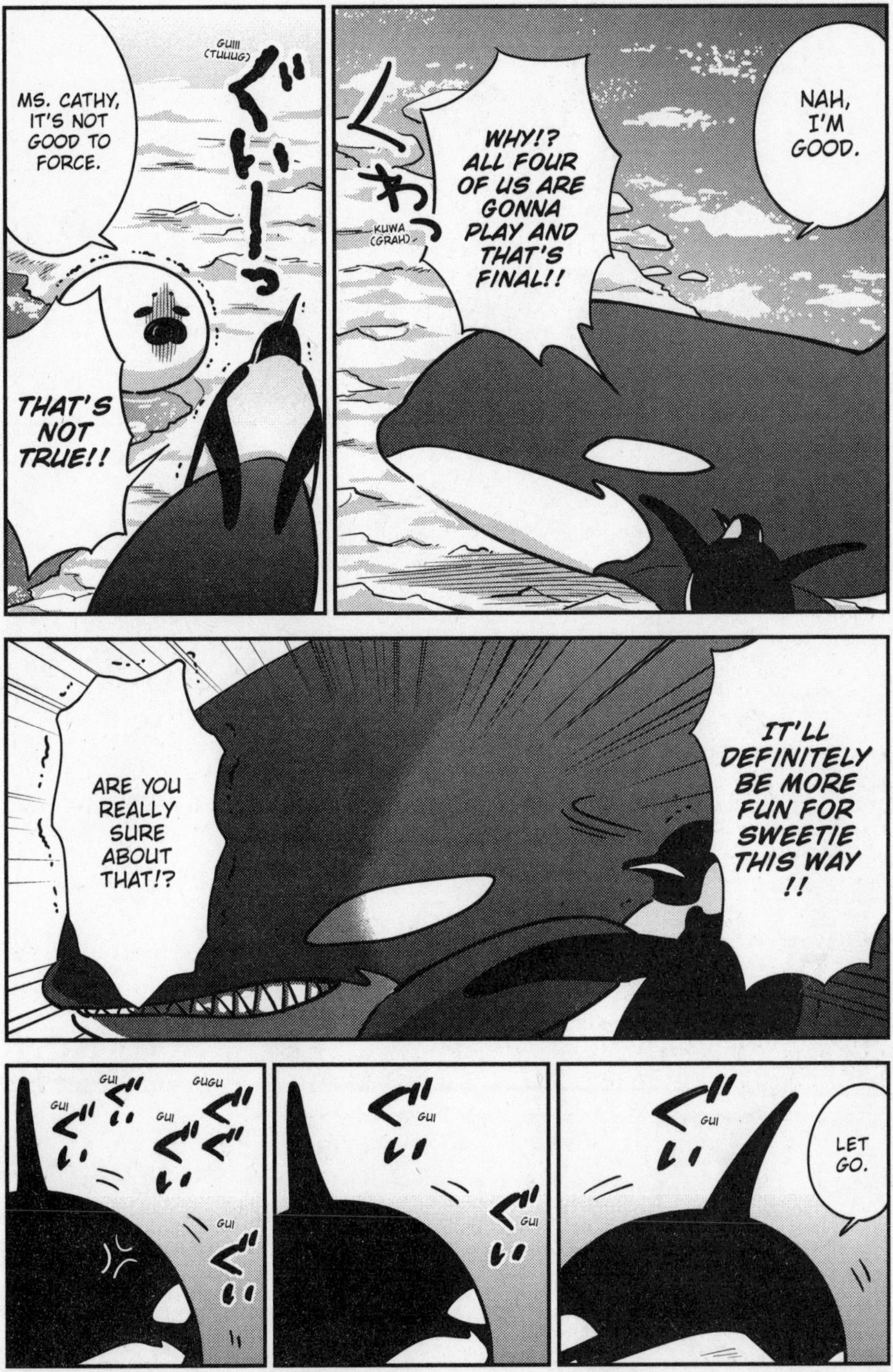

NAH, I'M GOOD.
WHY!? ALL FOUR OF US ARE GONNA PLAY AND THAT'S FINAL!!
KUWA (GRAH)
GUIII (TUUUG)
MS. CATHY, IT'S NOT GOOD TO FORCE.
THAT'S NOT TRUE!!
IT'LL DEFINITELY BE MORE FUN FOR SWEETIE THIS WAY!!
ARE YOU REALLY SURE ABOUT THAT!?
LET GO.
GUI
GUI
GUI
GUGU
GUI
GUI
GUI
GUI

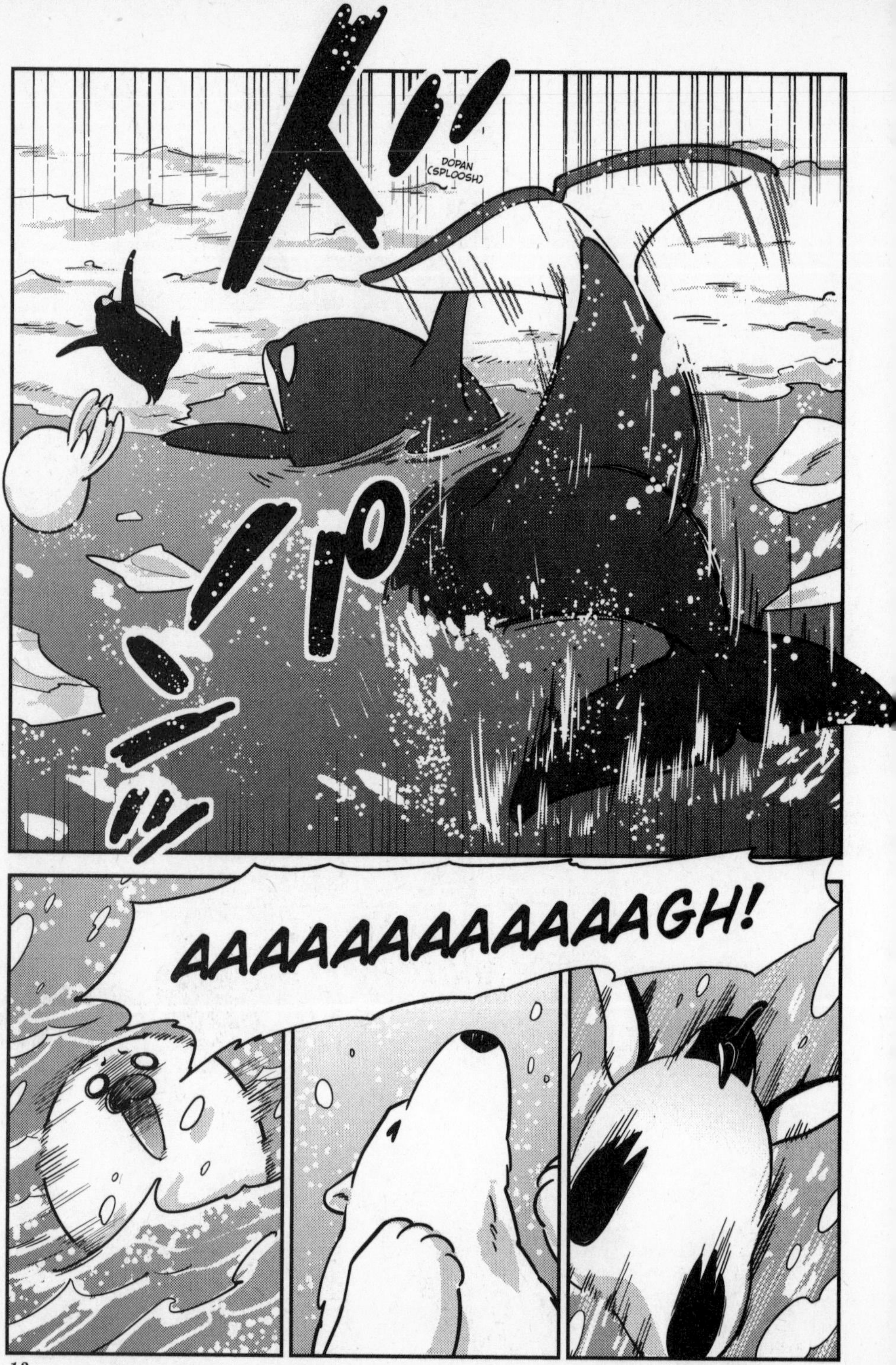
DOPAN
(SPLOOSH)
AAAAAAAAAAAAGH!

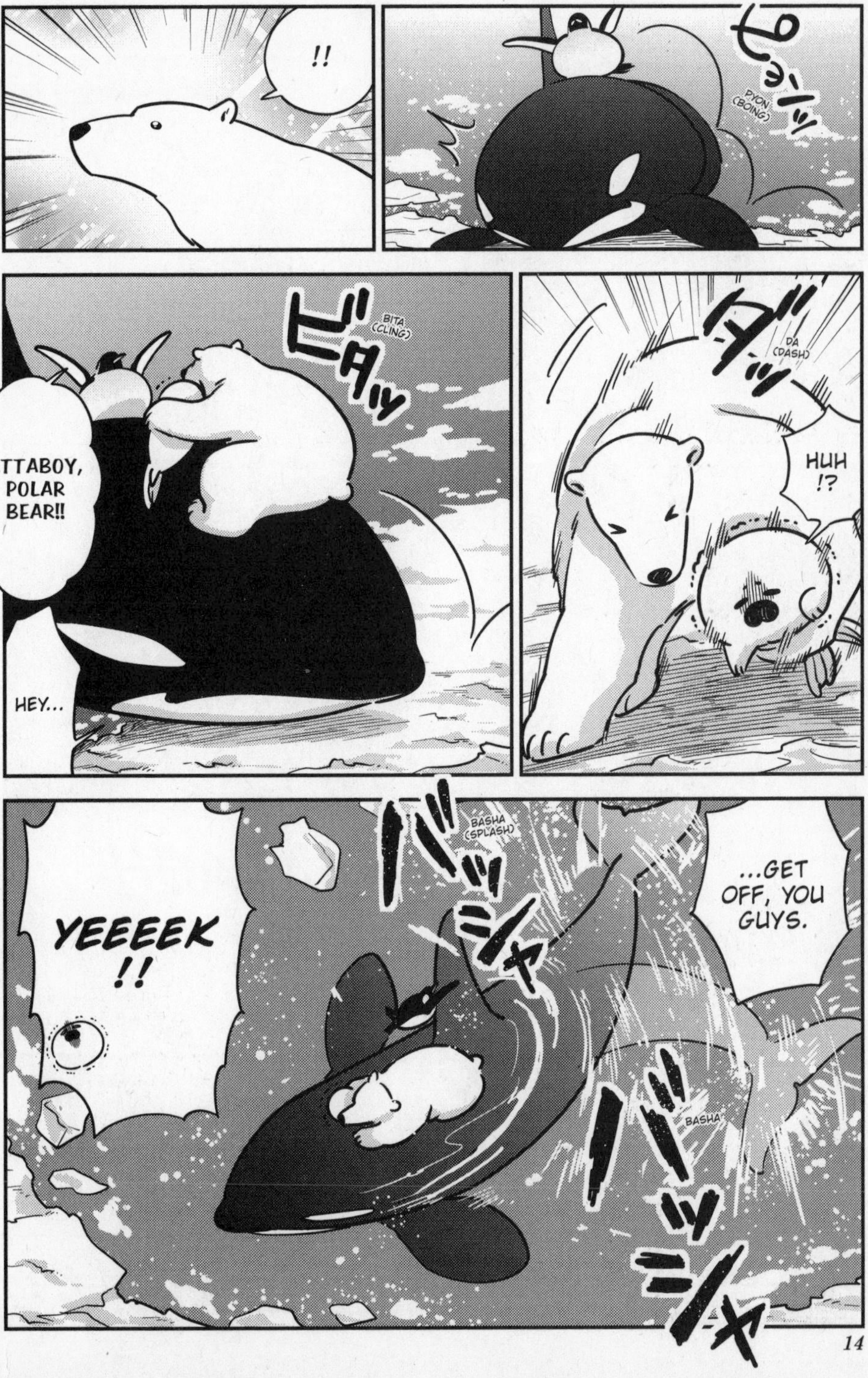
PYON (BOING)
!!
ダッ
DA (DASH)
HUH !?
ビタッ
BITA (CLING)
ATTABOY, POLAR BEAR!!
HEY...
...GET OFF, YOU GUYS.
バシャッ
BASHA (SPLASH)
YEEEEK !!
バシャッ
BASHA

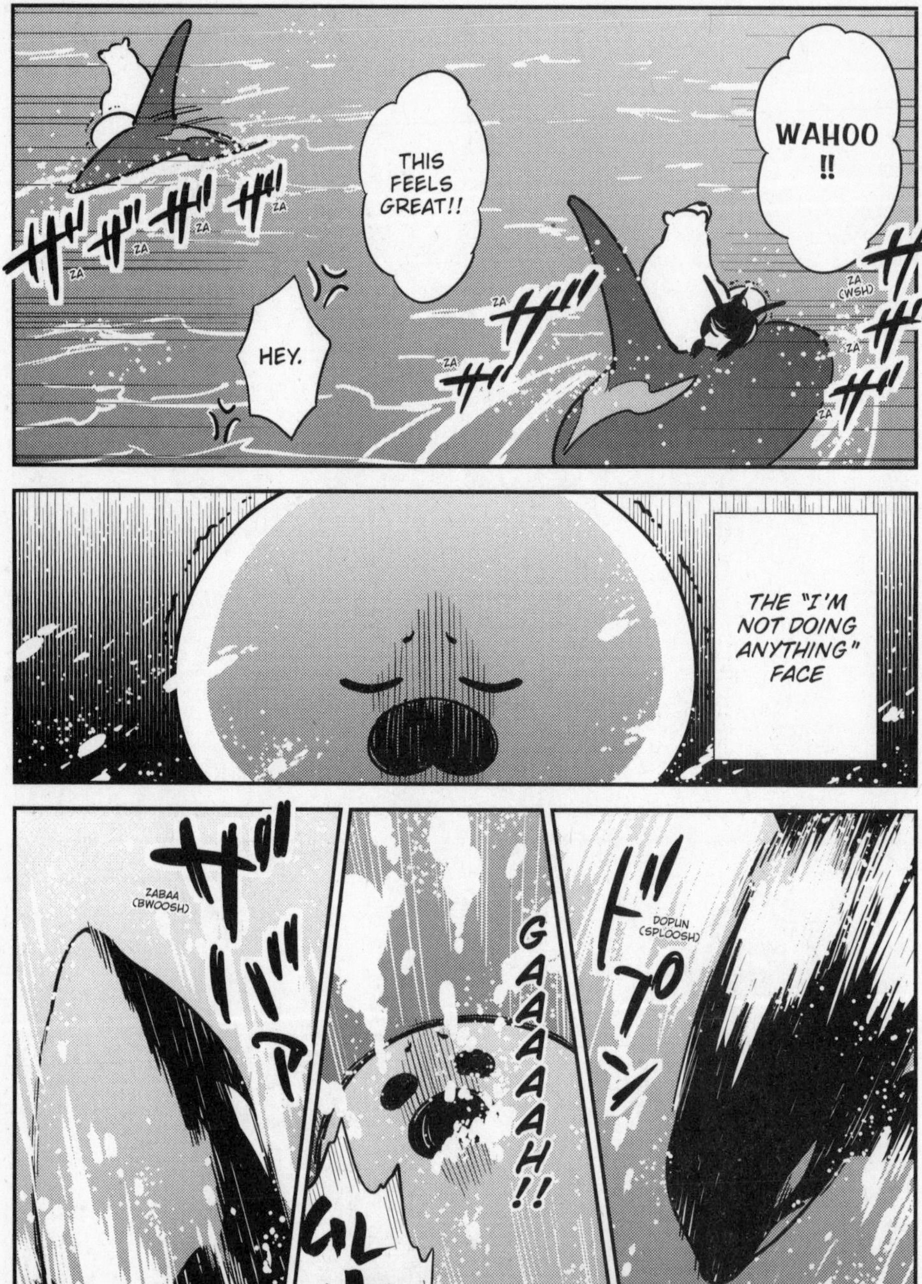
WAHOO!!
ZA (WSH)
ZA
ZA
ZA
ZA
THIS FEELS GREAT!!
HEY.
ZA
ZA
ZA
ZA
THE "I'M NOT DOING ANYTHING" FACE
DOPUN (SPLOOSH)
GAAAAAAH!!
GLUB!
ZABAA (BWOOSH)

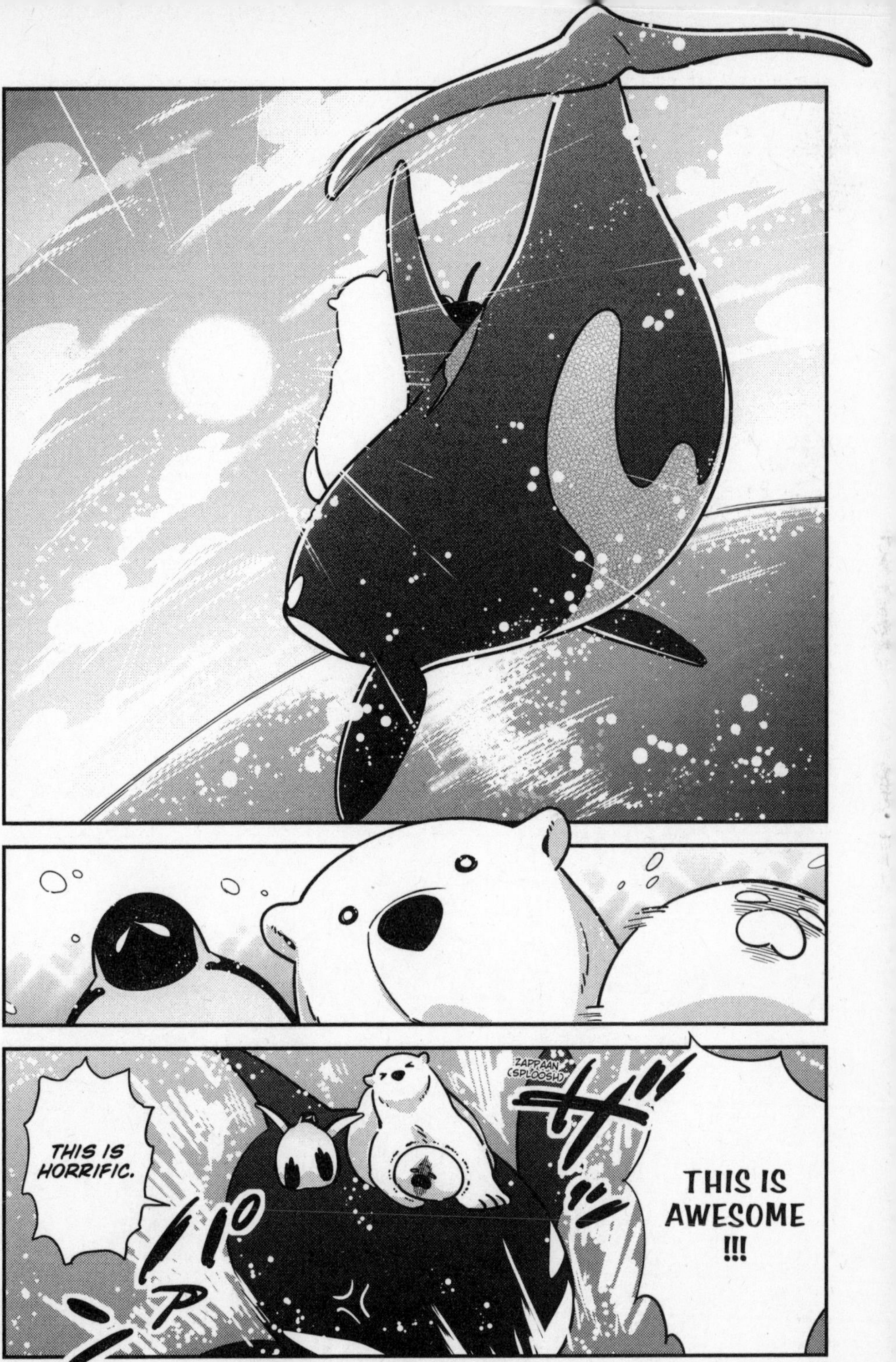
ZAPPAAN (SPLOOSH)
THIS IS AWESOME !!!
THIS IS HORRIFIC.

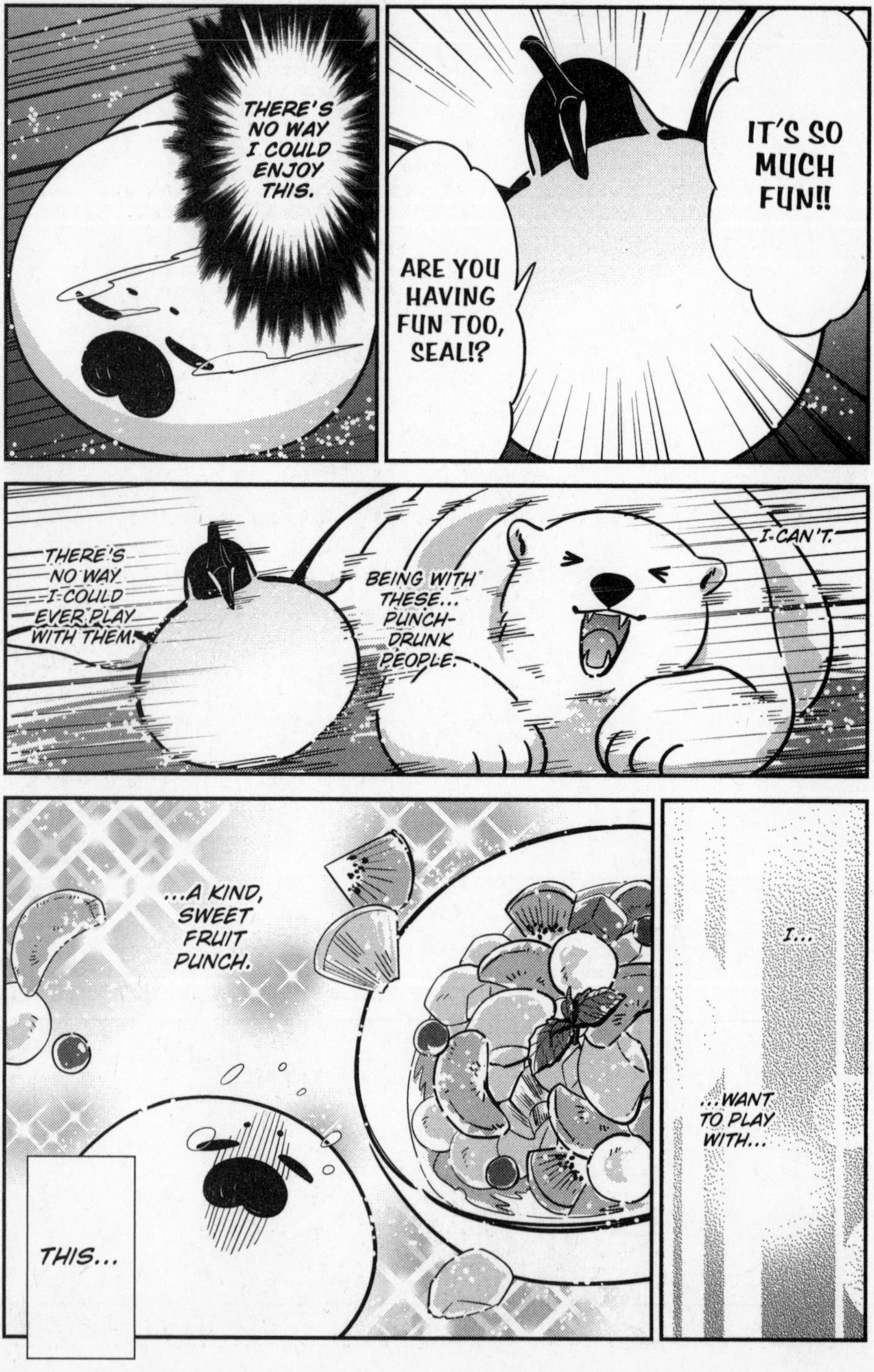
IT'S SO MUCH FUN!!
ARE YOU HAVING FUN TOO, SEAL!?
THERE'S NO WAY I COULD ENJOY THIS.
I-CAN'T.
BEING WITH THESE... PUNCH-DRUNK PEOPLE.
THERE'S NO WAY I COULD EVER PLAY WITH THEM.
I...
...WANT TO PLAY WITH...
...A KIND, SWEET FRUIT PUNCH.
THIS...

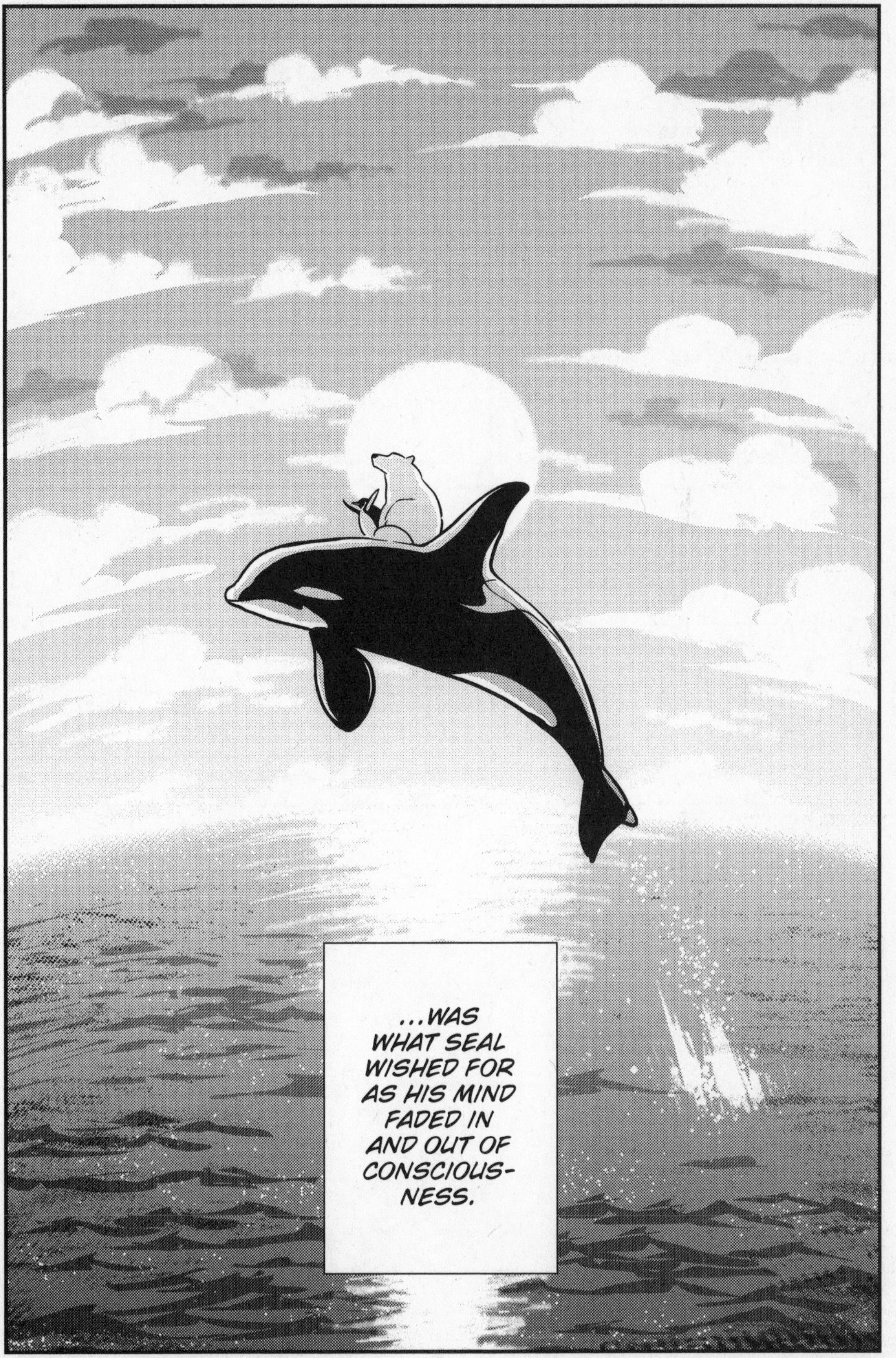
...WAS WHAT SEAL WISHED FOR AS HIS MIND FADED IN AND OUT OF CONSCIOUS-NESS.

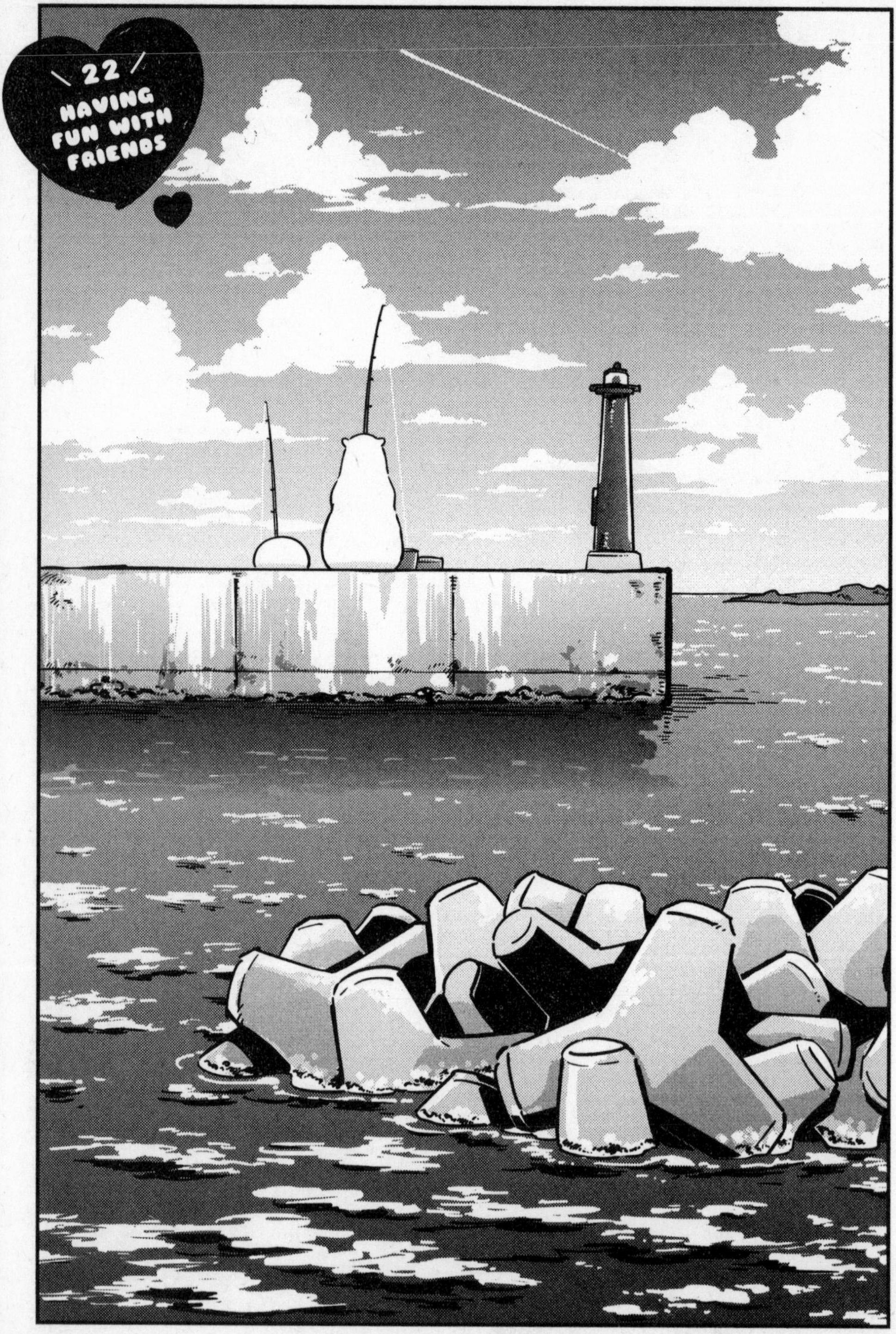
22
HAVING FUN WITH FRIENDS

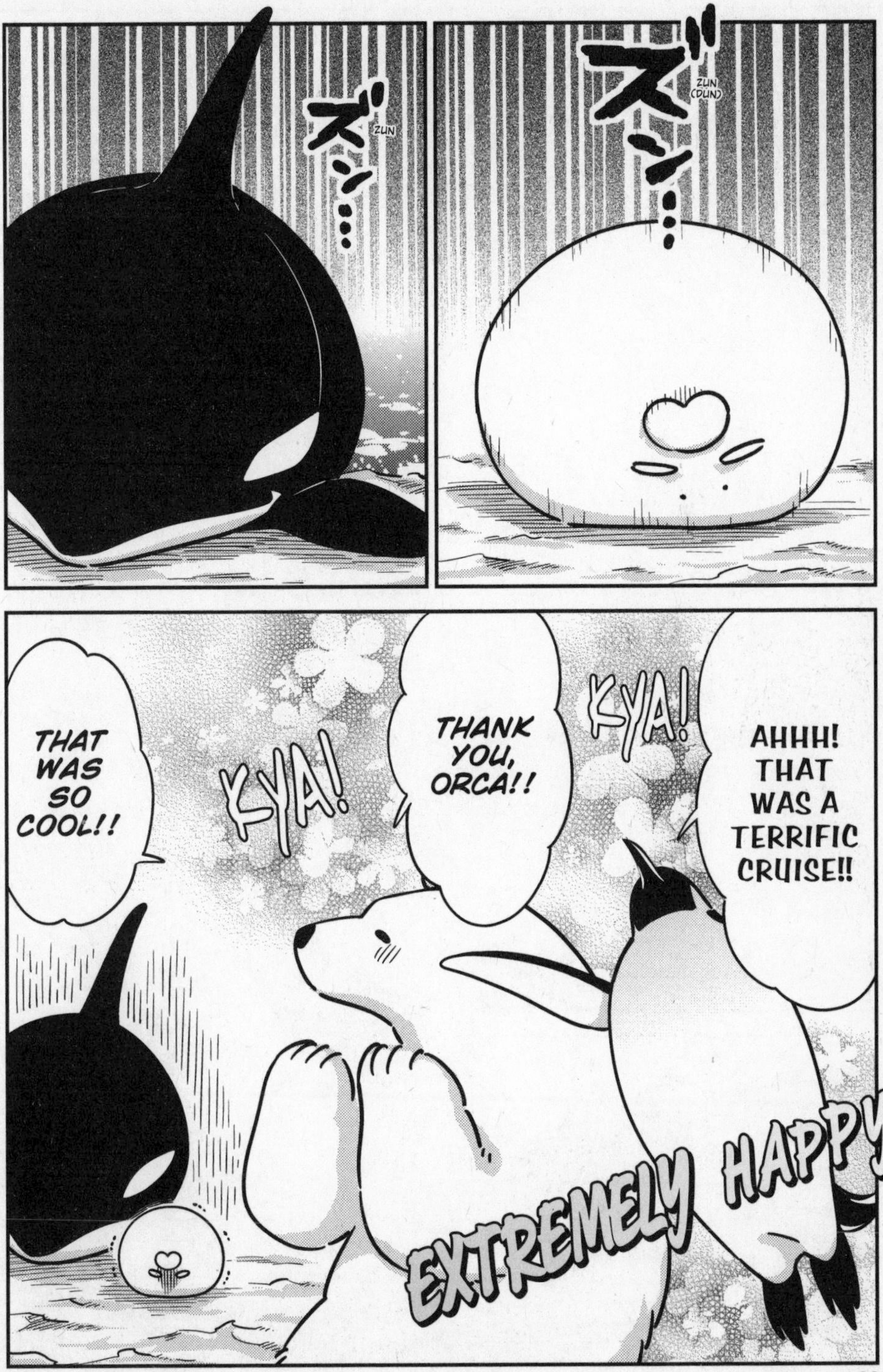
ズン…
ZUN (DUN)
ズン…
ZUN
AHHH! THAT WAS A TERRIFIC CRUISE!!
KYA!
THANK YOU, ORCA!!
KYA!
THAT WAS SO COOL!!
EXTREMELY HAPPY

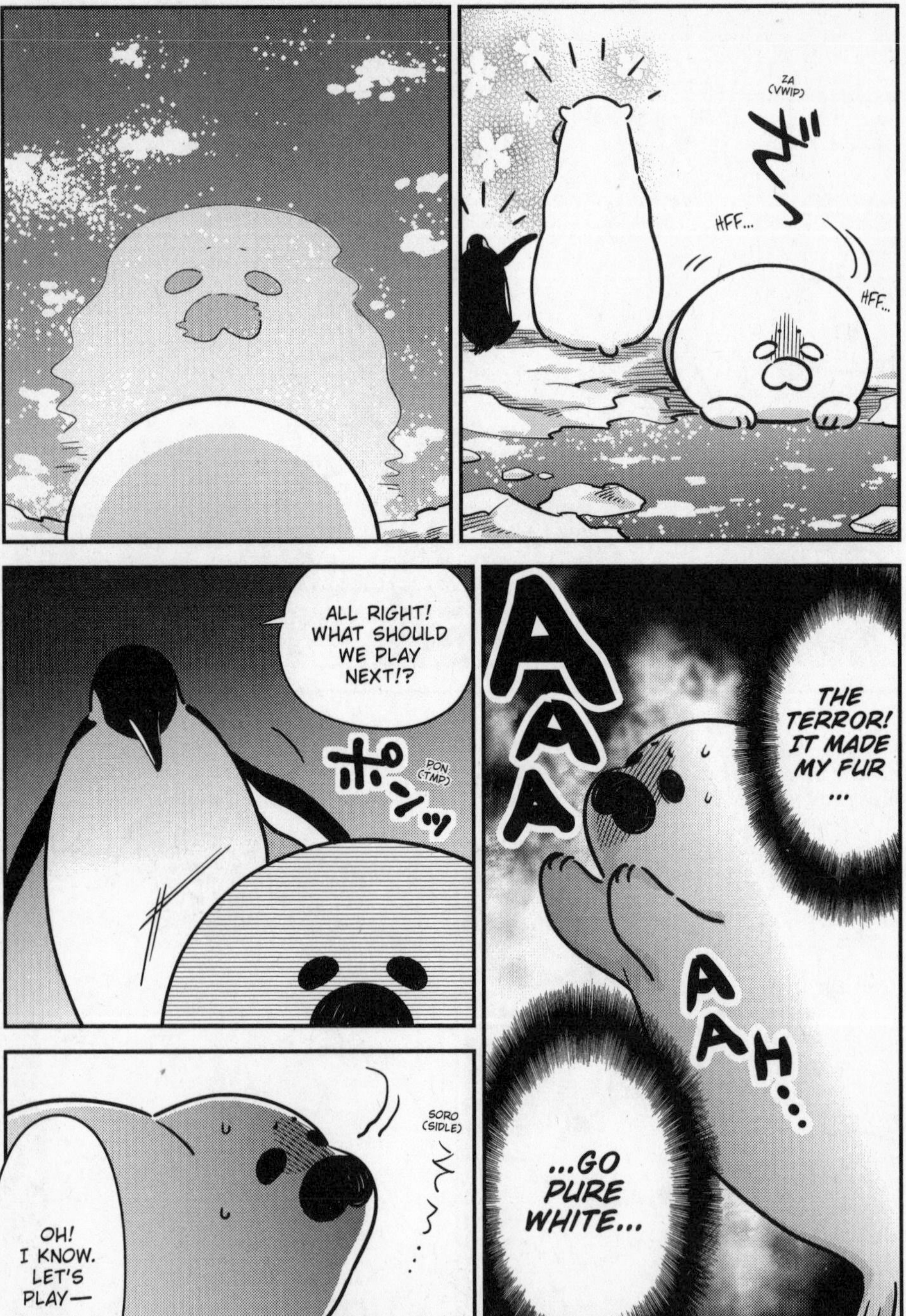

ザッ
ZA (VWIP)
HFF...
HFF...
AAAA
THE TERROR! IT MADE MY FUR ...
AAH...
...GO PURE WHITE...
ALL RIGHT! WHAT SHOULD WE PLAY NEXT!?
ポンッ
PON (TMP)
SORO (SIDLE)
OH! I KNOW. LET'S PLAY—

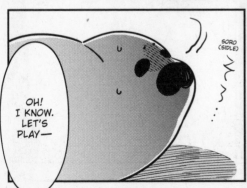

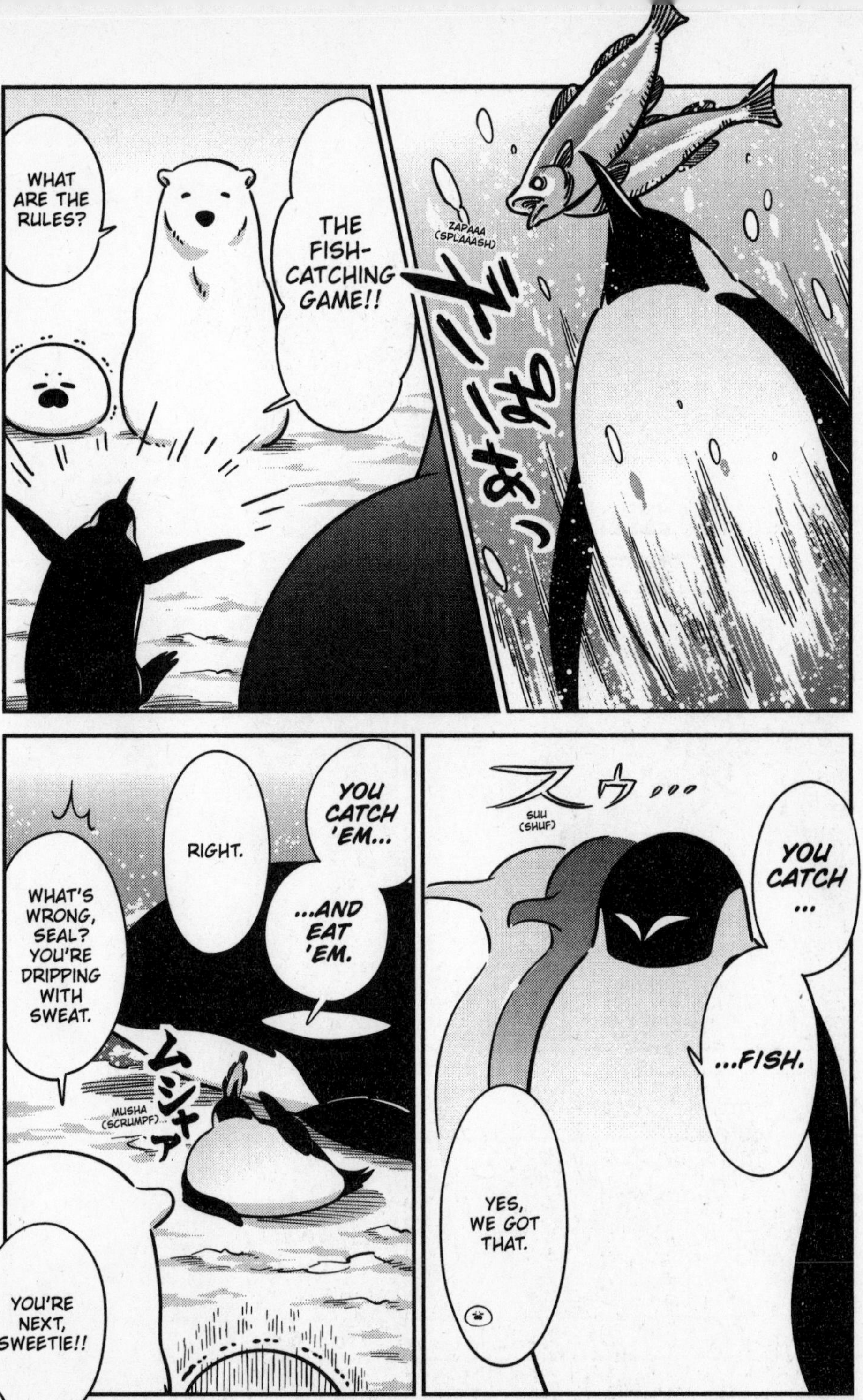
ZAPAAA
(SPLAAASH)
THE FISH-CATCHING GAME!!
WHAT ARE THE RULES?
スゥ…
SUU
(SHUF)
YOU CATCH ...
...FISH.
YES, WE GOT THAT.
YOU CATCH 'EM...
RIGHT.
...AND EAT 'EM.
WHAT'S WRONG, SEAL? YOU'RE DRIPPING WITH SWEAT.
ムシャア
MUSHA
(SCRUMPF)
YOU'RE NEXT, SWEETIE!!

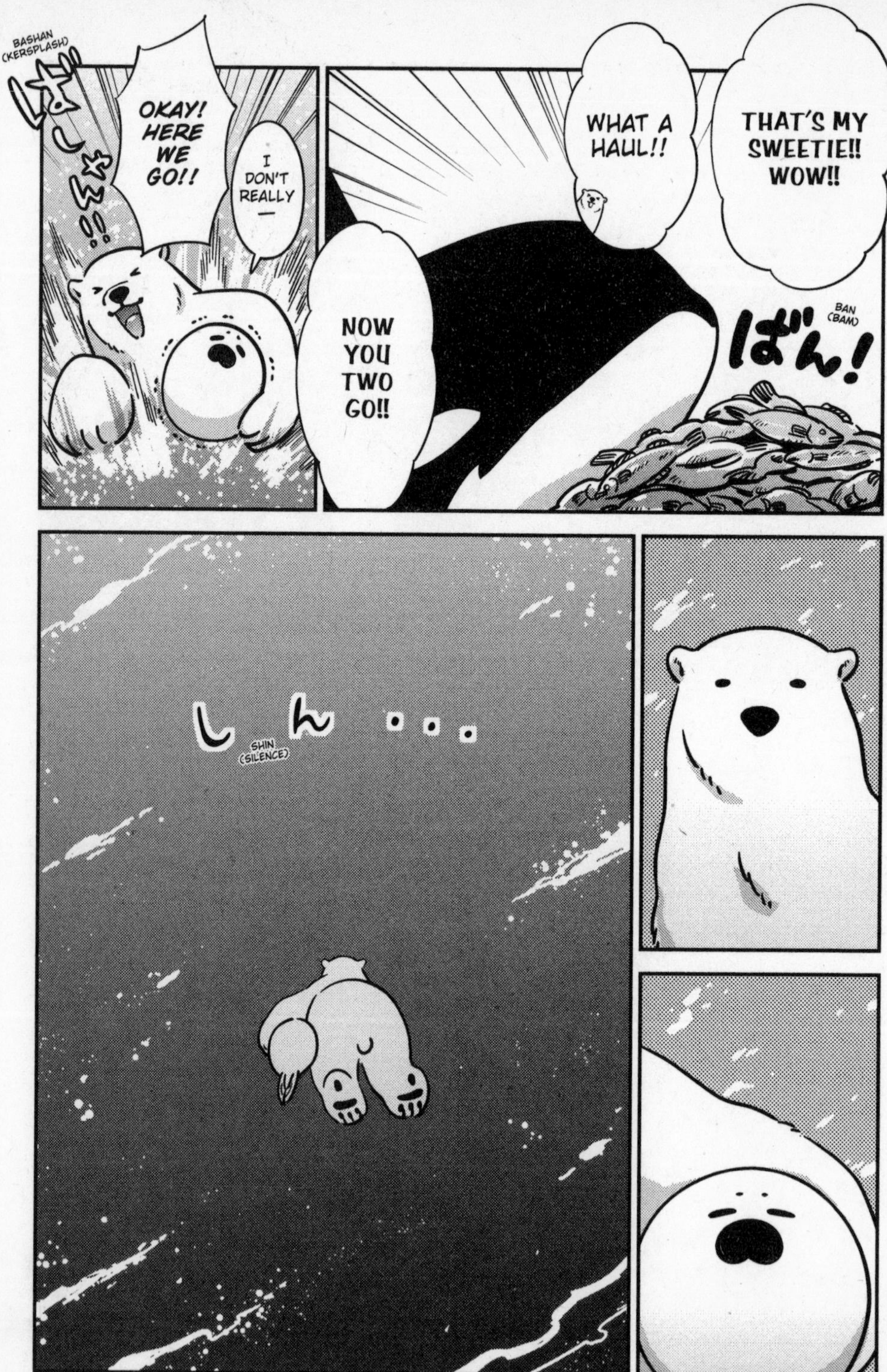
THAT'S MY SWEETIE!! WOW!!
WHAT A HAUL!!
BAN (BAM)
ばん!
NOW YOU TWO GO!!
BASHAN (KERSPLASH)
ばしゃん!!
OKAY! HERE WE GO!!
I DON'T REALLY —
しん...
SHIN (SILENCE)

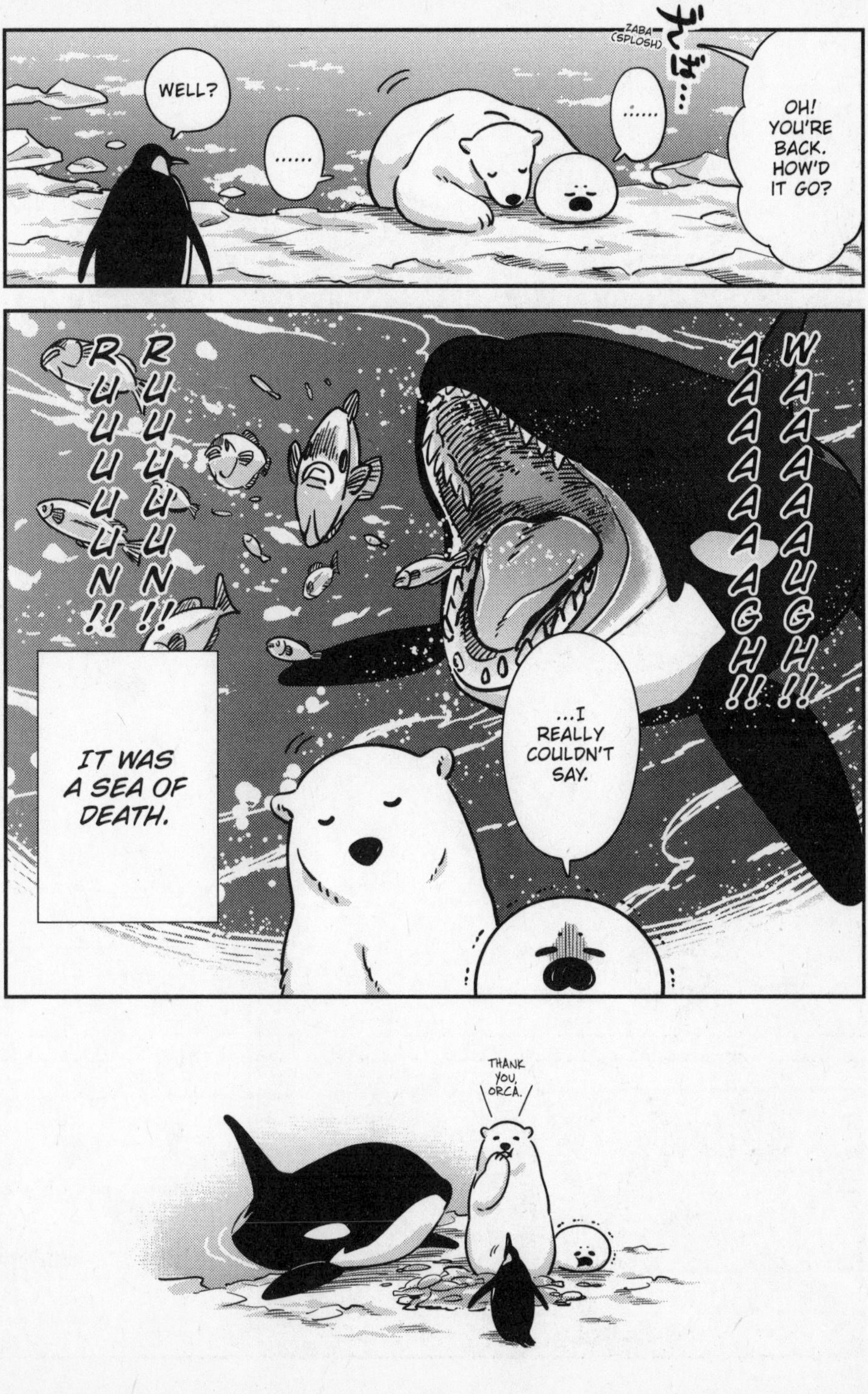
OH! YOU'RE BACK. HOW'D IT GO?
ZABA (SPLOSH)
......
......
WELL?
WAAAAAAAUGH!!
AAAAAAAAAGH!!
RUUUUUUN!!
RUUUUUUN!!
...I REALLY COULDN'T SAY.
IT WAS A SEA OF DEATH.
THANK YOU, ORCA.

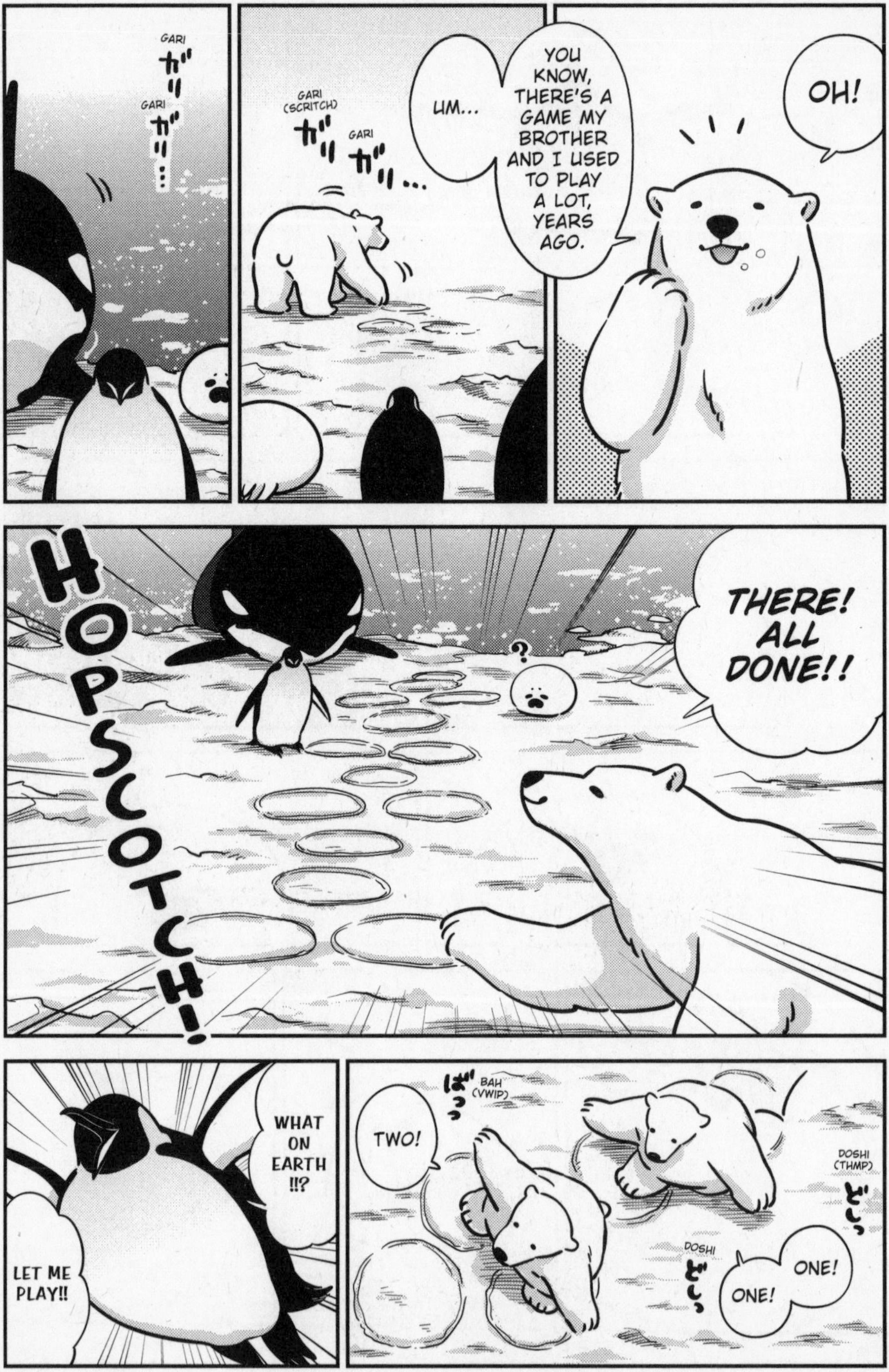
OH!
YOU KNOW, THERE'S A GAME MY BROTHER AND I USED TO PLAY A LOT, YEARS AGO.
UM...
GARI (SCRITCH)
ガリ
GARI
ガリ...
GARI
ガリ
GARI
ガリ...
THERE! ALL DONE!!
HOPSCOTCH!
DOSHI (THMP)
どしっ
ONE!
DOSHI
どしっ
ONE!
BAH (VWIP)
ばっ
TWO!
WHAT ON EARTH!!?
LET ME PLAY!!

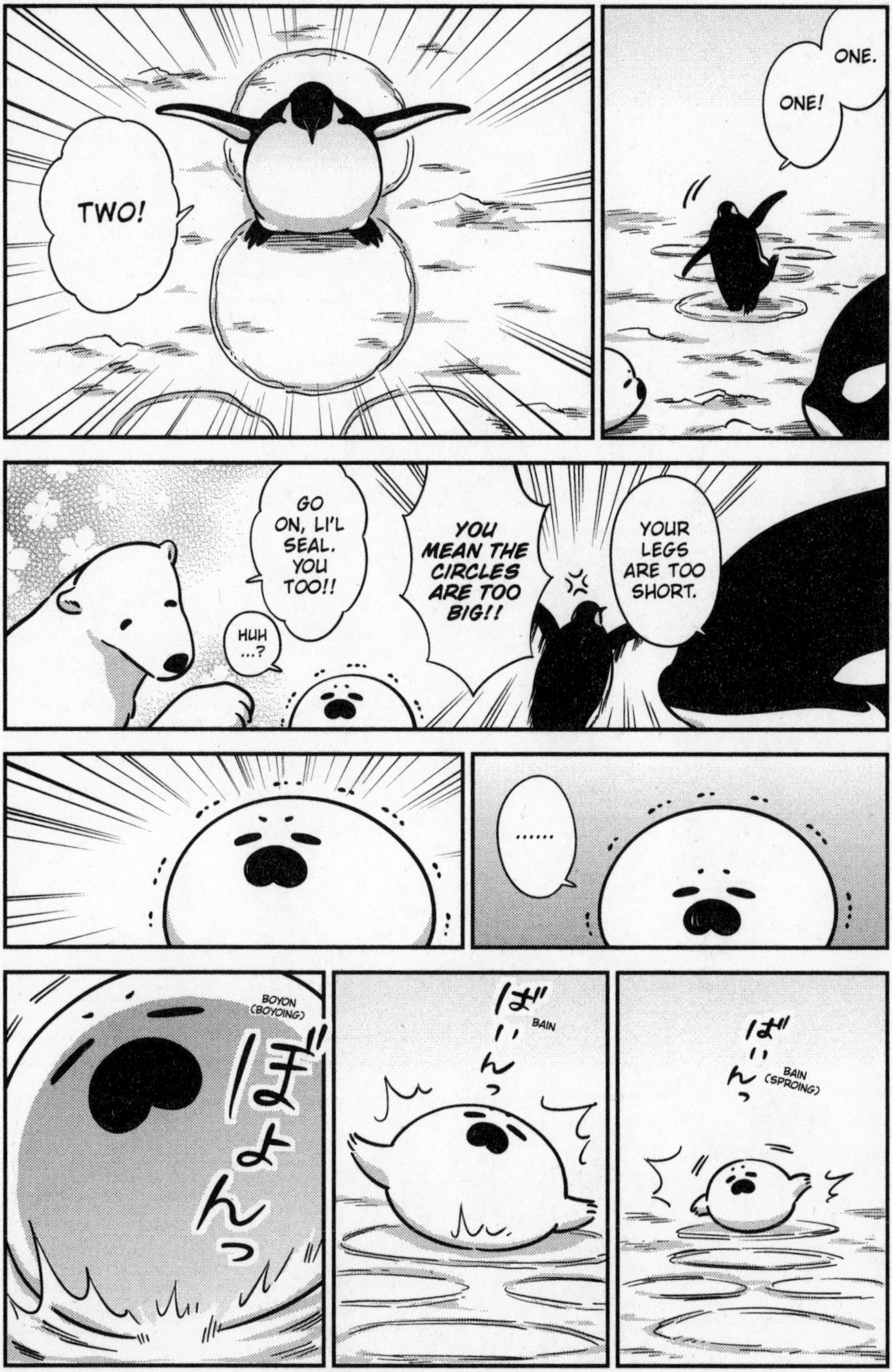
ONE.
ONE!
TWO!
YOUR LEGS ARE TOO SHORT.
YOU MEAN THE CIRCLES ARE TOO BIG!!
GO ON, LI'L SEAL. YOU TOO!!
HUH ...?
......
ばいんっ
BAIN (SPROING)
ばいんっ
BAIN
BOYON (BOYOING)
ぼよんっ

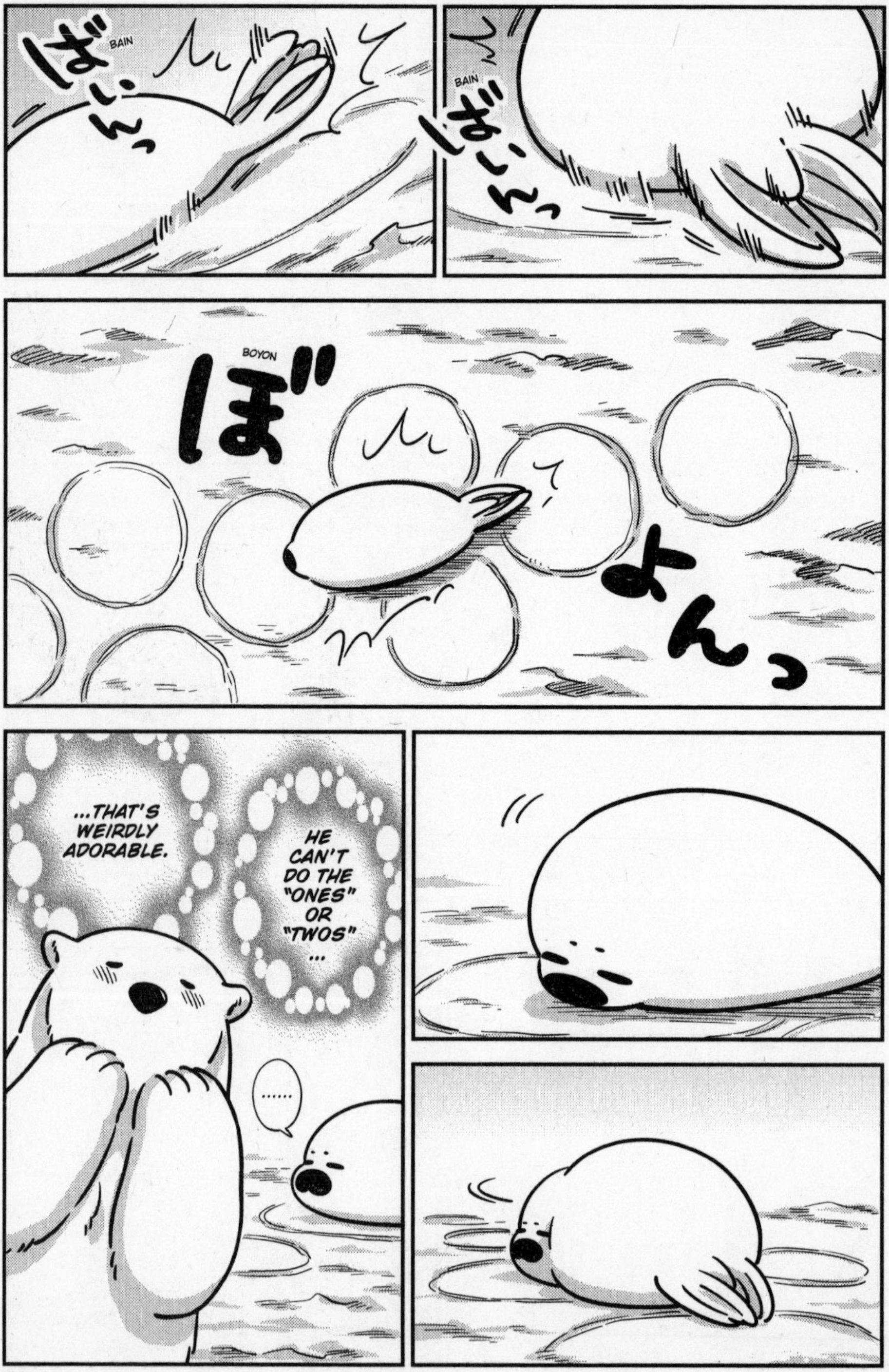
ばいんっ
BAIN
ばいんっ
BAIN
ぼよんっ
BOYON
HE CAN'T DO THE "ONES" OR "TWOS" ...
...THAT'S WEIRDLY ADORABLE.
......

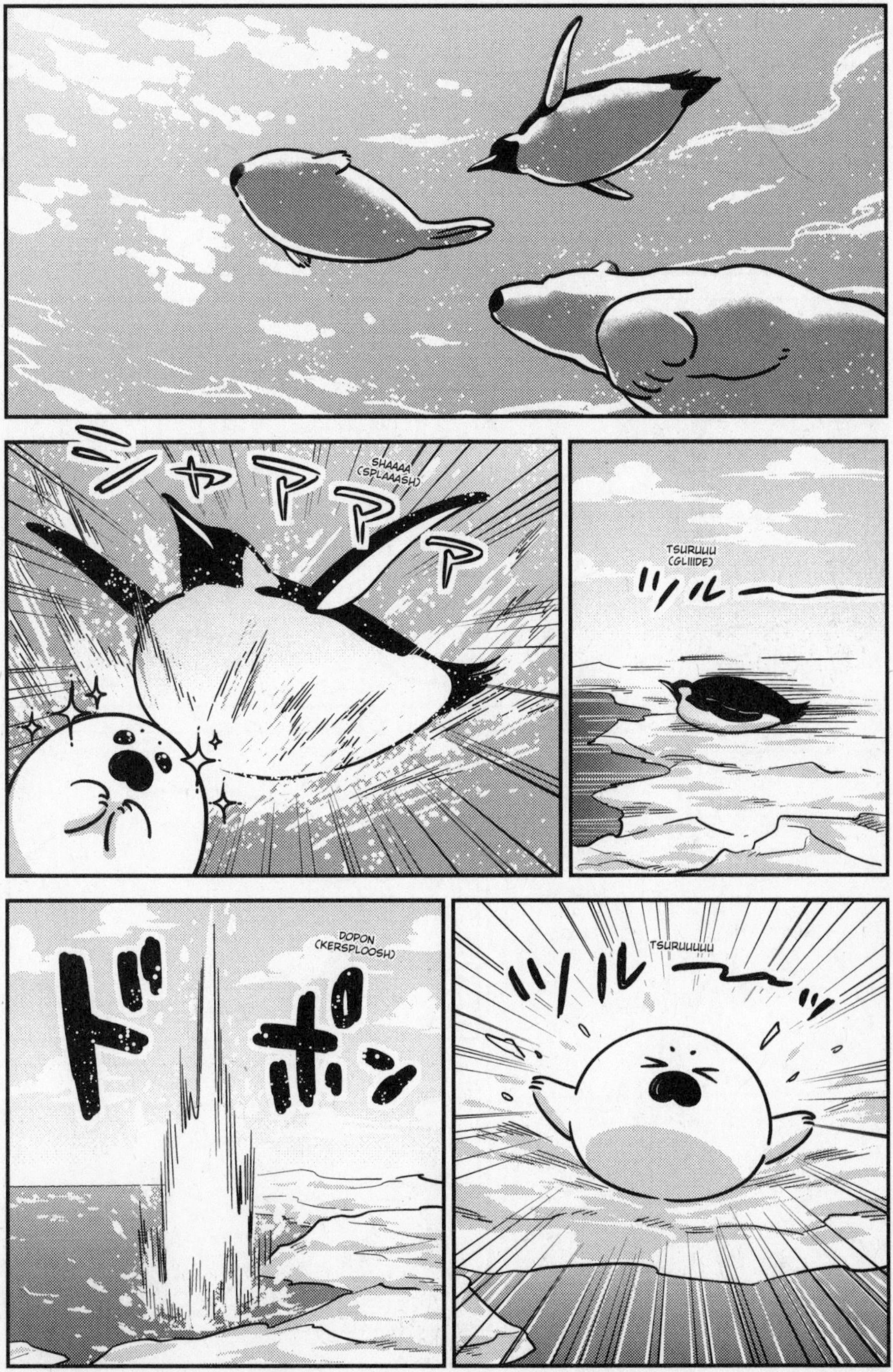

TSURUUU (GLIIIDE)
ツルー
SHAAAA (SPLAAASH)
シャアアアア
TSURUUUUU
ツルー
DOPON (KERSPLOOSH)
ドポン

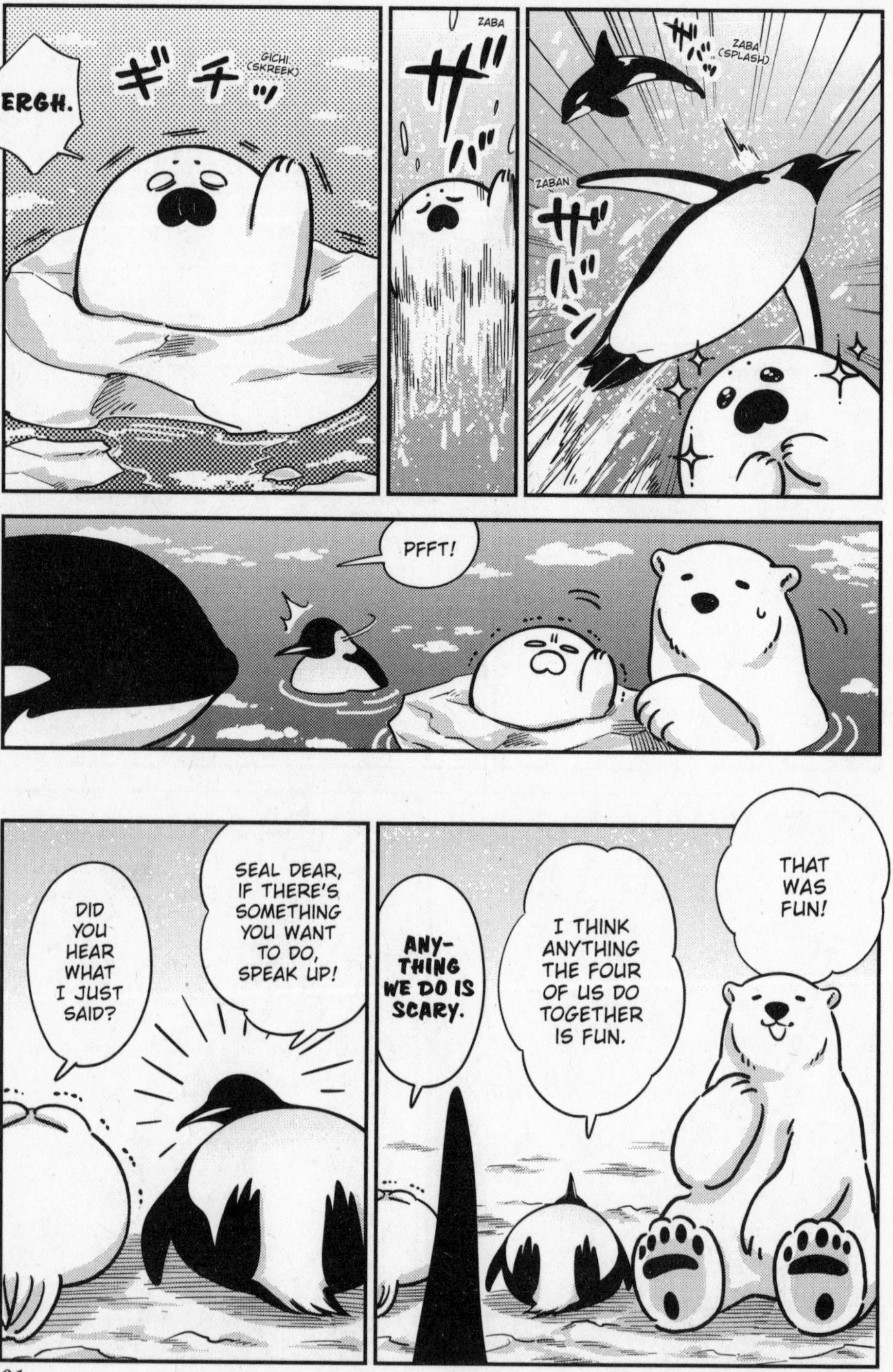
ザバッ
ZABA (SPLASH)
ZABAN
ザバン
ザバ
ZABA
ギチッ
GICHI (SKREEK)
ERGH.
PFFT!
THAT WAS FUN!
I THINK ANYTHING THE FOUR OF US DO TOGETHER IS FUN.
ANYTHING WE DO IS SCARY.
SEAL DEAR, IF THERE'S SOMETHING YOU WANT TO DO, SPEAK UP!
DID YOU HEAR WHAT I JUST SAID?

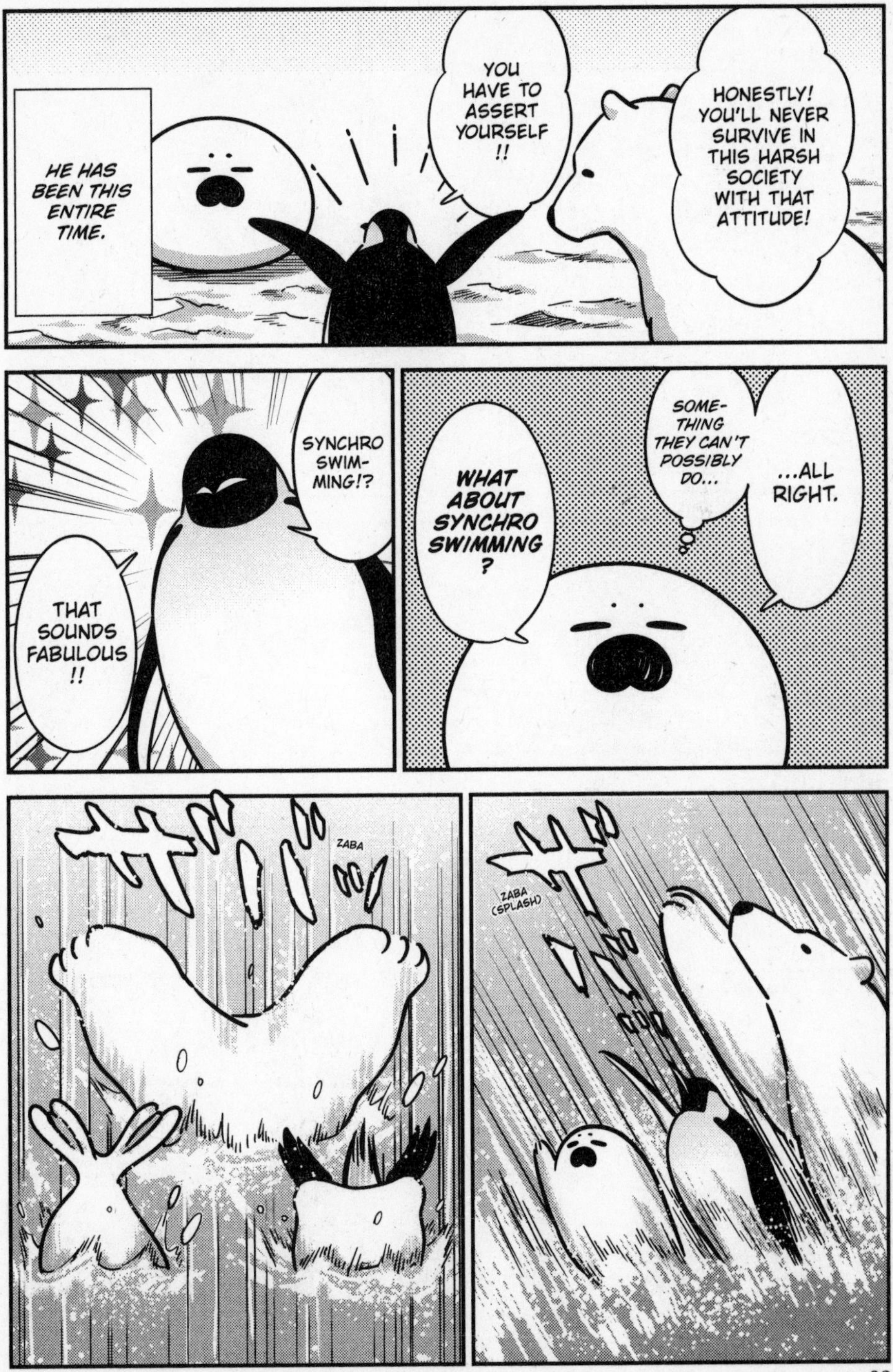
HONESTLY! YOU'LL NEVER SURVIVE IN THIS HARSH SOCIETY WITH THAT ATTITUDE!
YOU HAVE TO ASSERT YOURSELF !!
HE HAS BEEN THIS ENTIRE TIME.
...ALL RIGHT.
SOME-THING THEY CAN'T POSSIBLY DO...
WHAT ABOUT SYNCHRO SWIMMING ?
SYNCHRO SWIM-MING!?
THAT SOUNDS FABULOUS !!
ZABA (SPLASH)
ZABA

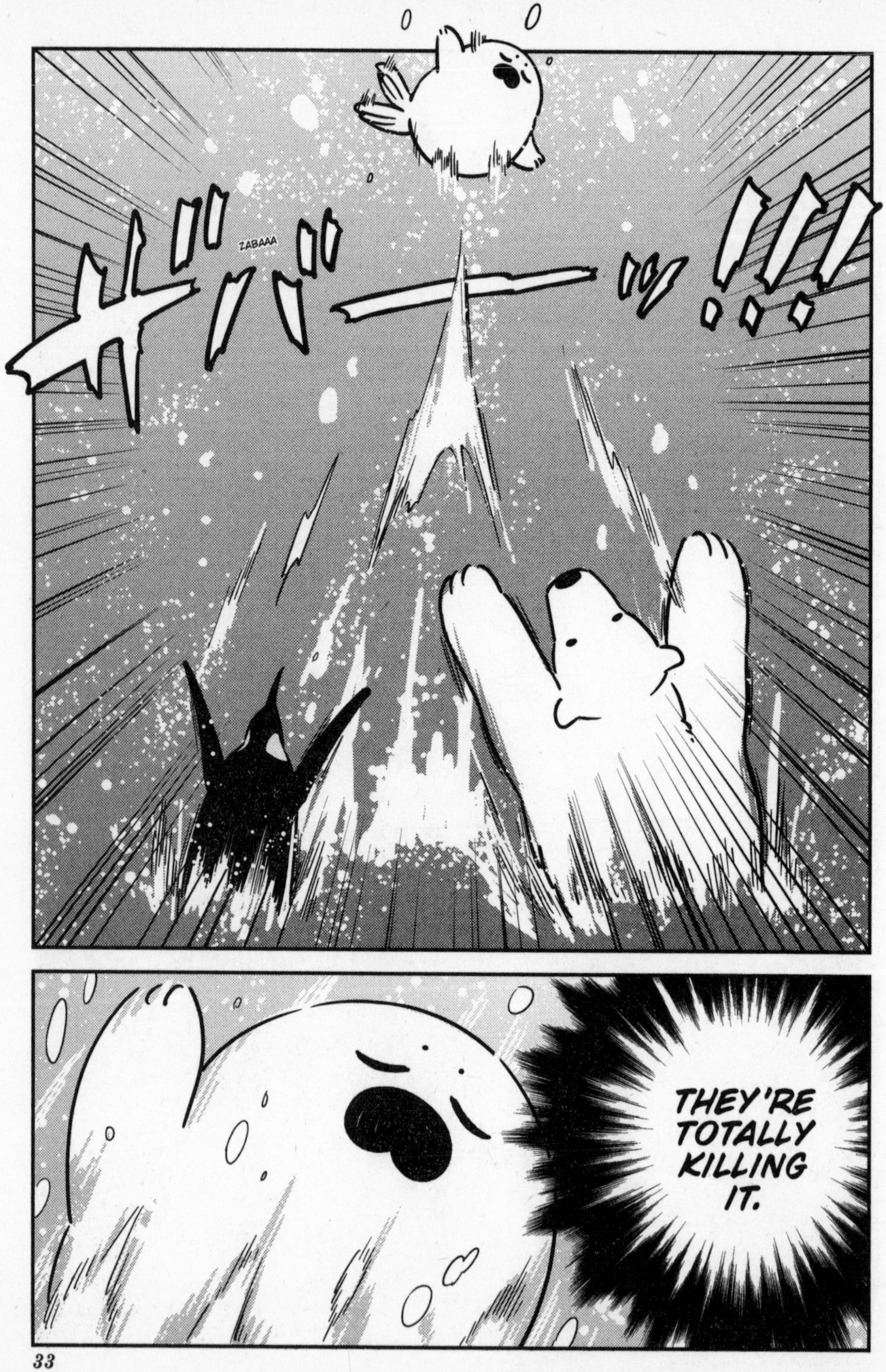
ザバーッ!!!!
ZABAAA
THEY'RE TOTALLY KILLING IT.

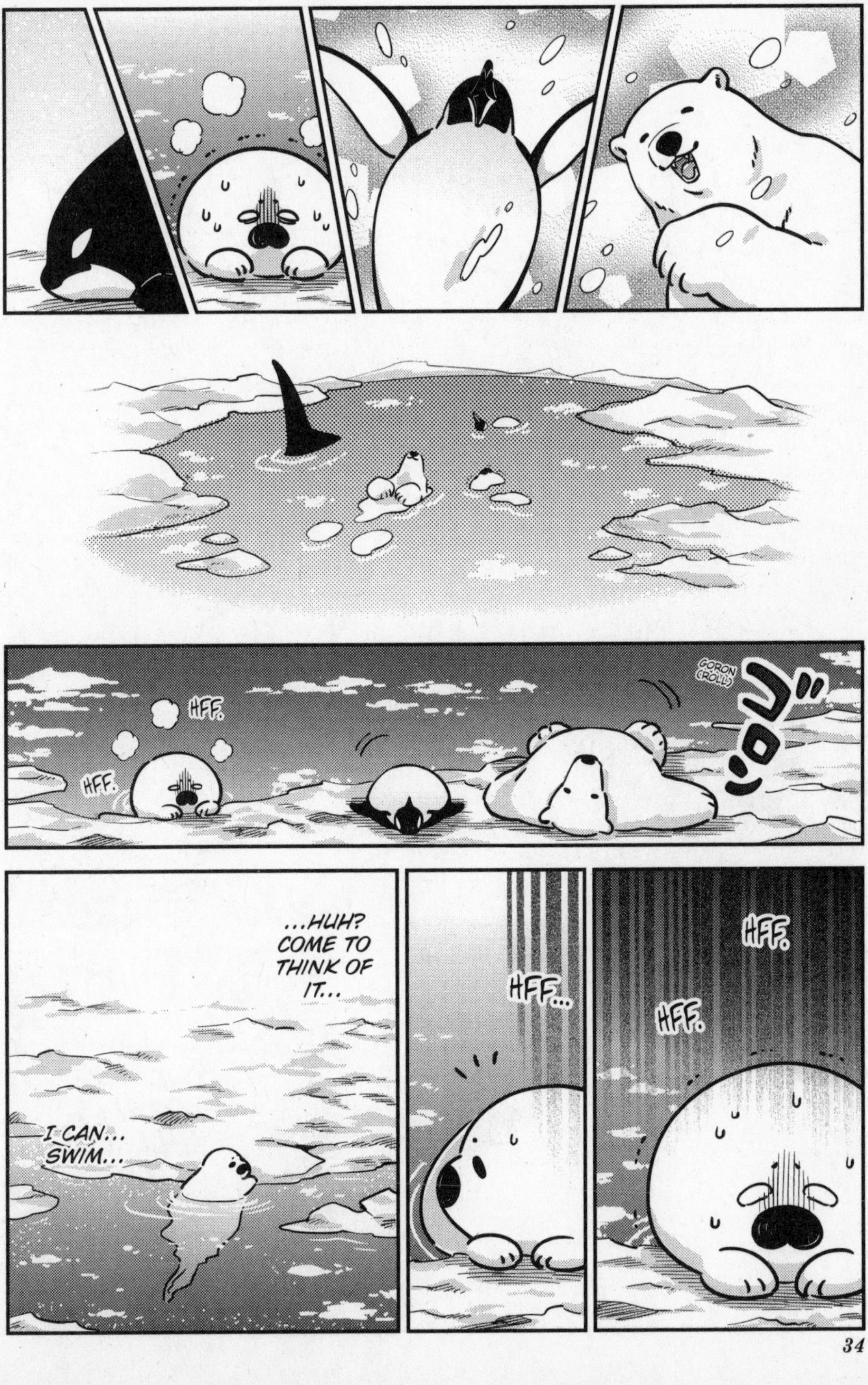
ゴロン
GORON (ROLL)
HFF.
HFF.
HFF.
HFF.
HFF...
...HUH? COME TO THINK OF IT...
I CAN... SWIM...

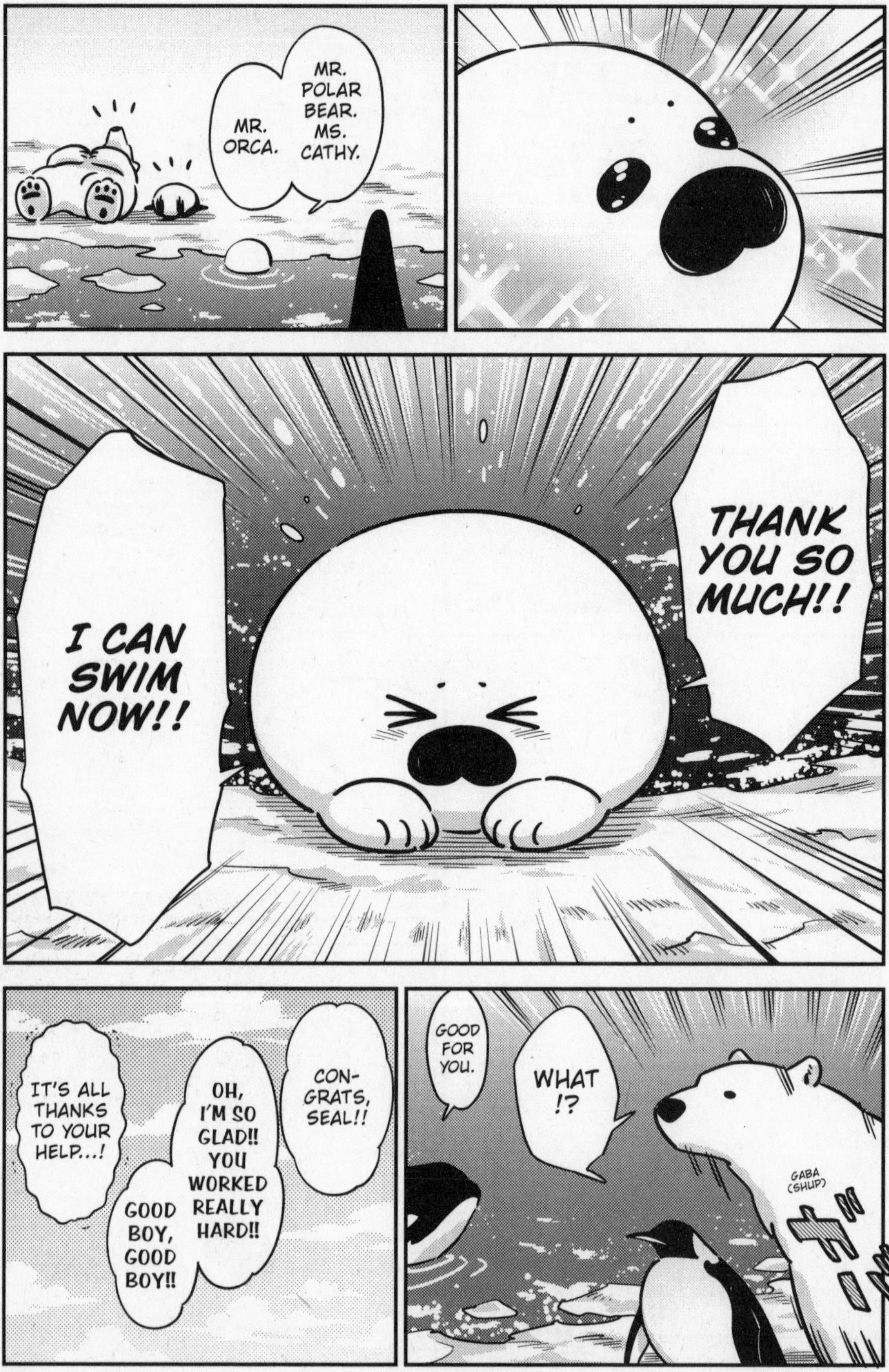
MR. ORCA. MR. POLAR BEAR. MS. CATHY.
THANK YOU SO MUCH!!
I CAN SWIM NOW!!
GOOD FOR YOU.
WHAT!?
GABA (SHUP)
CON-GRATS, SEAL!!
OH, I'M SO GLAD!! YOU WORKED REALLY HARD!!
GOOD BOY, GOOD BOY!!
IT'S ALL THANKS TO YOUR HELP...!

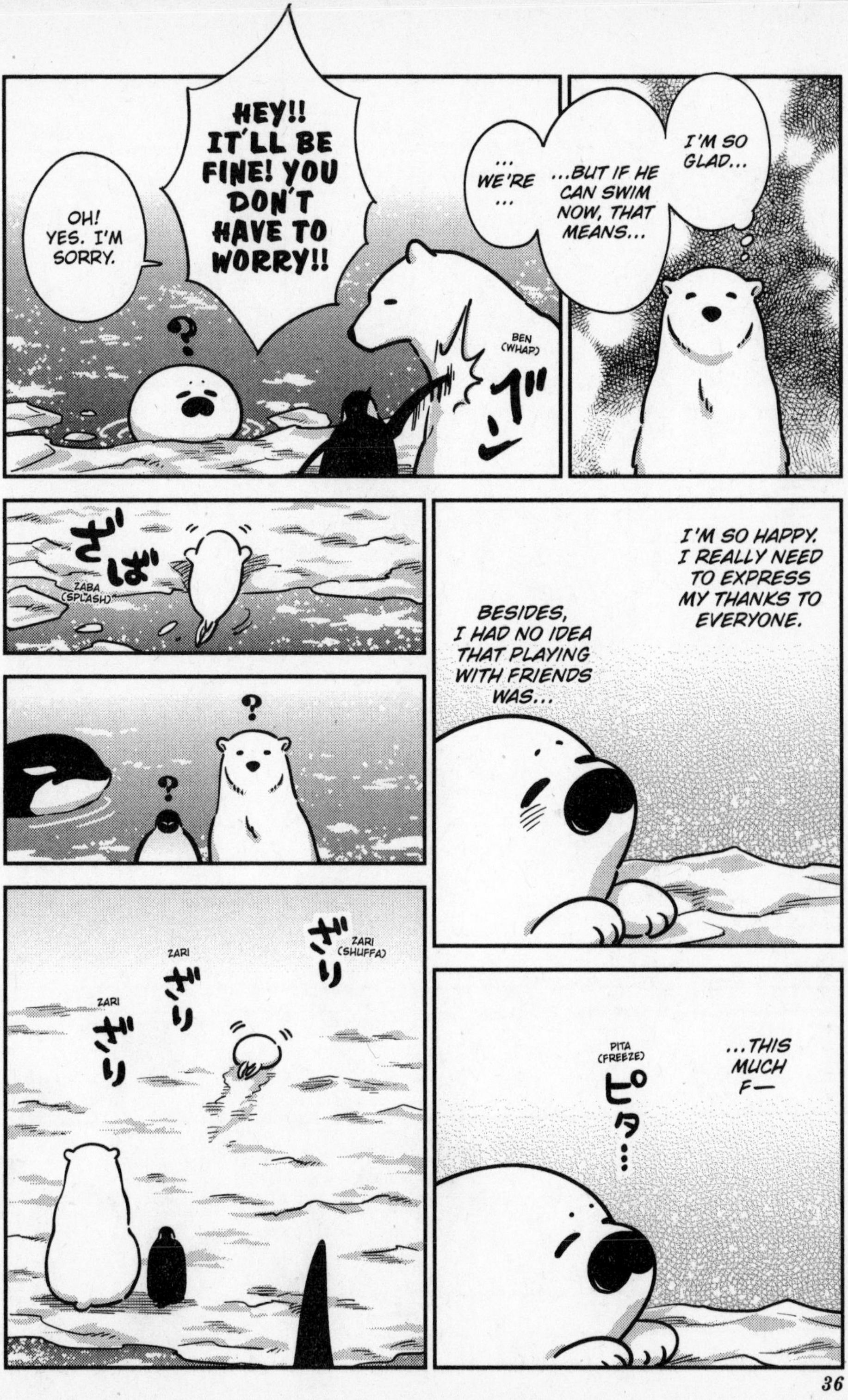
I'M SO GLAD...
...BUT IF HE CAN SWIM NOW, THAT MEANS...
... WE'RE ...
HEY!! IT'LL BE FINE! YOU DON'T HAVE TO WORRY!!
OH! YES. I'M SORRY.
?
BEN (WHAP)
ブン
I'M SO HAPPY. I REALLY NEED TO EXPRESS MY THANKS TO EVERYONE.
BESIDES, I HAD NO IDEA THAT PLAYING WITH FRIENDS WAS...
...THIS MUCH F—
PITA (FREEZE)
ピタ…
ざば
ZABA (SPLASH)
?
?
ざり
ZARI (SHUFFA)
ZARI
ざり
ZARI
ざり

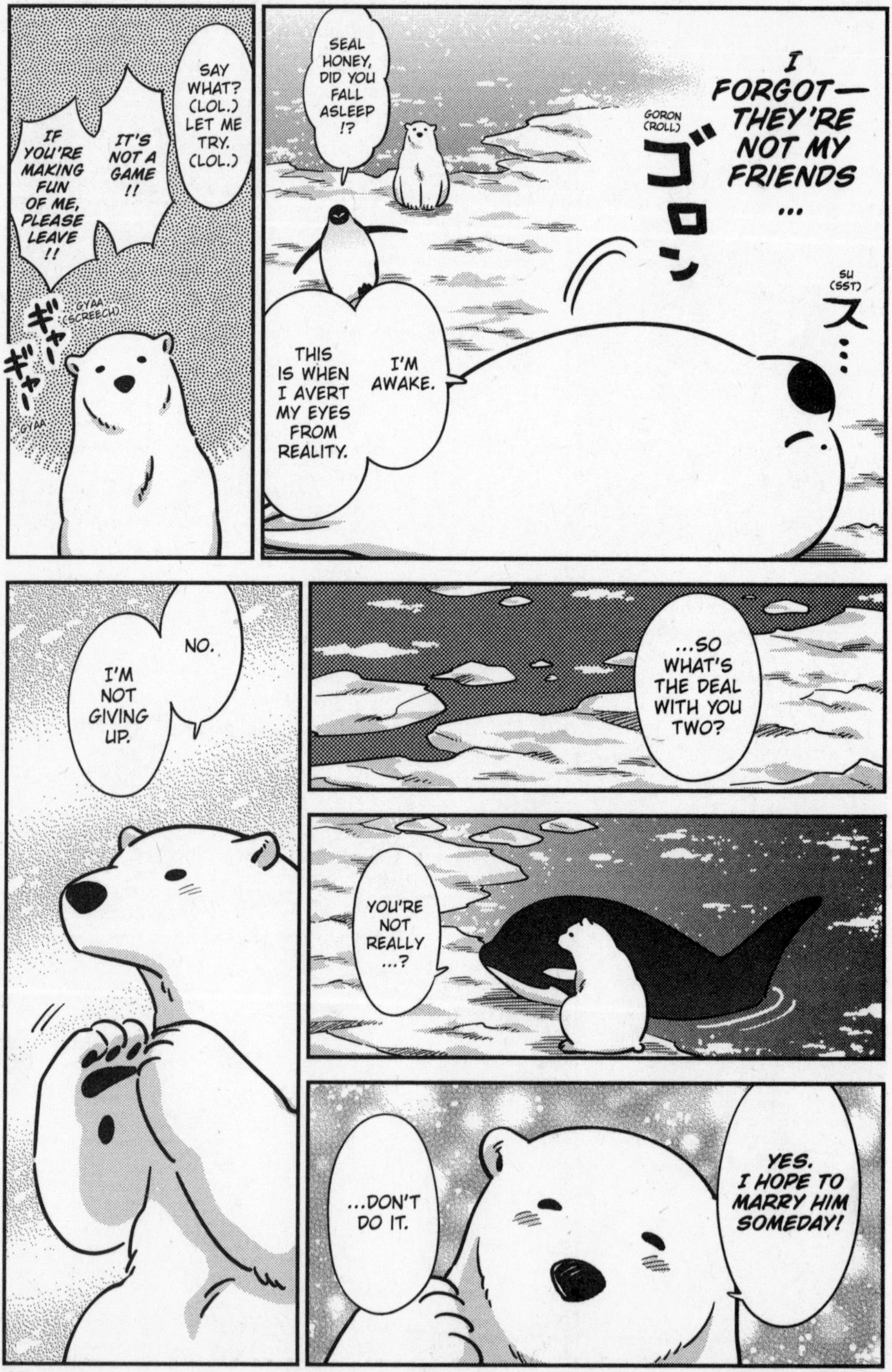
I FORGOT—THEY'RE NOT MY FRIENDS...
GORON (ROLL)
ゴロン
SEAL HONEY, DID YOU FALL ASLEEP!?
SU (SST)
ス…
I'M AWAKE.
THIS IS WHEN I AVERT MY EYES FROM REALITY.
SAY WHAT? (LOL.) LET ME TRY. (LOL.)
IT'S NOT A GAME!!
IF YOU'RE MAKING FUN OF ME, PLEASE LEAVE!!
GYAA (SCREECH)
ギャーギャー
GYAA
...SO WHAT'S THE DEAL WITH YOU TWO?
YOU'RE NOT REALLY...?
YES. I HOPE TO MARRY HIM SOMEDAY!
...DON'T DO IT.
NO.
I'M NOT GIVING UP.

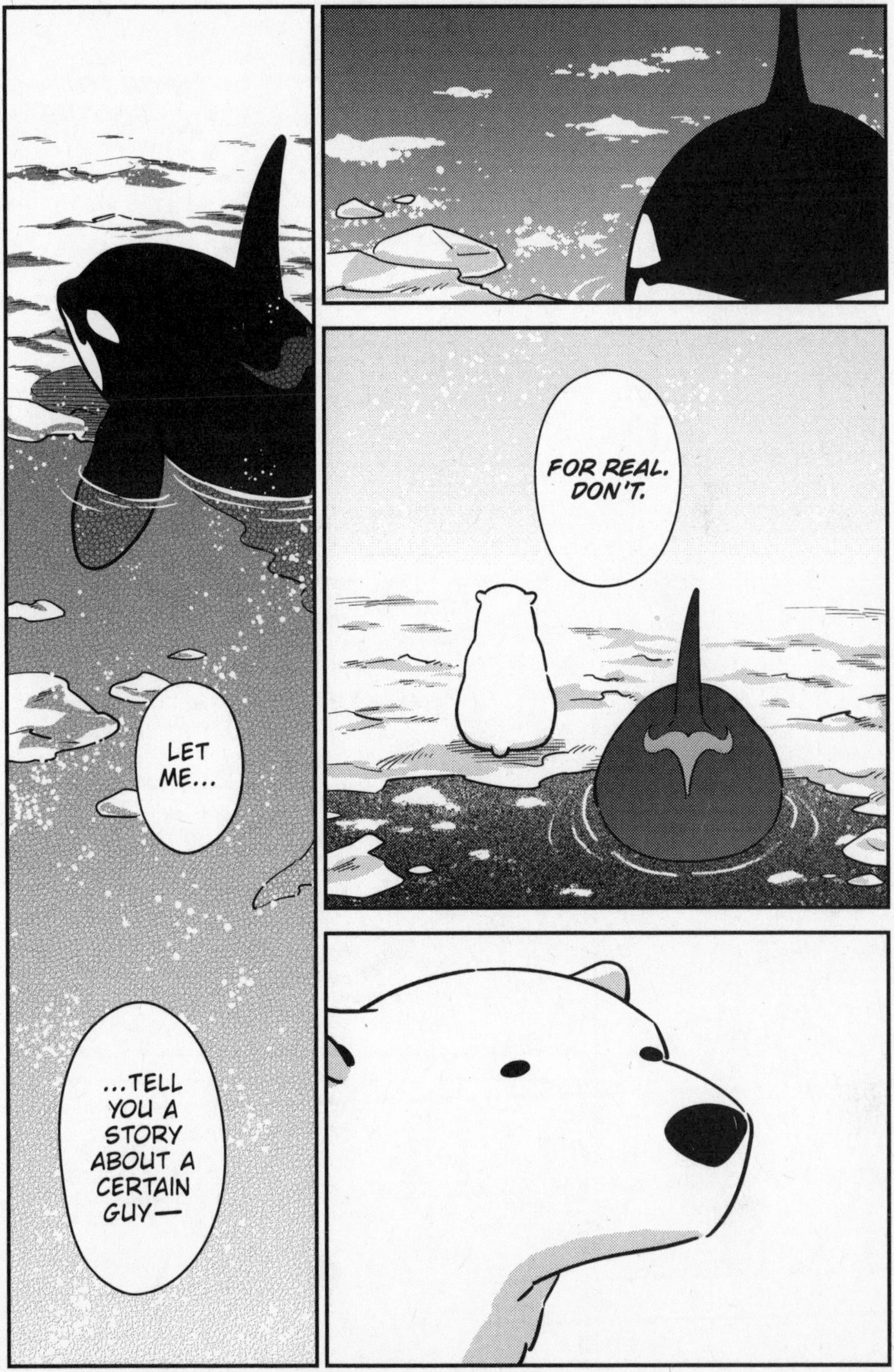
FOR REAL. DON'T.
LET ME...
...TELL YOU A STORY ABOUT A CERTAIN GUY—

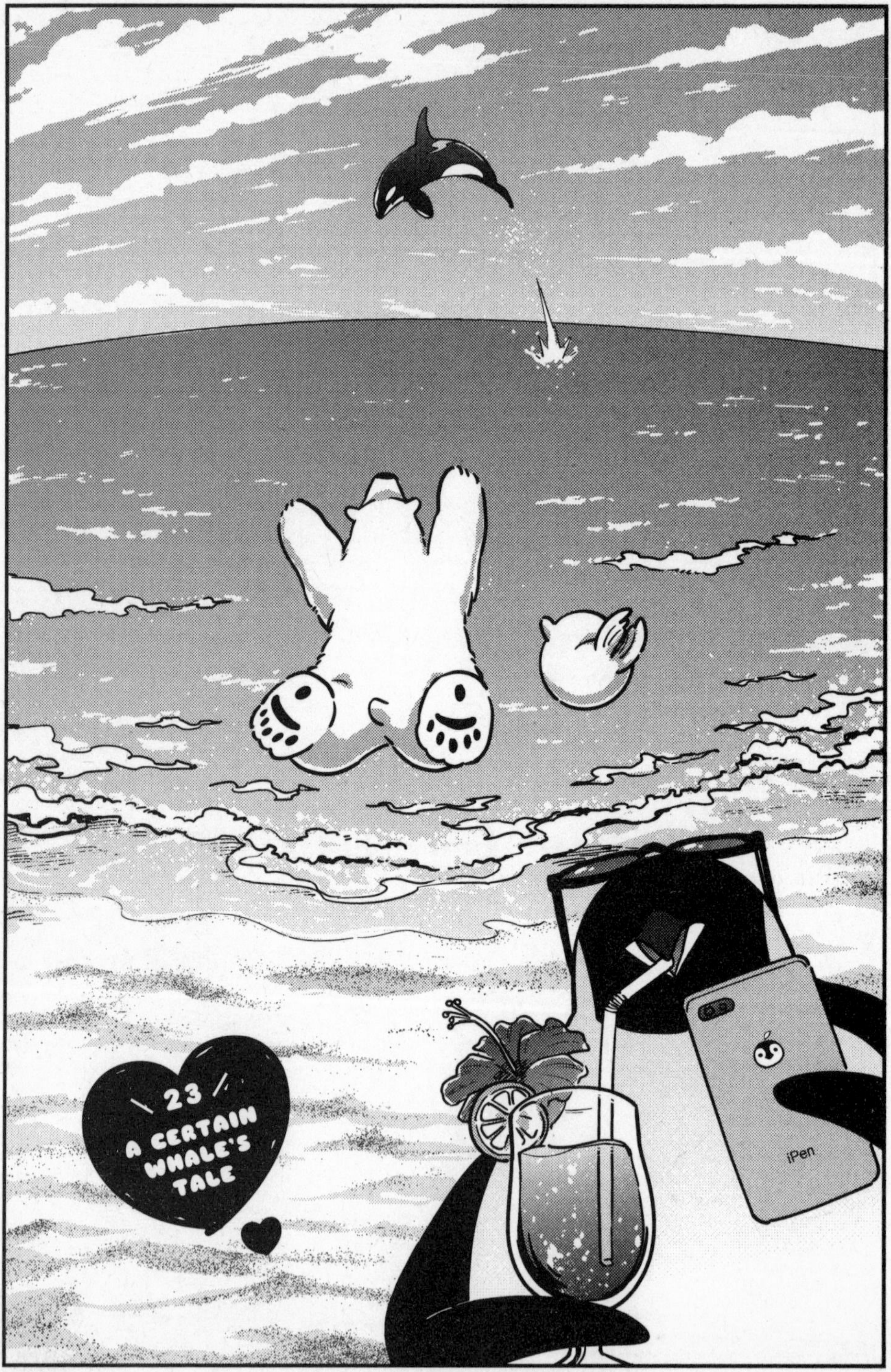
23
A CERTAIN WHALE'S TALE
iPen

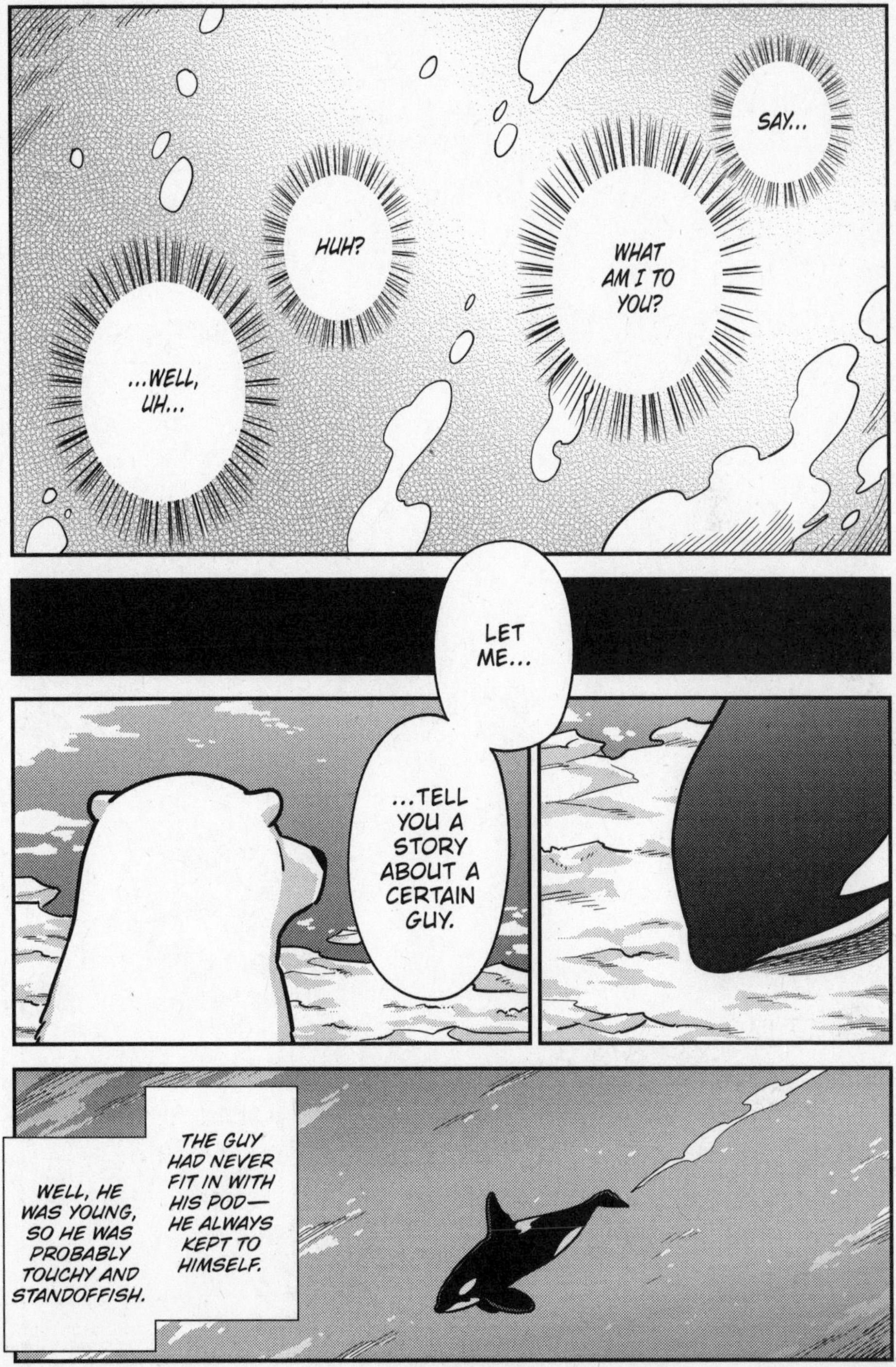
SAY...
WHAT AM I TO YOU?
HUH?
...WELL, UH...
LET ME...
...TELL YOU A STORY ABOUT A CERTAIN GUY.
THE GUY HAD NEVER FIT IN WITH HIS POD—HE ALWAYS KEPT TO HIMSELF.
WELL, HE WAS YOUNG, SO HE WAS PROBABLY TOUCHY AND STANDOFFISH.

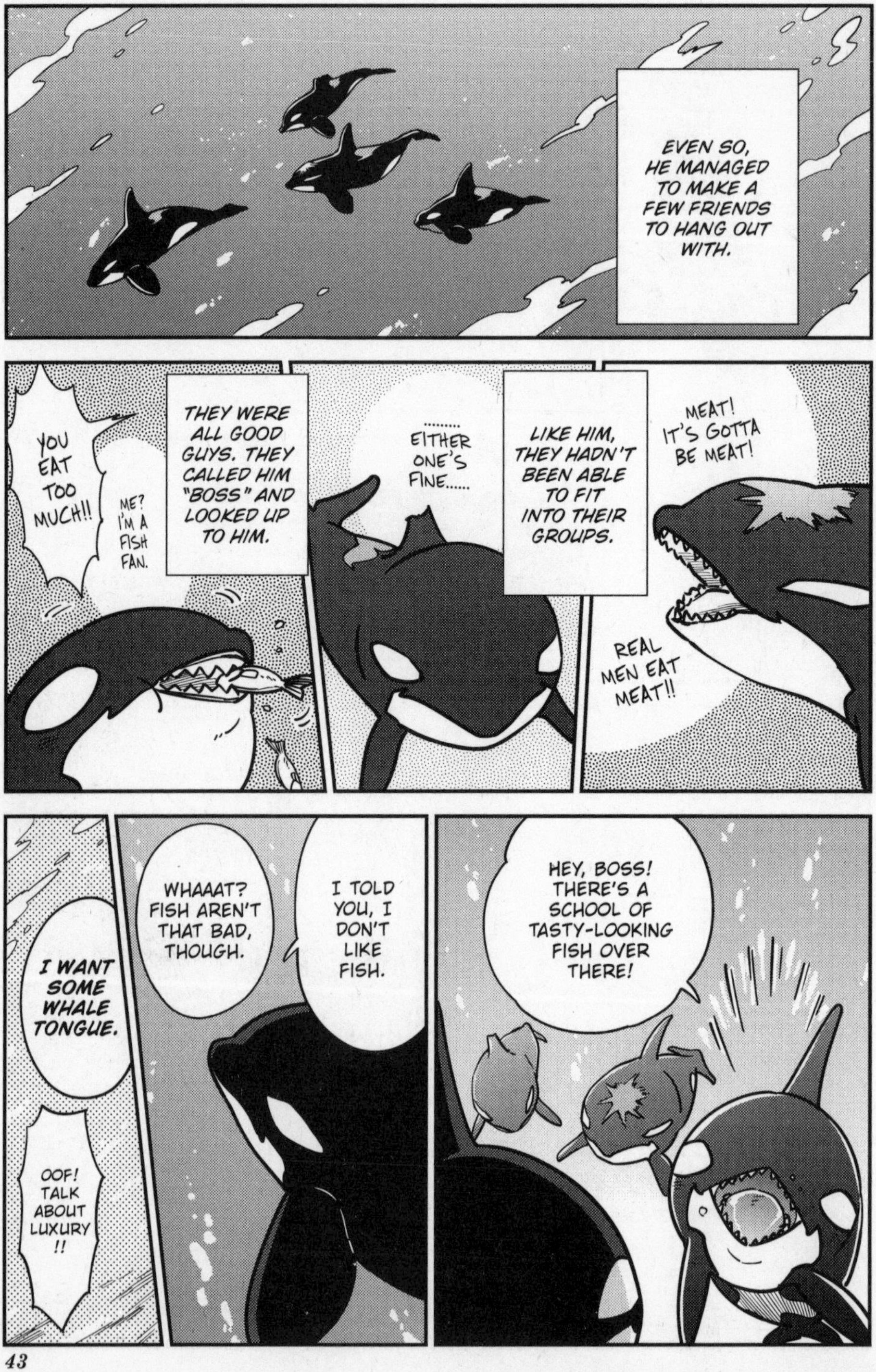
EVEN SO, HE MANAGED TO MAKE A FEW FRIENDS TO HANG OUT WITH.
MEAT! IT'S GOTTA BE MEAT!
REAL MEN EAT MEAT!!
LIKE HIM, THEY HADN'T BEEN ABLE TO FIT INTO THEIR GROUPS.
.... EITHER ONE'S FINE......
THEY WERE ALL GOOD GUYS. THEY CALLED HIM "BOSS" AND LOOKED UP TO HIM.
ME? I'M A FISH FAN.
YOU EAT TOO MUCH!!
HEY, BOSS! THERE'S A SCHOOL OF TASTY-LOOKING FISH OVER THERE!
I TOLD YOU, I DON'T LIKE FISH.
WHAAAT? FISH AREN'T THAT BAD, THOUGH.
I WANT SOME WHALE TONGUE.
OOF! TALK ABOUT LUXURY!!

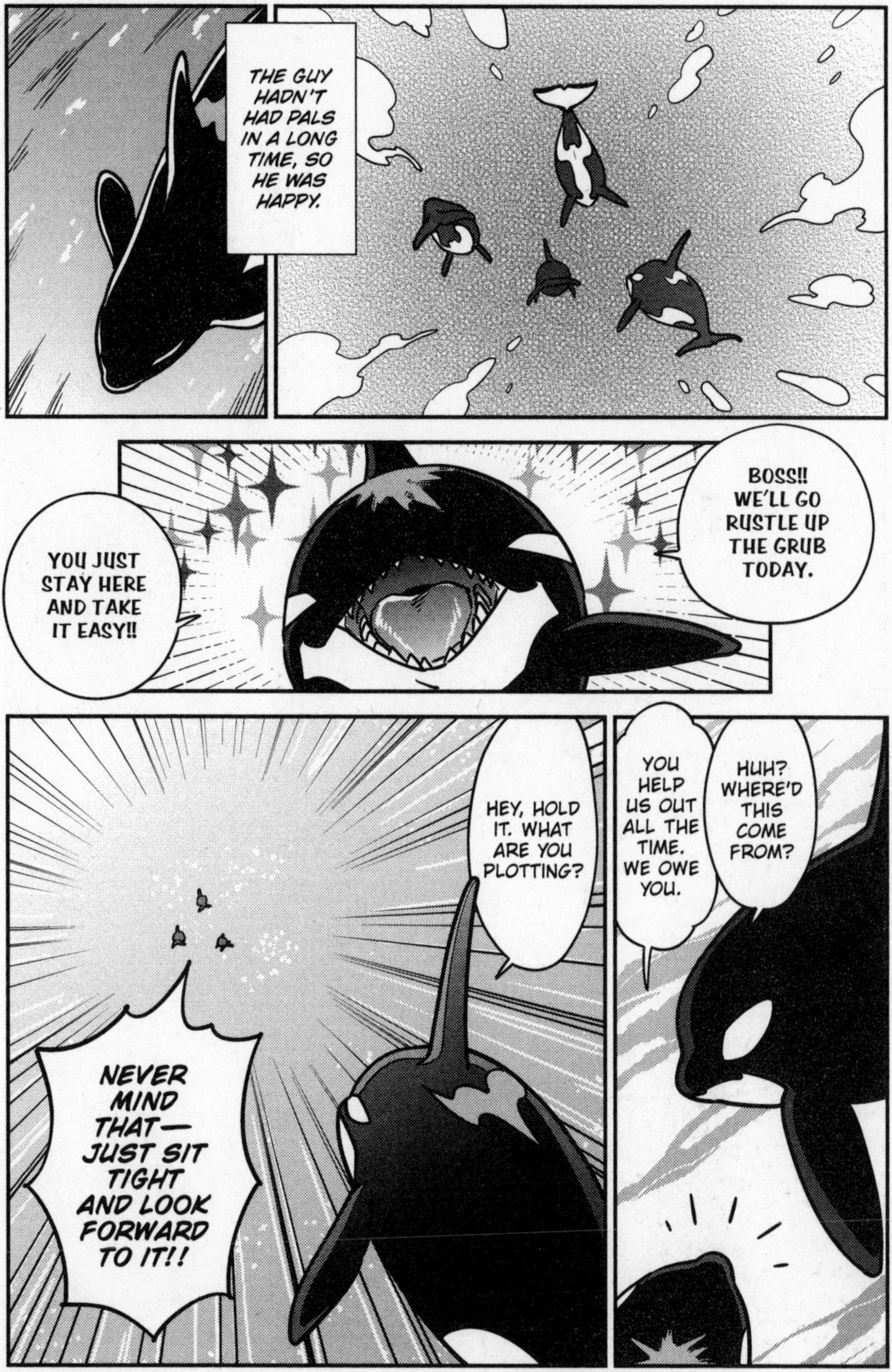
THE GUY HADN'T HAD PALS IN A LONG TIME, SO HE WAS HAPPY.
BOSS!! WE'LL GO RUSTLE UP THE GRUB TODAY.
YOU JUST STAY HERE AND TAKE IT EASY!!
HUH? WHERE'D THIS COME FROM?
YOU HELP US OUT ALL THE TIME. WE OWE YOU.
HEY, HOLD IT. WHAT ARE YOU PLOTTING?
NEVER MIND THAT— JUST SIT TIGHT AND LOOK FORWARD TO IT!!

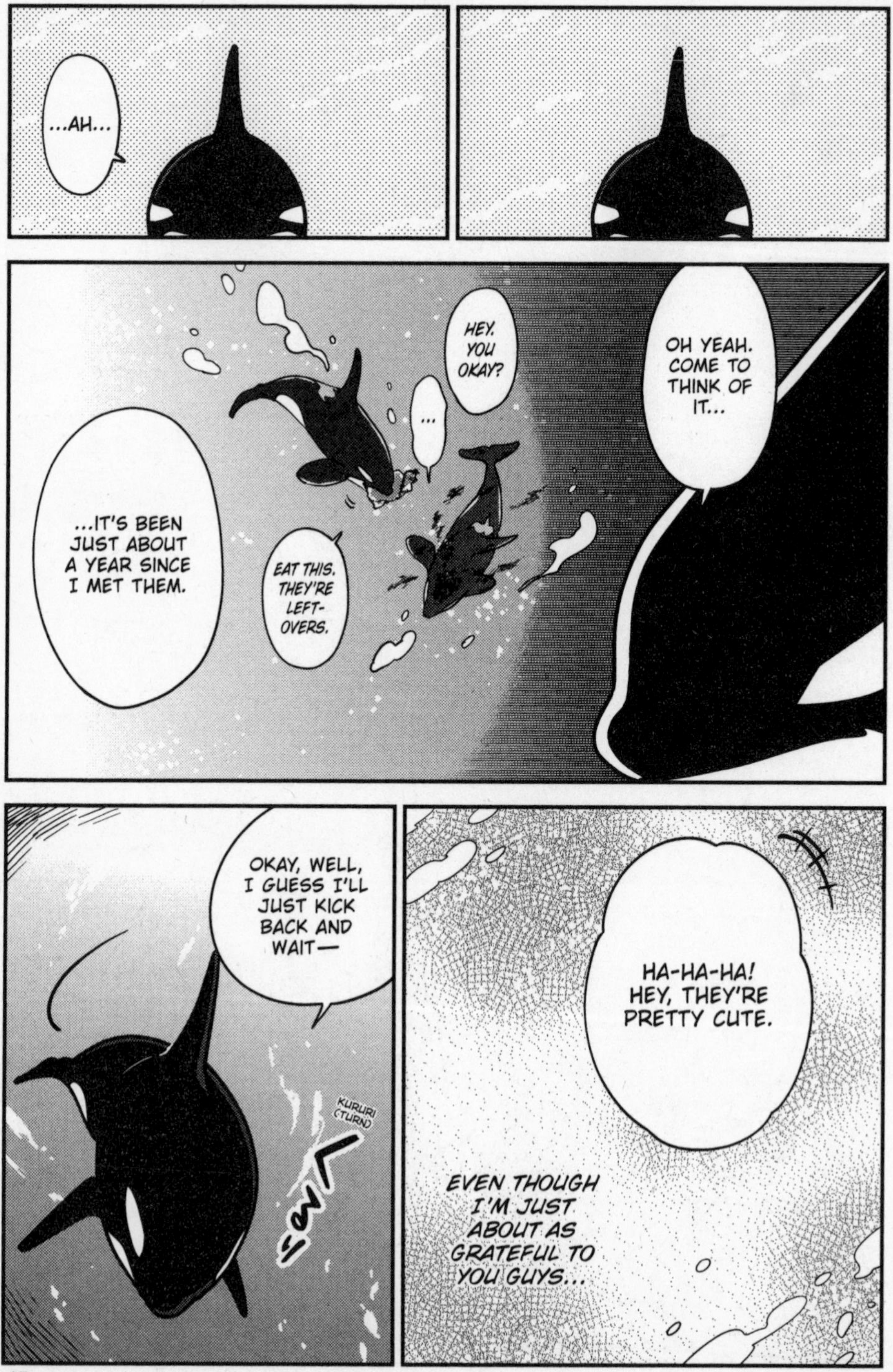

...AH...
OH YEAH. COME TO THINK OF IT...
HEY. YOU OKAY?
...
EAT THIS. THEY'RE LEFT-OVERS.
...IT'S BEEN JUST ABOUT A YEAR SINCE I MET THEM.
HA-HA-HA! HEY, THEY'RE PRETTY CUTE.
EVEN THOUGH I'M JUST ABOUT AS GRATEFUL TO YOU GUYS...
OKAY, WELL, I GUESS I'LL JUST KICK BACK AND WAIT—
KURURI (TURN)

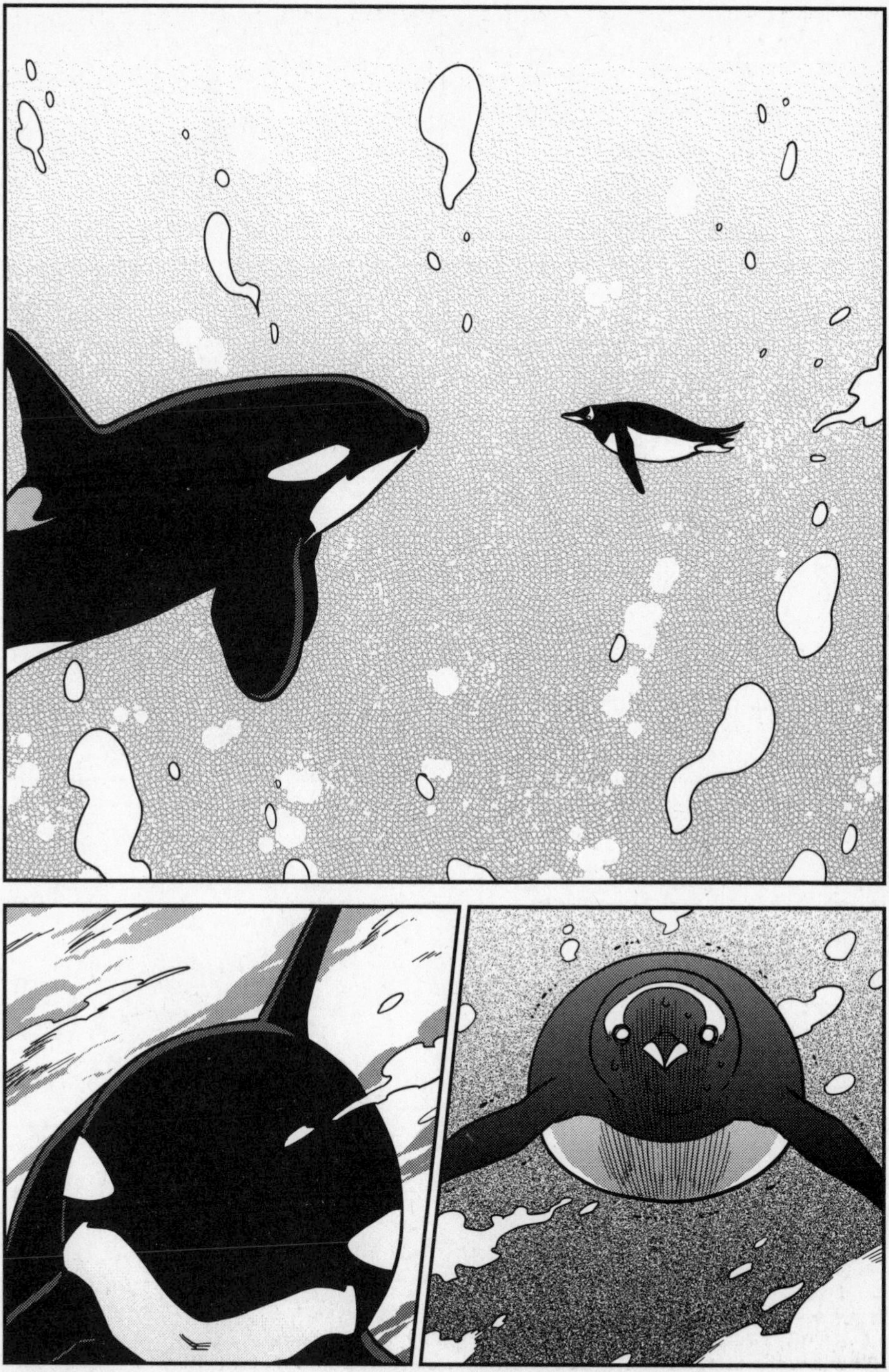

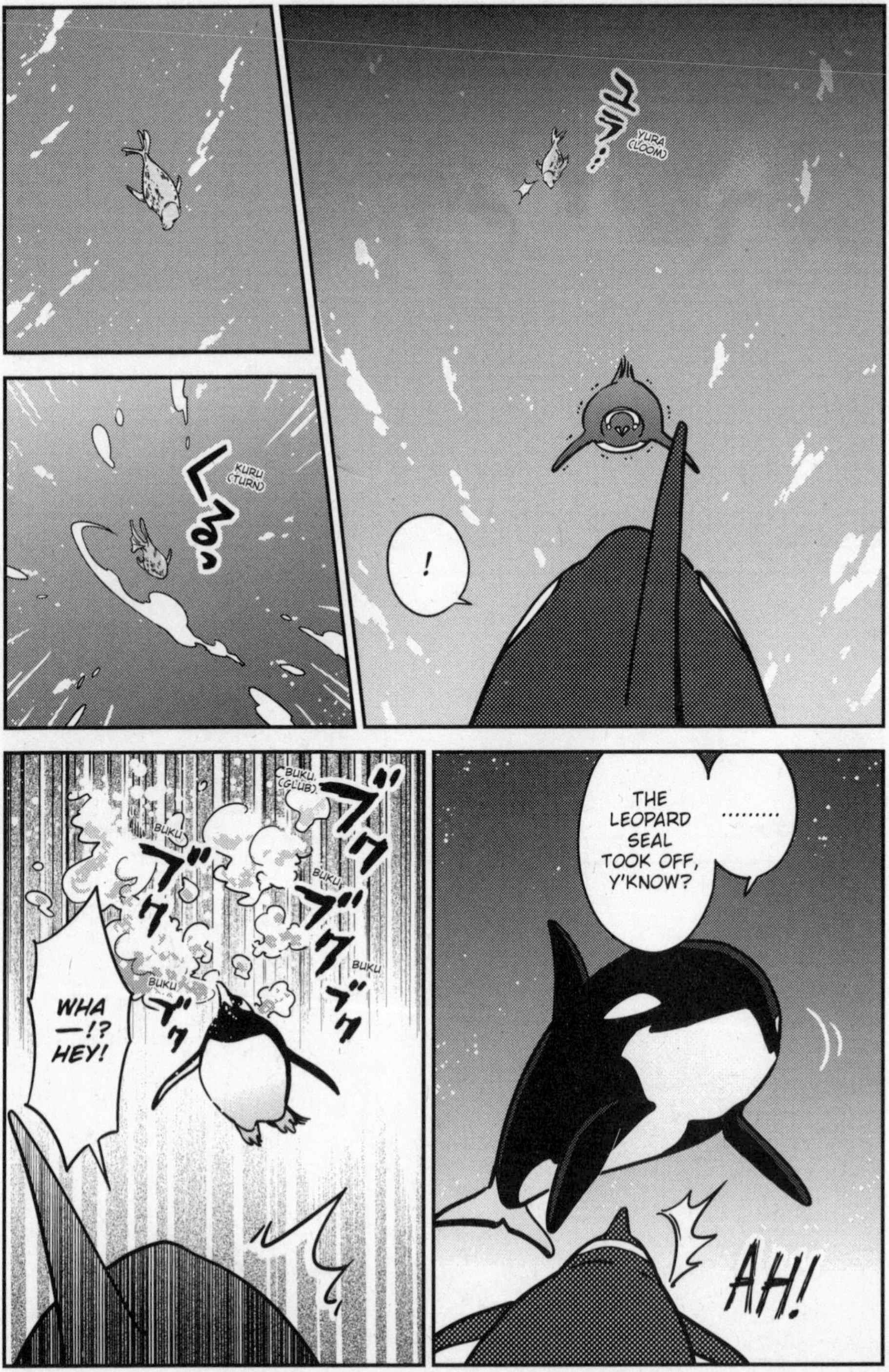
ユラ…
YURA (LOOM)
!
くるっ
KURU (TURN)
....
THE LEOPARD SEAL TOOK OFF, Y'KNOW?
AH!
ブクブクブクブク
BUKU (GLUB)
BUKU
BUKU
BUKU
BUKU
WHA—!? HEY!

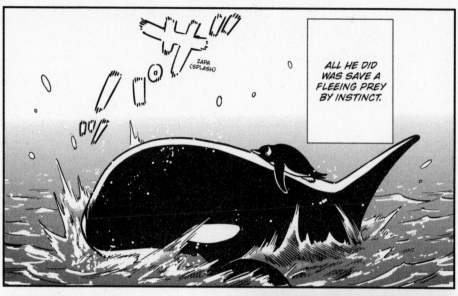

ZAPA
(SPLASH)

ALL HE DID WAS SAVE A FLEEING PREY BY INSTINCT.

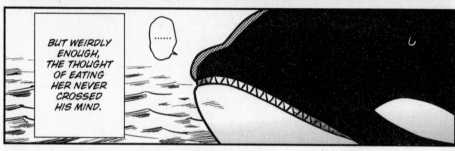

BUT WEIRDLY ENOUGH, THE THOUGHT OF EATING HER NEVER CROSSED HIS MIND.

......

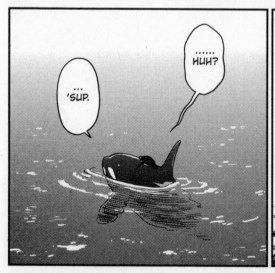

...... HUH?

... 'SUP.

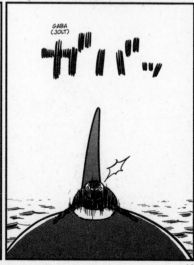

GABA
(JOLT)

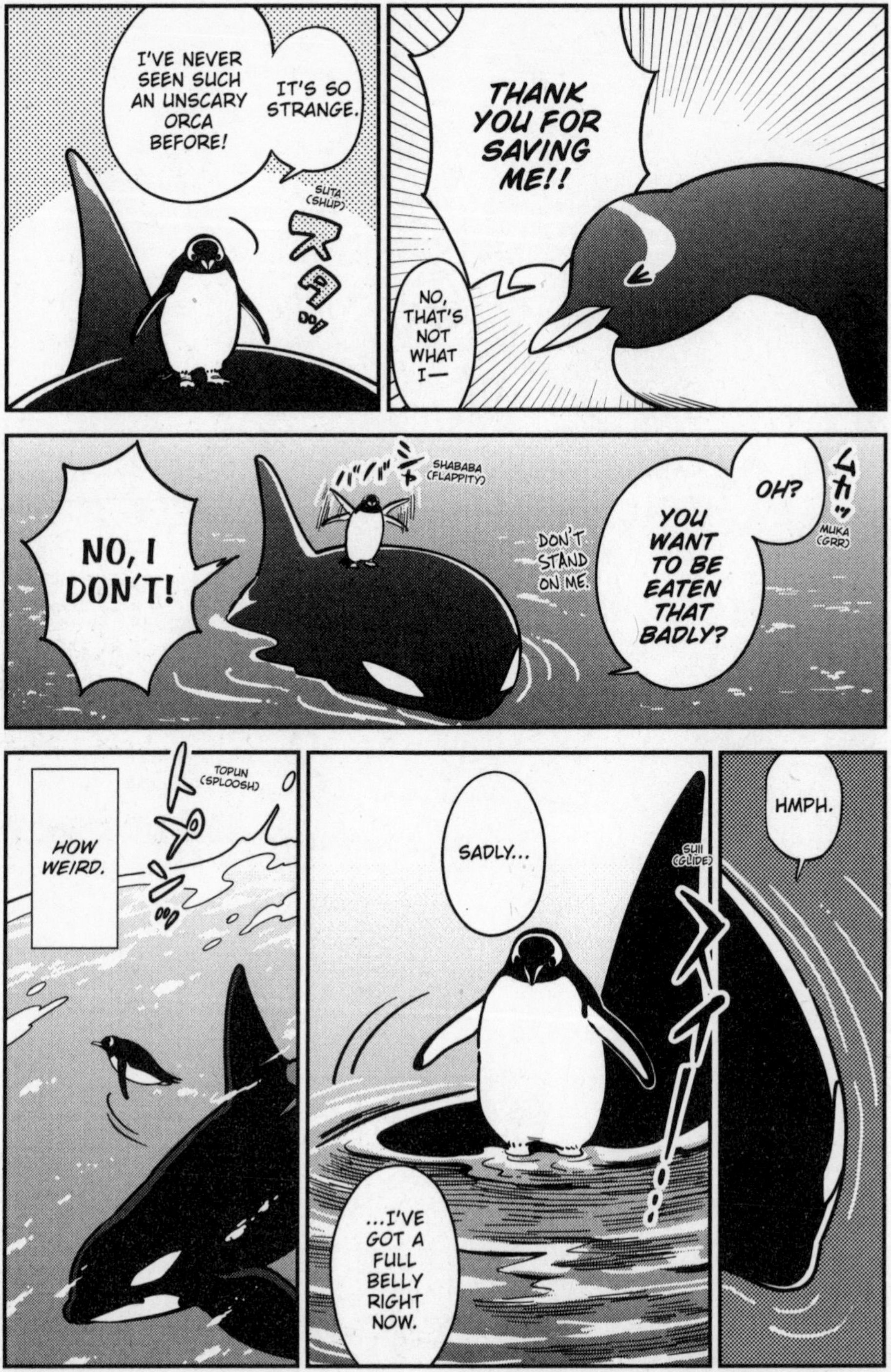
THANK YOU FOR SAVING ME!!
NO, THAT'S NOT WHAT I—
IT'S SO STRANGE.
I'VE NEVER SEEN SUCH AN UNSCARY ORCA BEFORE!
SUTA (SHUP)
MUKA (GRR)
OH?
YOU WANT TO BE EATEN THAT BADLY?
DON'T STAND ON ME.
SHABABA (FLAPPITY)
NO, I DON'T!
HMPH.
SUII (GLIDE)
SADLY...
...I'VE GOT A FULL BELLY RIGHT NOW.
TOPUN (SPLOOSH)
HOW WEIRD.

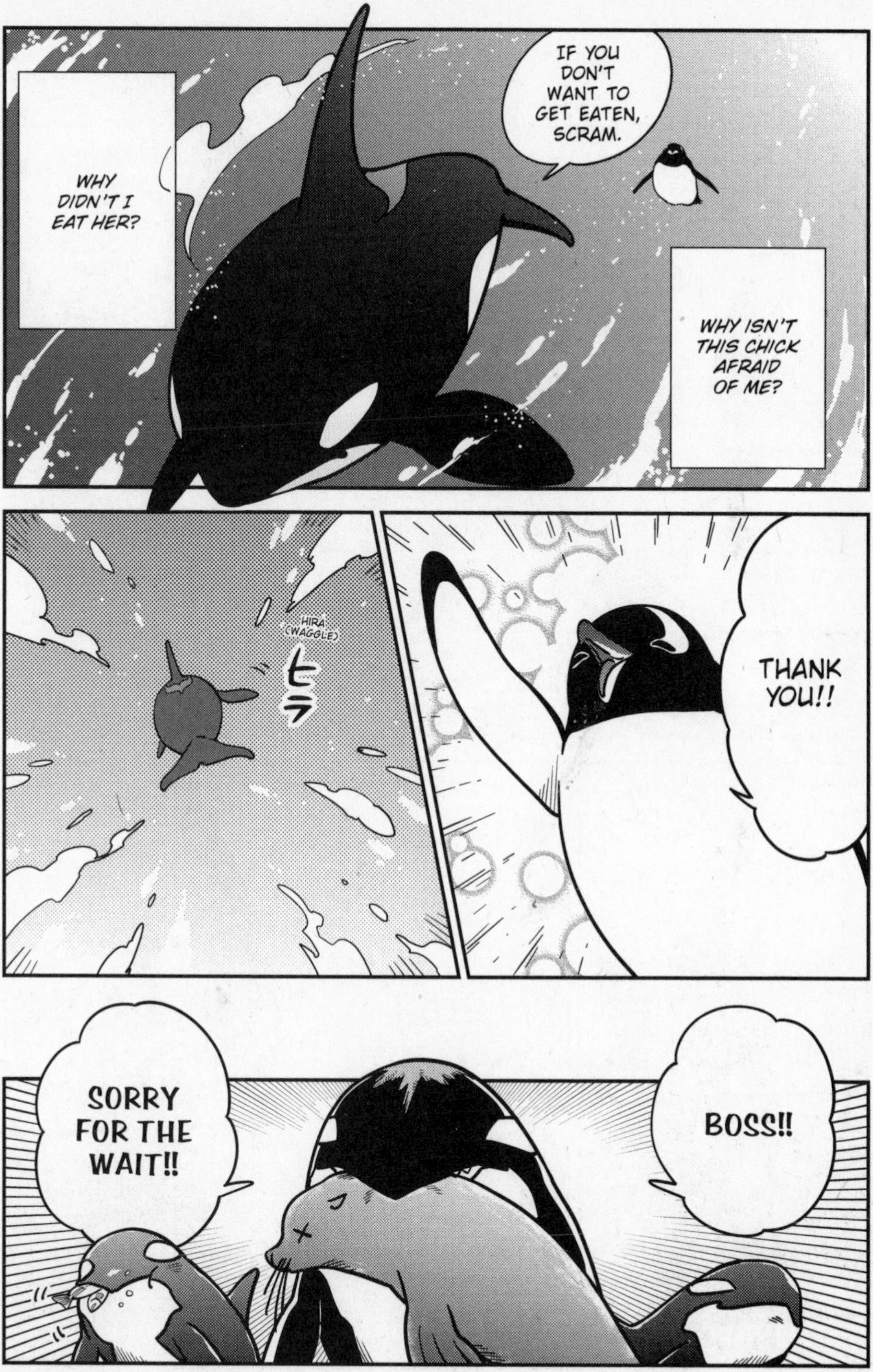
IF YOU DON'T WANT TO GET EATEN, SCRAM.
WHY ISN'T THIS CHICK AFRAID OF ME?
WHY DIDN'T I EAT HER?
THANK YOU!!
HIRA (WAGGLE)
ヒラ
BOSS!!
SORRY FOR THE WAIT!!

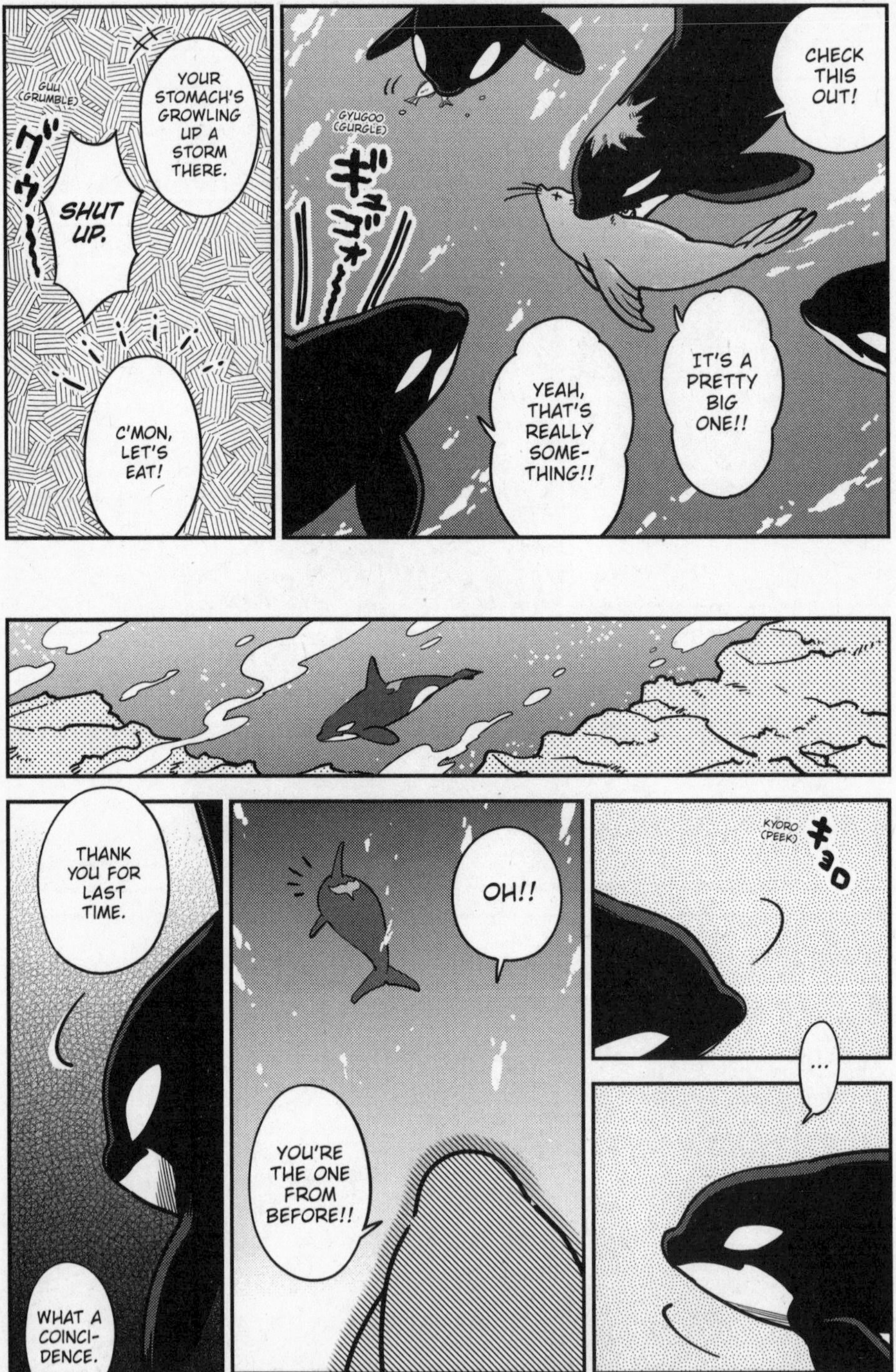
CHECK THIS OUT!
GYUGOO (GURGLE)
ギュゴォー
IT'S A PRETTY BIG ONE!!
YEAH, THAT'S REALLY SOMETHING!!
YOUR STOMACH'S GROWLING UP A STORM THERE.
GUU (GRUMBLE)
グゥ〜
SHUT UP.
C'MON, LET'S EAT!
KYORO (PEEK)
キョロ
...
OH!!
YOU'RE THE ONE FROM BEFORE!!
THANK YOU FOR LAST TIME.
WHAT A COINCIDENCE.

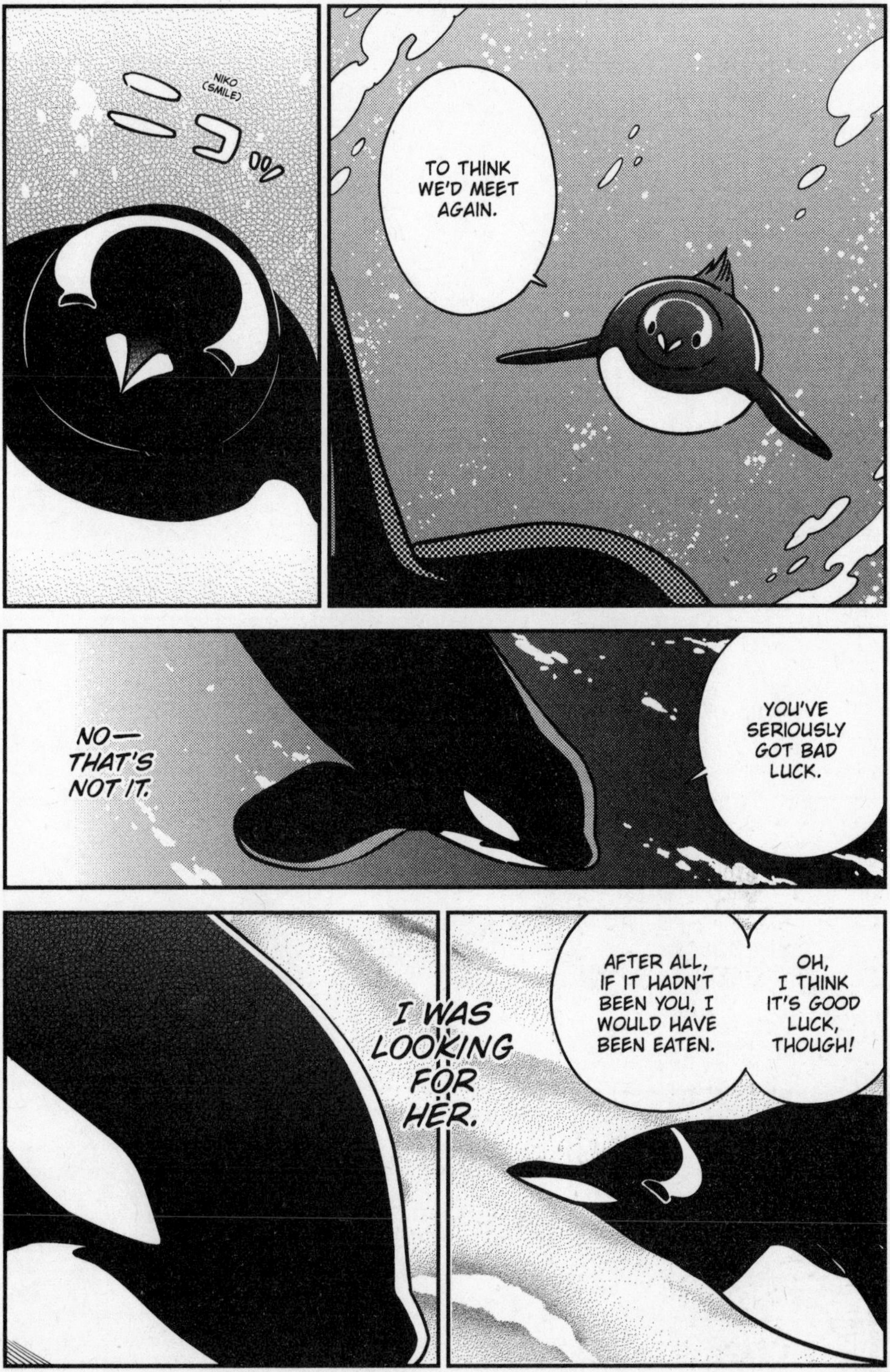
TO THINK WE'D MEET AGAIN.
NIKO (SMILE)
YOU'VE SERIOUSLY GOT BAD LUCK.
NO— THAT'S NOT IT.
OH, I THINK IT'S GOOD LUCK, THOUGH!
AFTER ALL, IF IT HADN'T BEEN YOU, I WOULD HAVE BEEN EATEN.
I WAS LOOKING FOR HER.

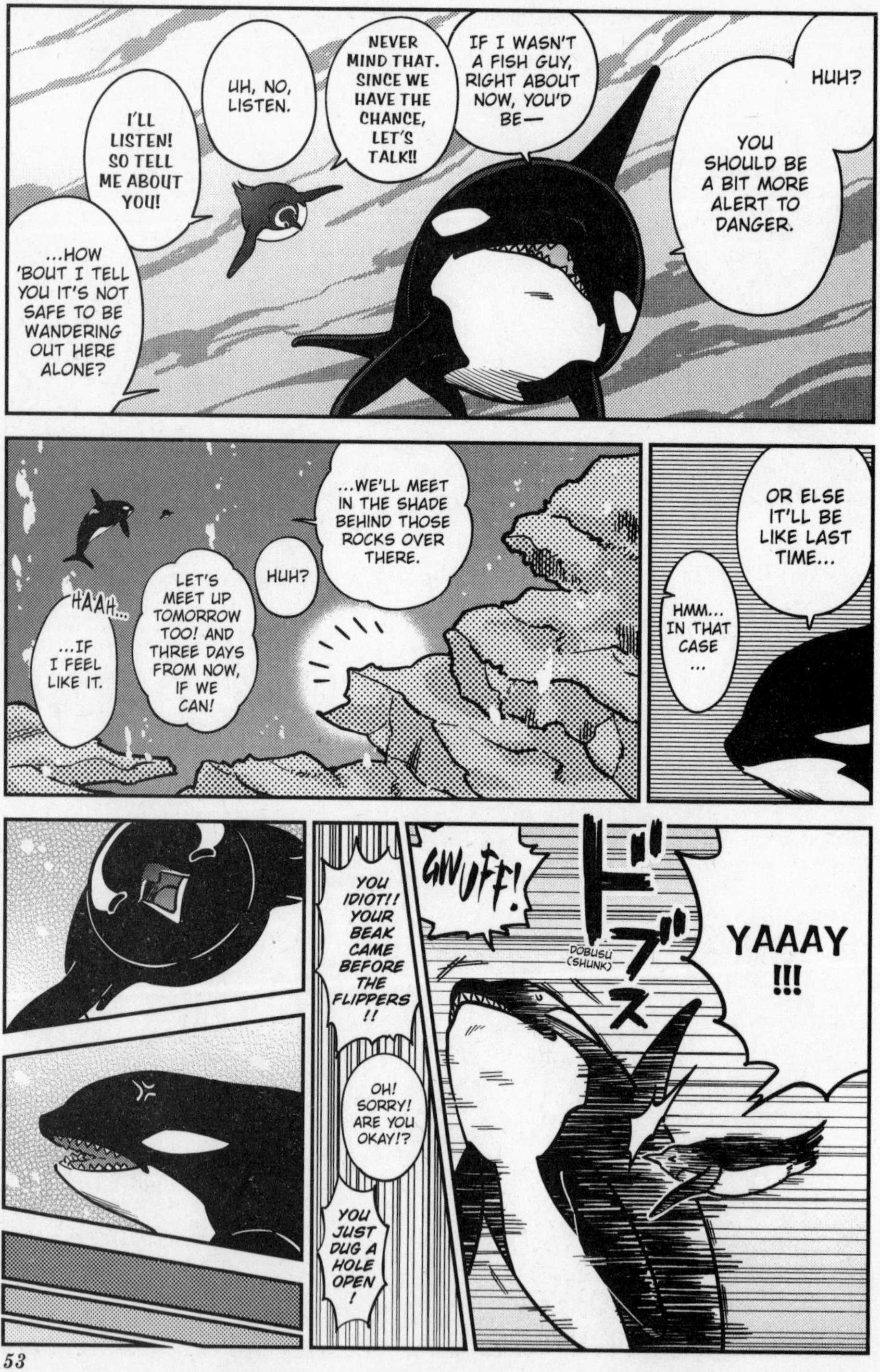
HUH?
YOU SHOULD BE A BIT MORE ALERT TO DANGER.
IF I WASN'T A FISH GUY, RIGHT ABOUT NOW, YOU'D BE—
NEVER MIND THAT. SINCE WE HAVE THE CHANCE, LET'S TALK!!
UH, NO, LISTEN.
I'LL LISTEN! SO TELL ME ABOUT YOU!
...HOW 'BOUT I TELL YOU IT'S NOT SAFE TO BE WANDERING OUT HERE ALONE?
OR ELSE IT'LL BE LIKE LAST TIME...
HMM... IN THAT CASE...
...WE'LL MEET IN THE SHADE BEHIND THOSE ROCKS OVER THERE.
HUH?
LET'S MEET UP TOMORROW TOO! AND THREE DAYS FROM NOW, IF WE CAN!
HAAH...
...IF I FEEL LIKE IT.
YAAAY!!!
ドブス
DOBUSU (SHUNK)
GWUFF!
YOU IDIOT!! YOUR BEAK CAME BEFORE THE FLIPPERS!!
OH! SORRY! ARE YOU OKAY!?
YOU JUST DUG A HOLE OPEN!

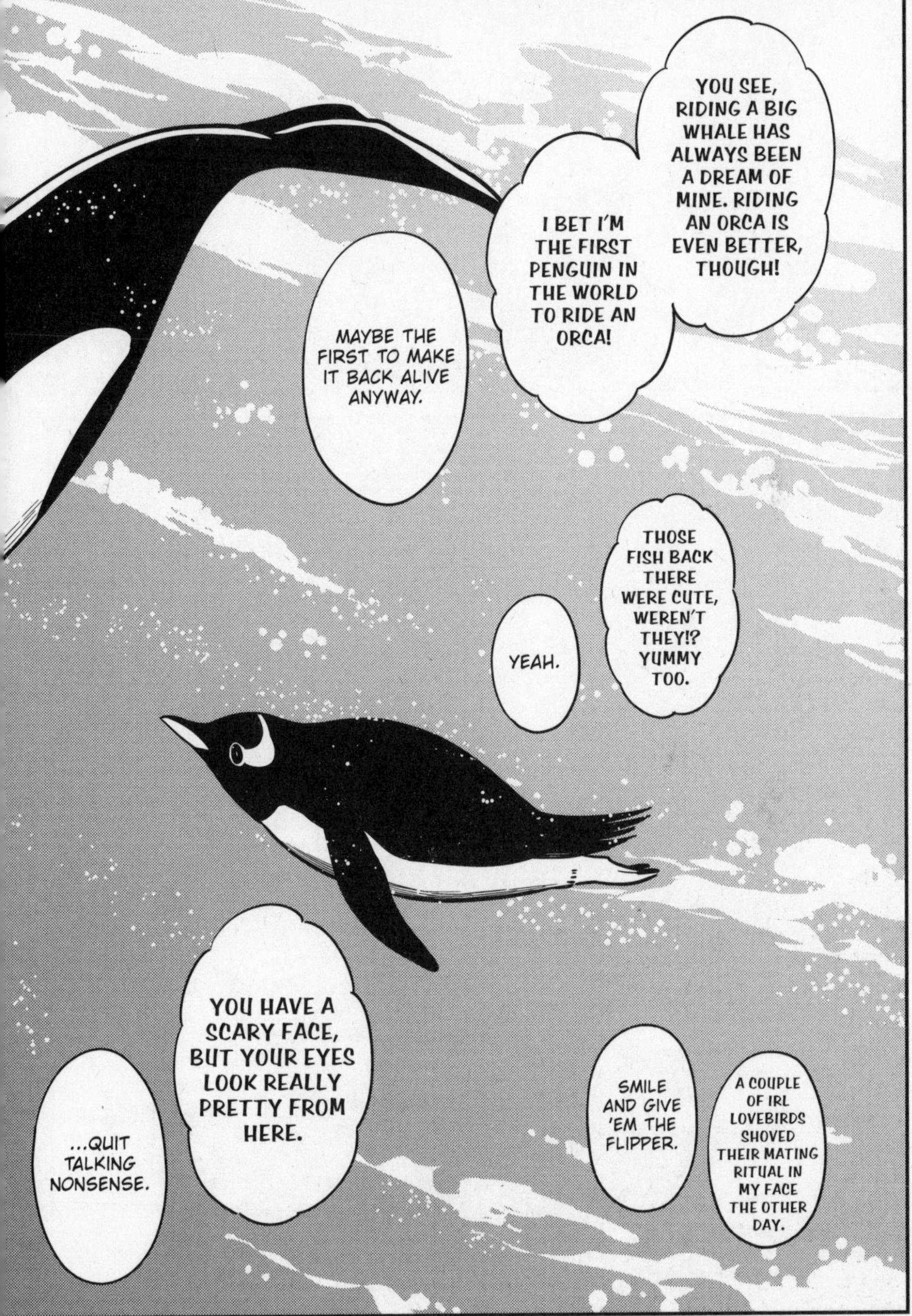
YOU SEE, RIDING A BIG WHALE HAS ALWAYS BEEN A DREAM OF MINE. RIDING AN ORCA IS EVEN BETTER, THOUGH!
I BET I'M THE FIRST PENGUIN IN THE WORLD TO RIDE AN ORCA!
MAYBE THE FIRST TO MAKE IT BACK ALIVE ANYWAY.
THOSE FISH BACK THERE WERE CUTE, WEREN'T THEY!? YUMMY TOO.
YEAH.
A COUPLE OF IRL LOVEBIRDS SHOVED THEIR MATING RITUAL IN MY FACE THE OTHER DAY.
SMILE AND GIVE 'EM THE FLIPPER.
YOU HAVE A SCARY FACE, BUT YOUR EYES LOOK REALLY PRETTY FROM HERE.
...QUIT TALKING NONSENSE.

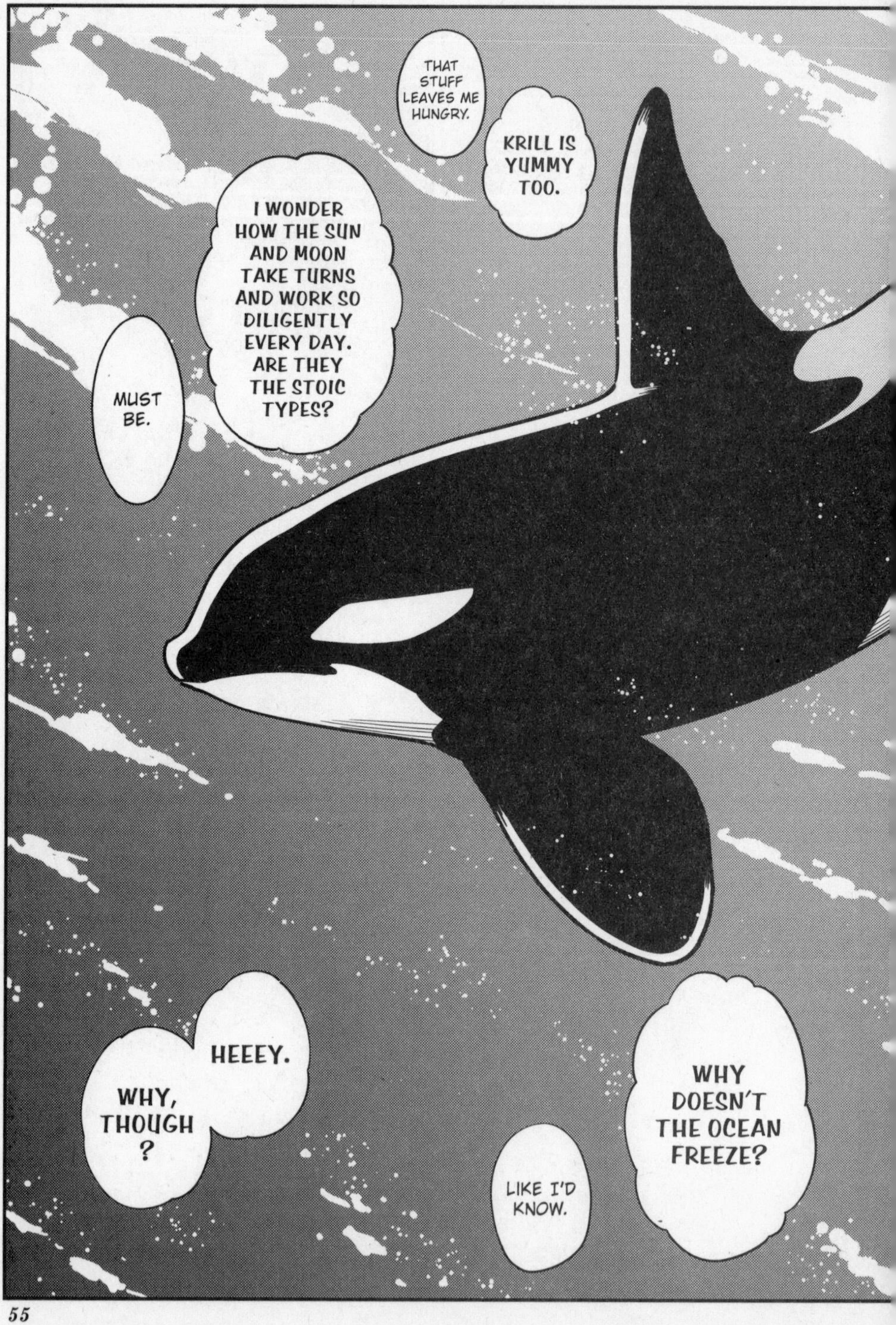
KRILL IS YUMMY TOO.
THAT STUFF LEAVES ME HUNGRY.
I WONDER HOW THE SUN AND MOON TAKE TURNS AND WORK SO DILIGENTLY EVERY DAY. ARE THEY THE STOIC TYPES?
MUST BE.
WHY DOESN'T THE OCEAN FREEZE?
LIKE I'D KNOW.
HEEEY.
WHY, THOUGH?

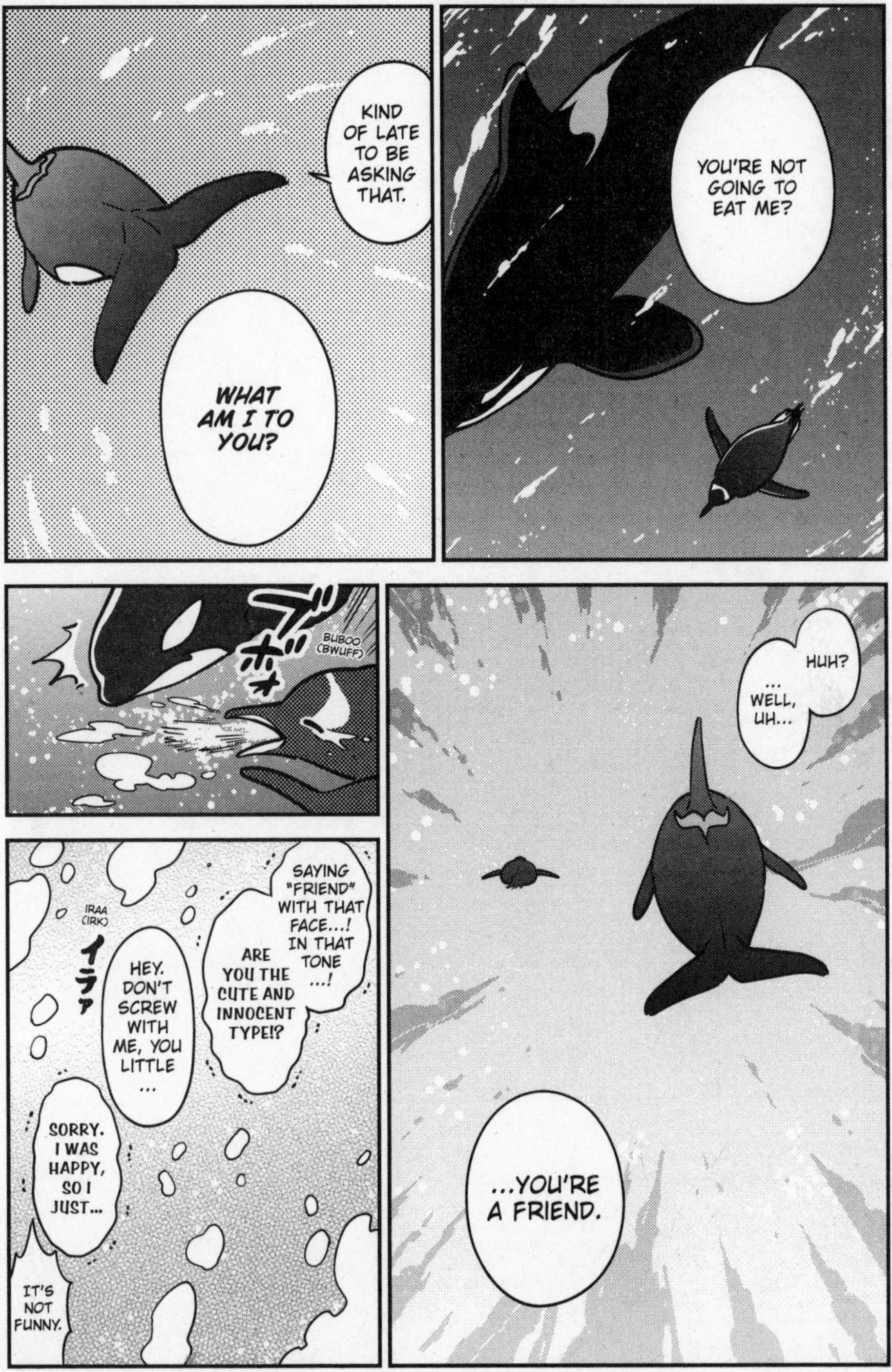
YOU'RE NOT GOING TO EAT ME?
KIND OF LATE TO BE ASKING THAT.
WHAT AM I TO YOU?
HUH?
... WELL, UH...
...YOU'RE A FRIEND.
ブボォ
BUBOO (BWUFF)
SAYING "FRIEND" WITH THAT FACE...! IN THAT TONE...!
ARE YOU THE CUTE AND INNOCENT TYPE!?
HEY. DON'T SCREW WITH ME, YOU LITTLE...
IRAA (IRK)
イラァ
SORRY. I WAS HAPPY, SO I JUST...
IT'S NOT FUNNY.

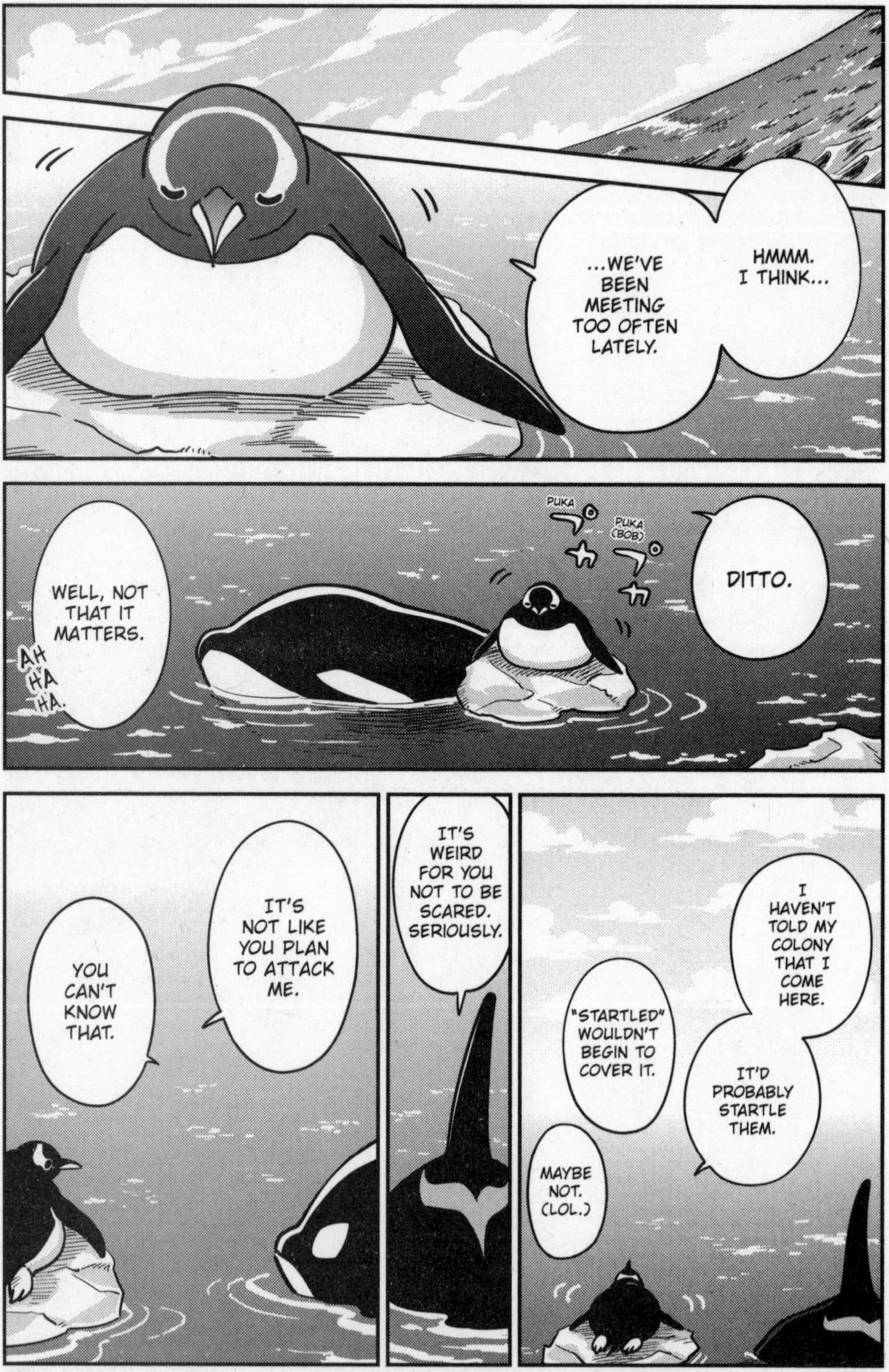
HMMM. I THINK...
...WE'VE BEEN MEETING TOO OFTEN LATELY.
DITTO.
PUKA
PUKA (BOB)
WELL, NOT THAT IT MATTERS.
AH HA HA.
I HAVEN'T TOLD MY COLONY THAT I COME HERE.
IT'D PROBABLY STARTLE THEM.
"STARTLED" WOULDN'T BEGIN TO COVER IT.
MAYBE NOT. (LOL.)
IT'S WEIRD FOR YOU NOT TO BE SCARED. SERIOUSLY.
IT'S NOT LIKE YOU PLAN TO ATTACK ME.
YOU CAN'T KNOW THAT.

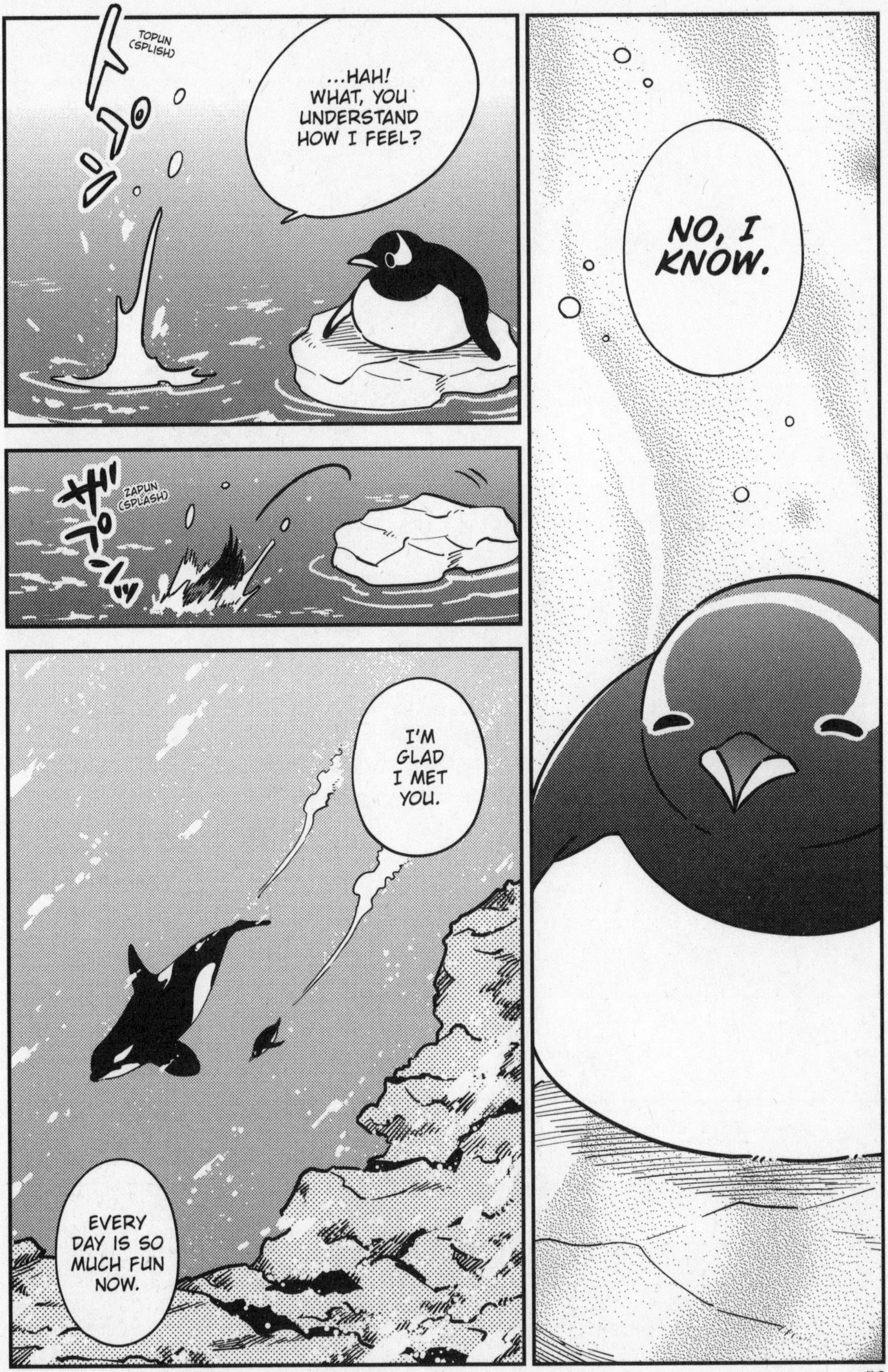
NO, I KNOW.
TOPUN (SPLISH)
...HAH! WHAT, YOU UNDERSTAND HOW I FEEL?
ZAPUN (SPLASH)
I'M GLAD I MET YOU.
EVERY DAY IS SO MUCH FUN NOW.

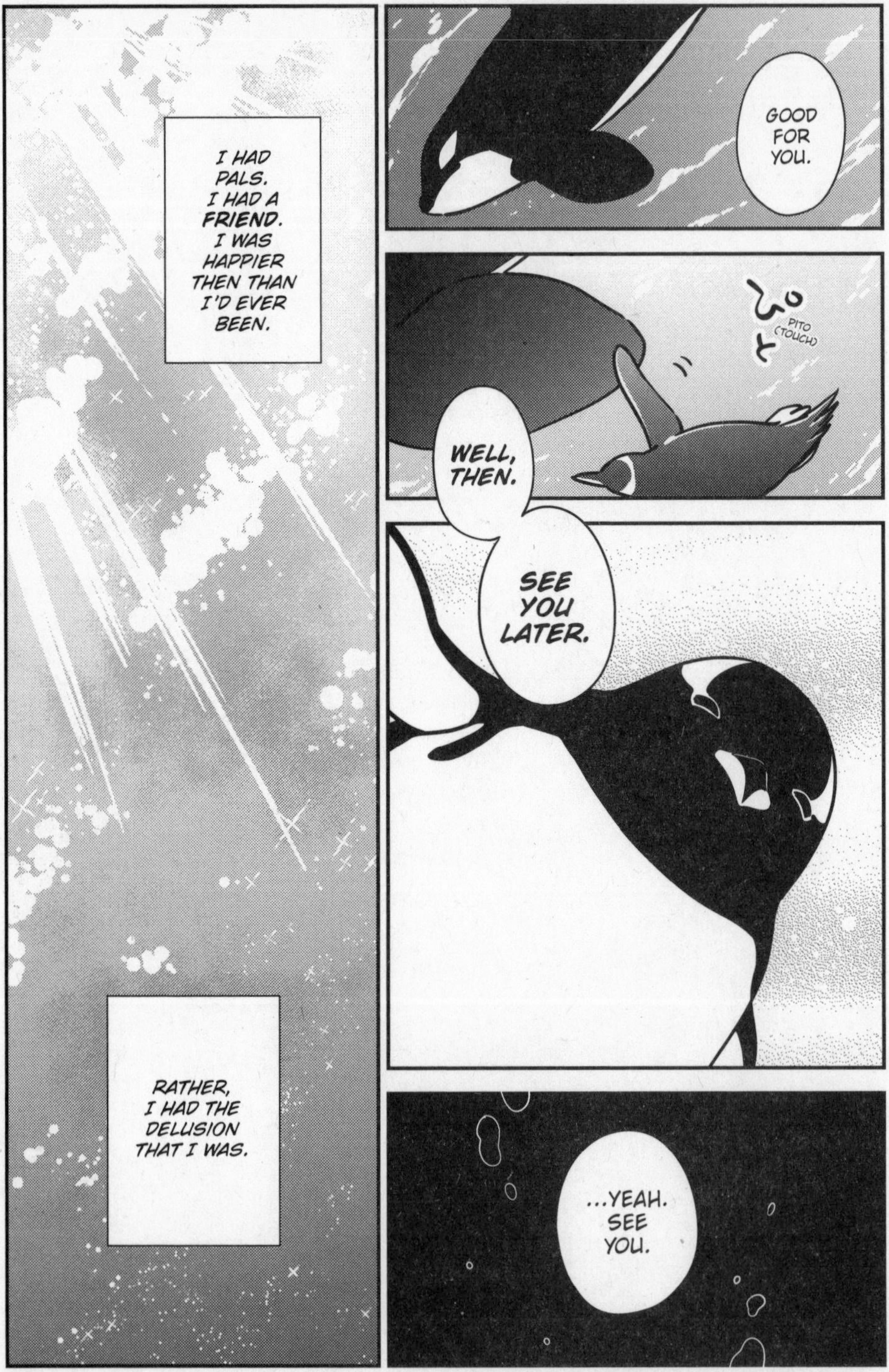
GOOD FOR YOU.
ぴと
PITO (TOUCH)
WELL, THEN.
SEE YOU LATER.
...YEAH. SEE YOU.
I HAD PALS. I HAD A **FRIEND**. I WAS HAPPIER THEN THAN I'D EVER BEEN.
RATHER, I HAD THE DELUSION THAT I WAS.

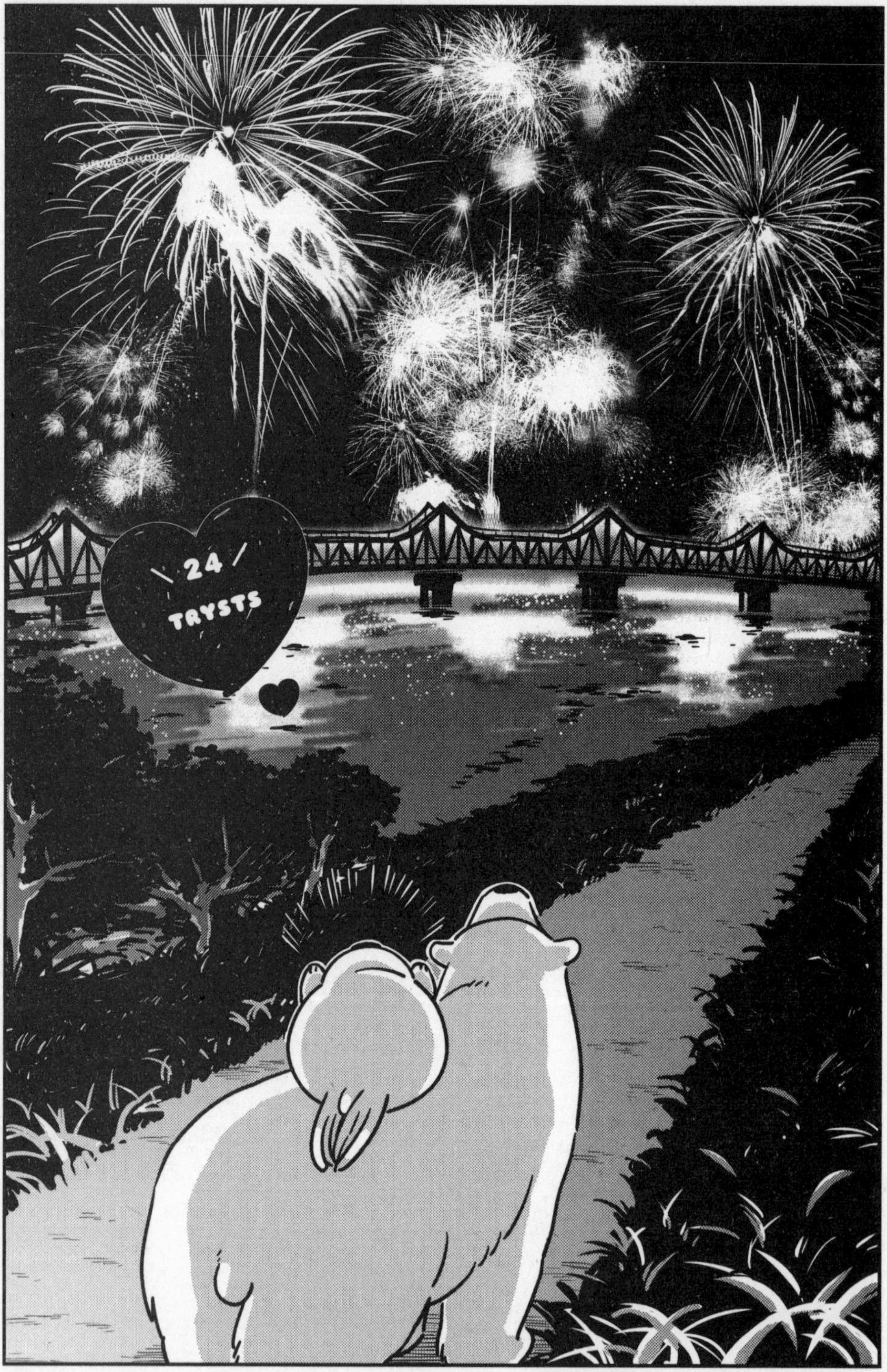
24
TRYSTS

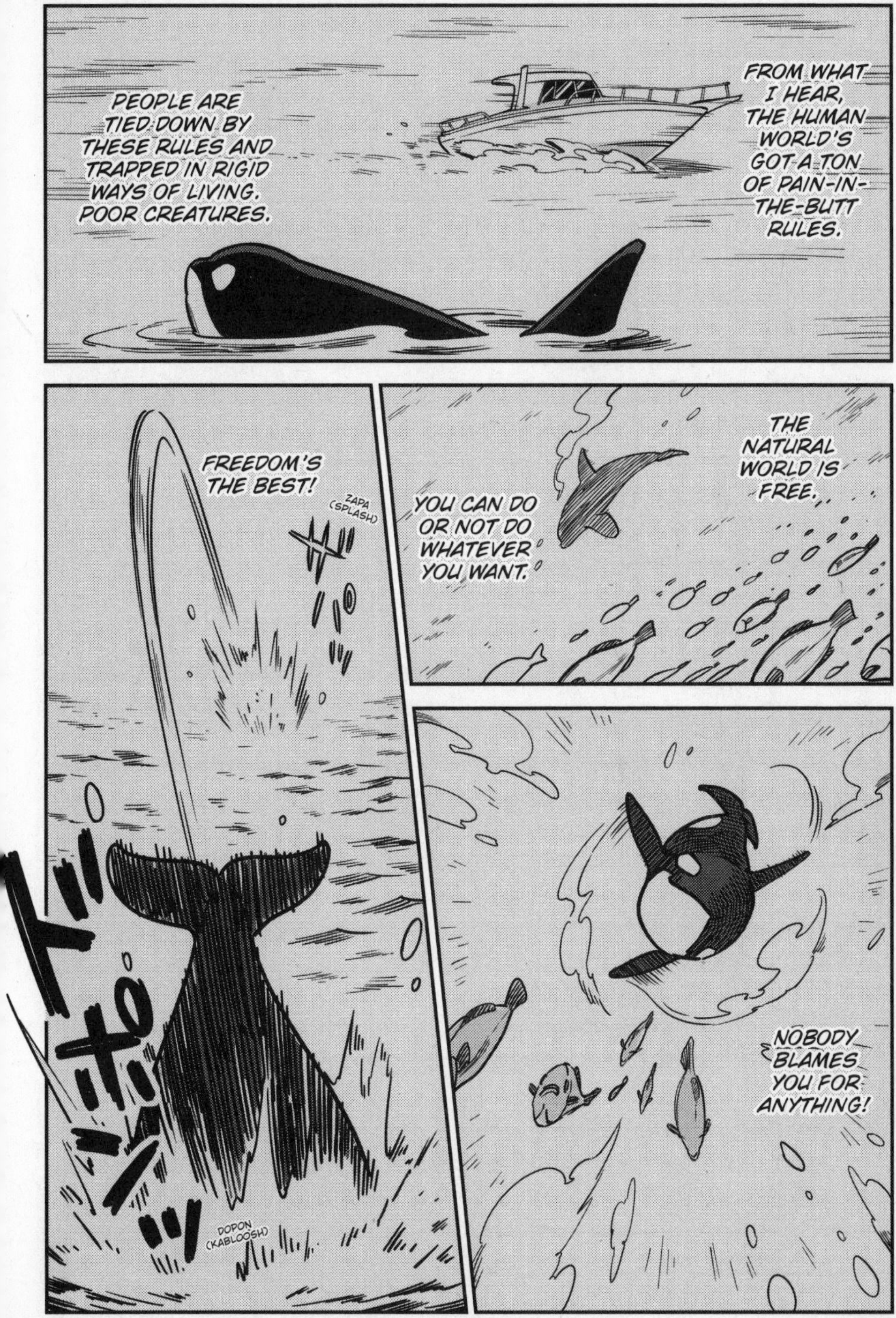
FROM WHAT I HEAR, THE HUMAN WORLD'S GOT A TON OF PAIN-IN-THE-BUTT RULES.
PEOPLE ARE TIED DOWN BY THESE RULES AND TRAPPED IN RIGID WAYS OF LIVING. POOR CREATURES.
THE NATURAL WORLD IS FREE.
YOU CAN DO OR NOT DO WHATEVER YOU WANT.
NOBODY BLAMES YOU FOR ANYTHING!
FREEDOM'S THE BEST!
ZAPA (SPLASH)
DOPON (KABLOOSH)

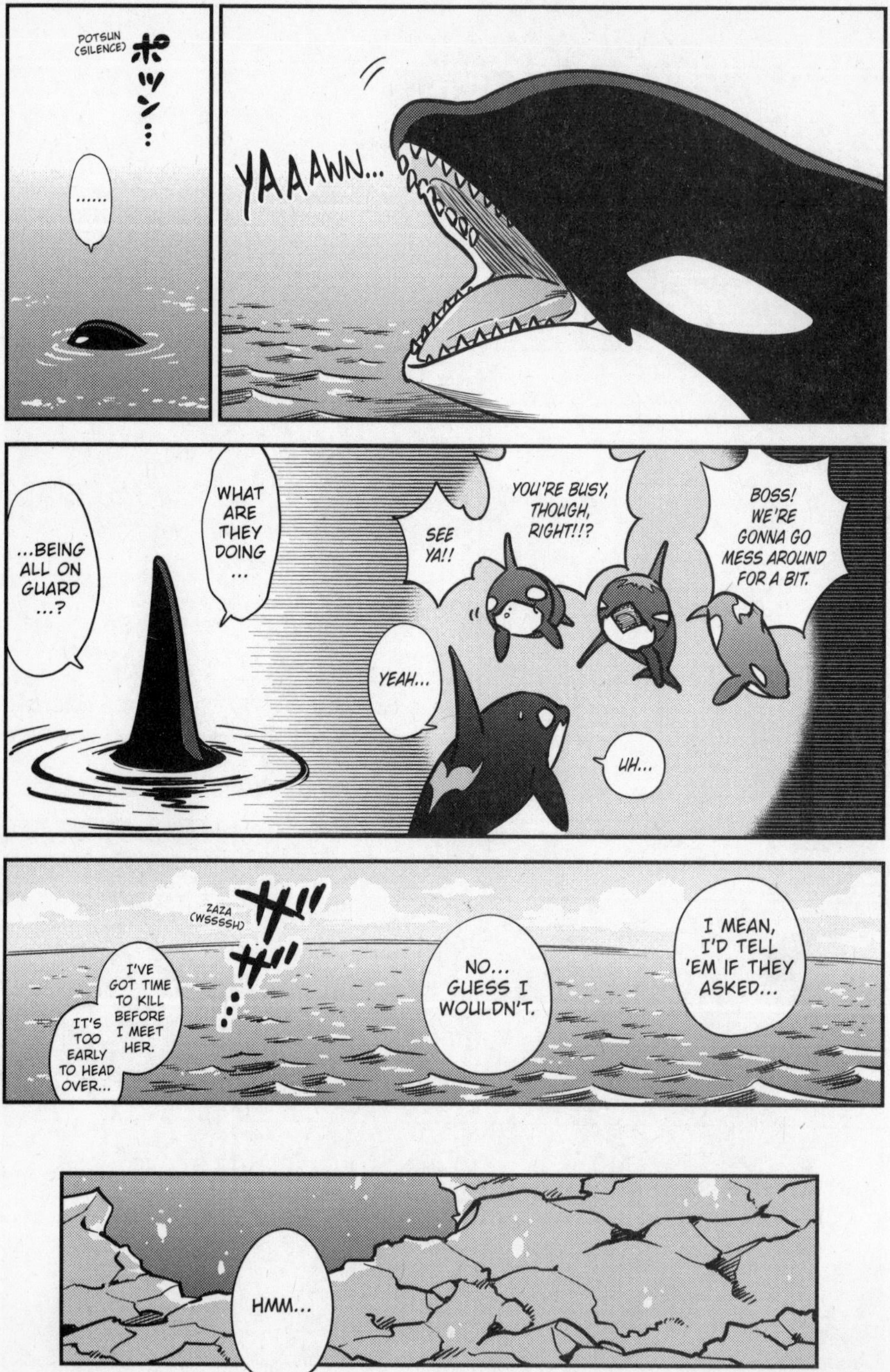
YAAAWN...
POTSUN (SILENCE) ポツン…
......
BOSS! WE'RE GONNA GO MESS AROUND FOR A BIT.
YOU'RE BUSY, THOUGH, RIGHT!!?
SEE YA!!
UH...
YEAH...
WHAT ARE THEY DOING...
...BEING ALL ON GUARD...?
I MEAN, I'D TELL 'EM IF THEY ASKED...
NO... GUESS I WOULDN'T.
ZAZA (WSSSSH) ザザ…
I'VE GOT TIME TO KILL BEFORE I MEET HER.
IT'S TOO EARLY TO HEAD OVER...
HMM...

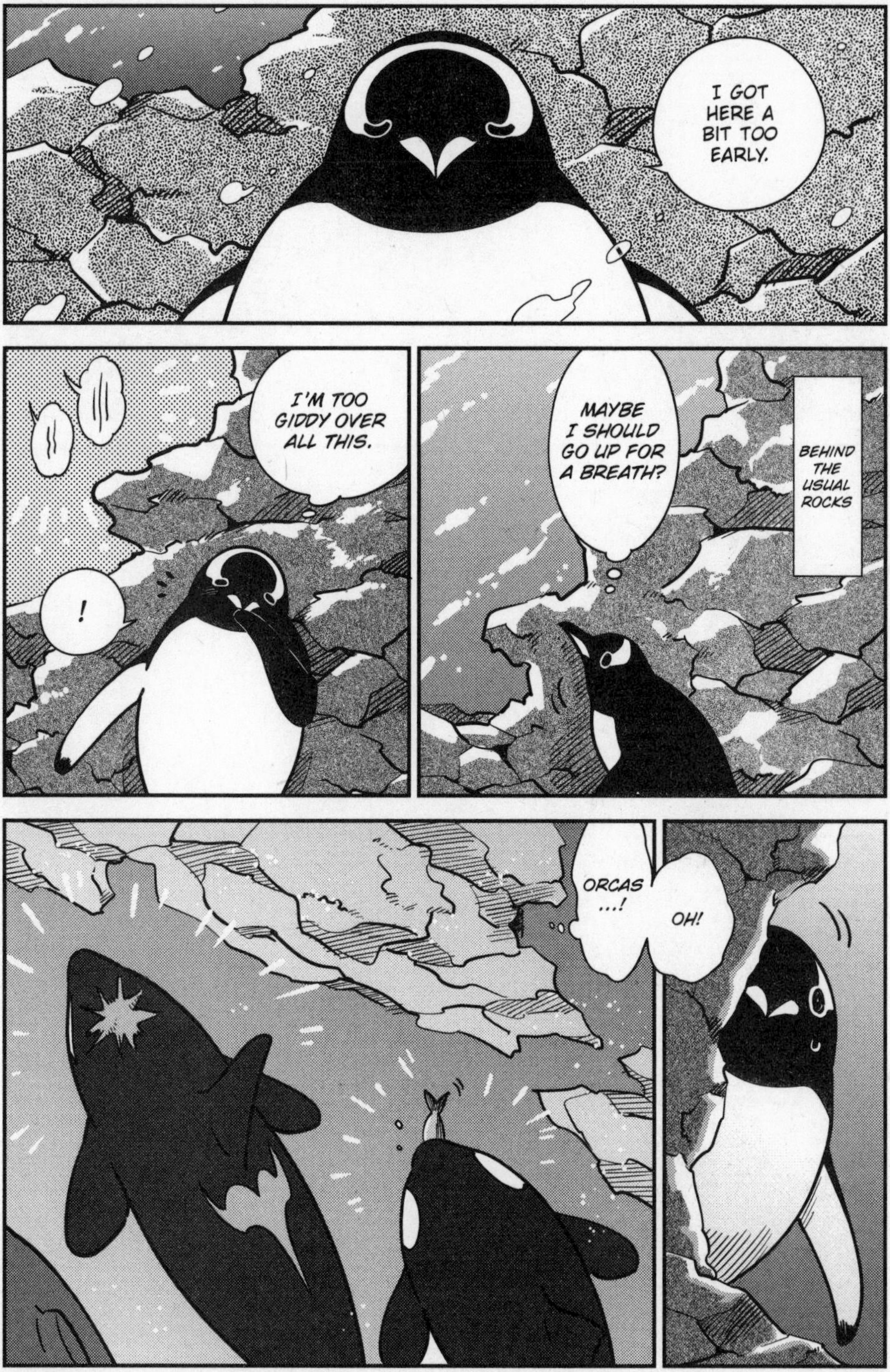
I GOT HERE A BIT TOO EARLY.
BEHIND THE USUAL ROCKS
MAYBE I SHOULD GO UP FOR A BREATH?
I'M TOO GIDDY OVER ALL THIS.
!
OH!
ORCAS ...!

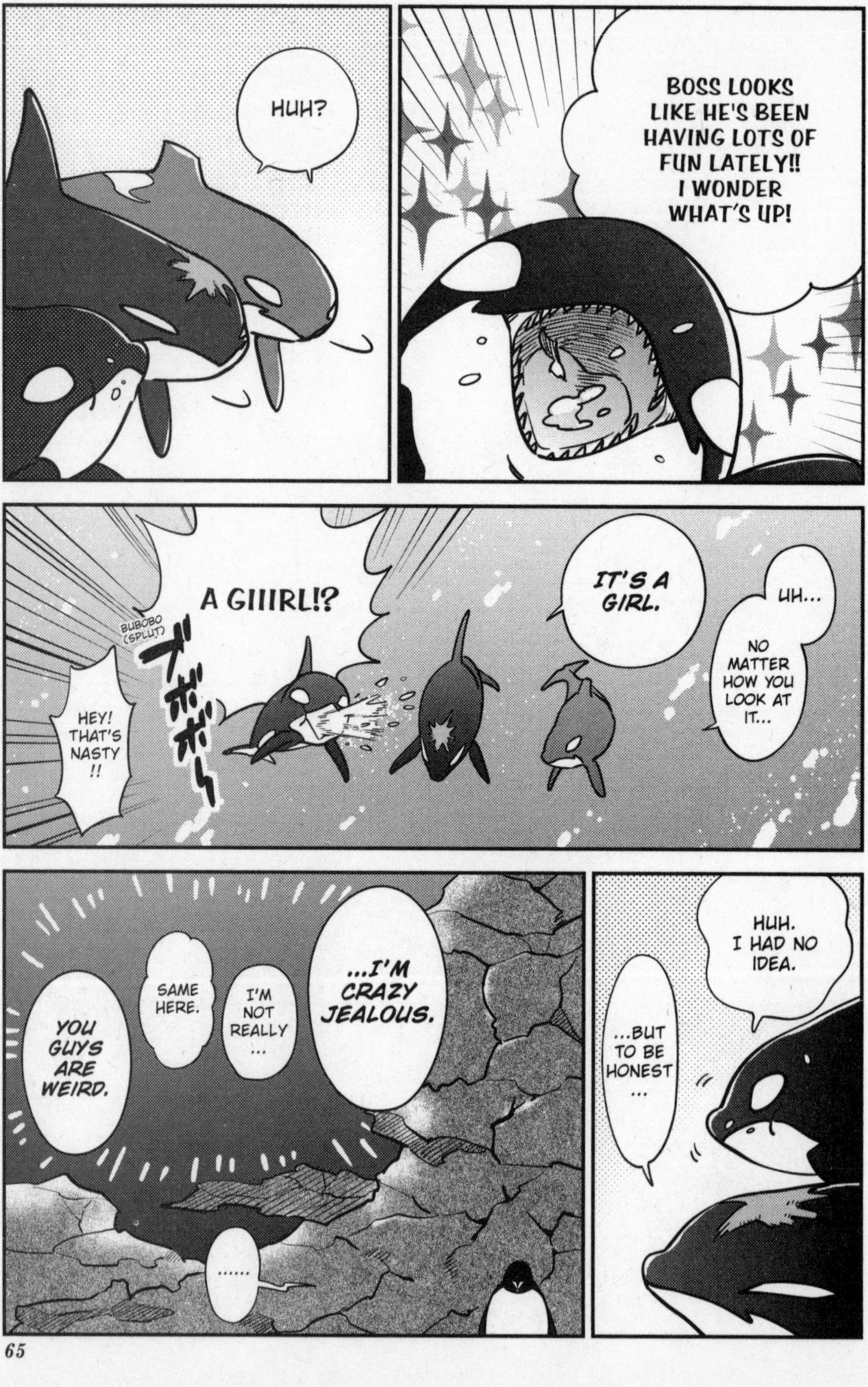
BOSS LOOKS LIKE HE'S BEEN HAVING LOTS OF FUN LATELY!! I WONDER WHAT'S UP!
HUH?
UH...
NO MATTER HOW YOU LOOK AT IT...
IT'S A GIRL.
A GIIIRL!?
BUBOBO (SPLUT)
HEY! THAT'S NASTY!!
HUH. I HAD NO IDEA.
...BUT TO BE HONEST...
...I'M CRAZY JEALOUS.
I'M NOT REALLY...
SAME HERE.
YOU GUYS ARE WEIRD.
......

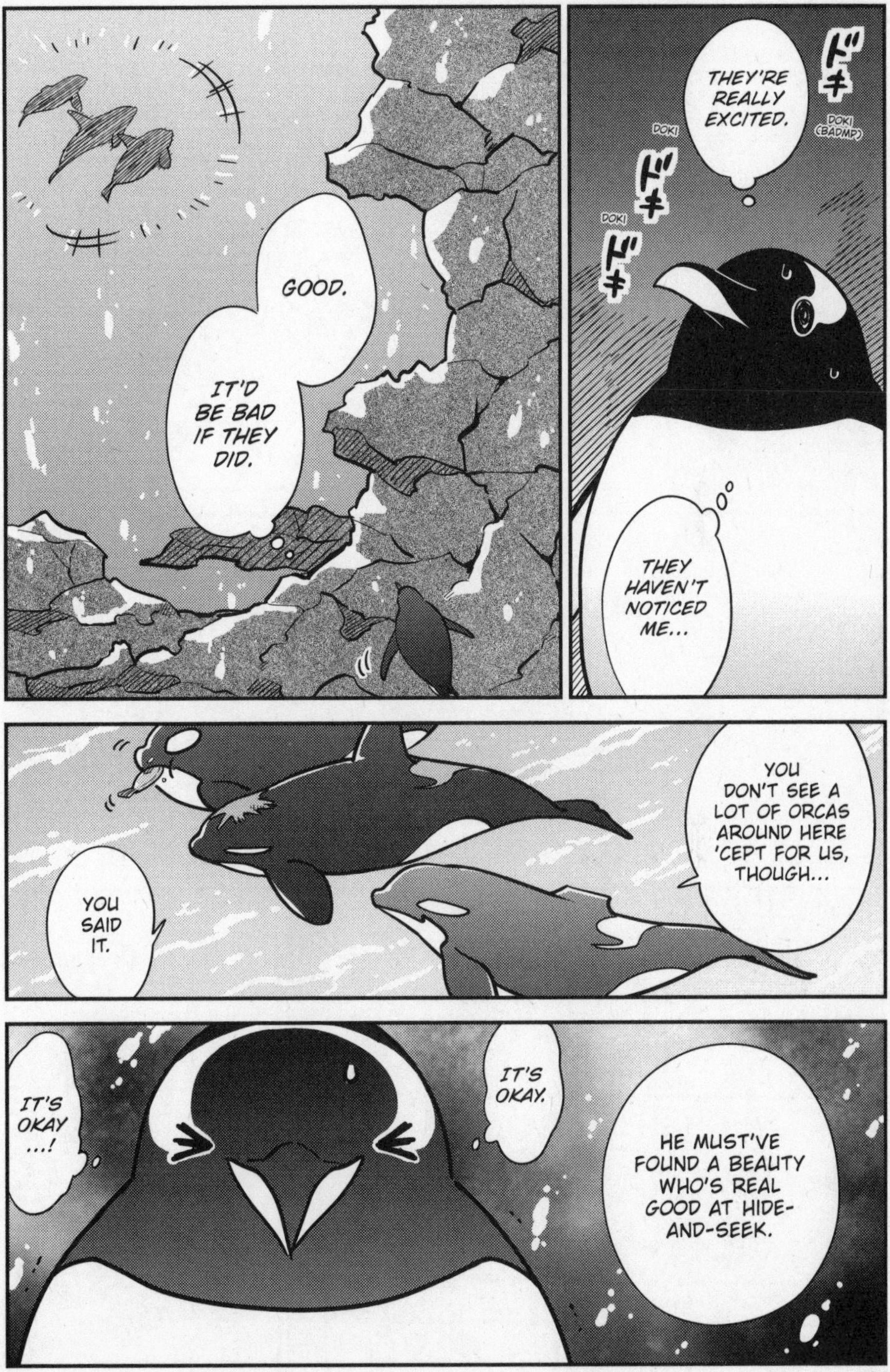
ドキ
DOKI (BADMP)
THEY'RE REALLY EXCITED.
ドキ
DOKI!
ドキ
DOKI
THEY HAVEN'T NOTICED ME...
GOOD.
IT'D BE BAD IF THEY DID.
YOU DON'T SEE A LOT OF ORCAS AROUND HERE 'CEPT FOR US, THOUGH...
YOU SAID IT.
HE MUST'VE FOUND A BEAUTY WHO'S REAL GOOD AT HIDE-AND-SEEK.
IT'S OKAY.
IT'S OKAY ...!

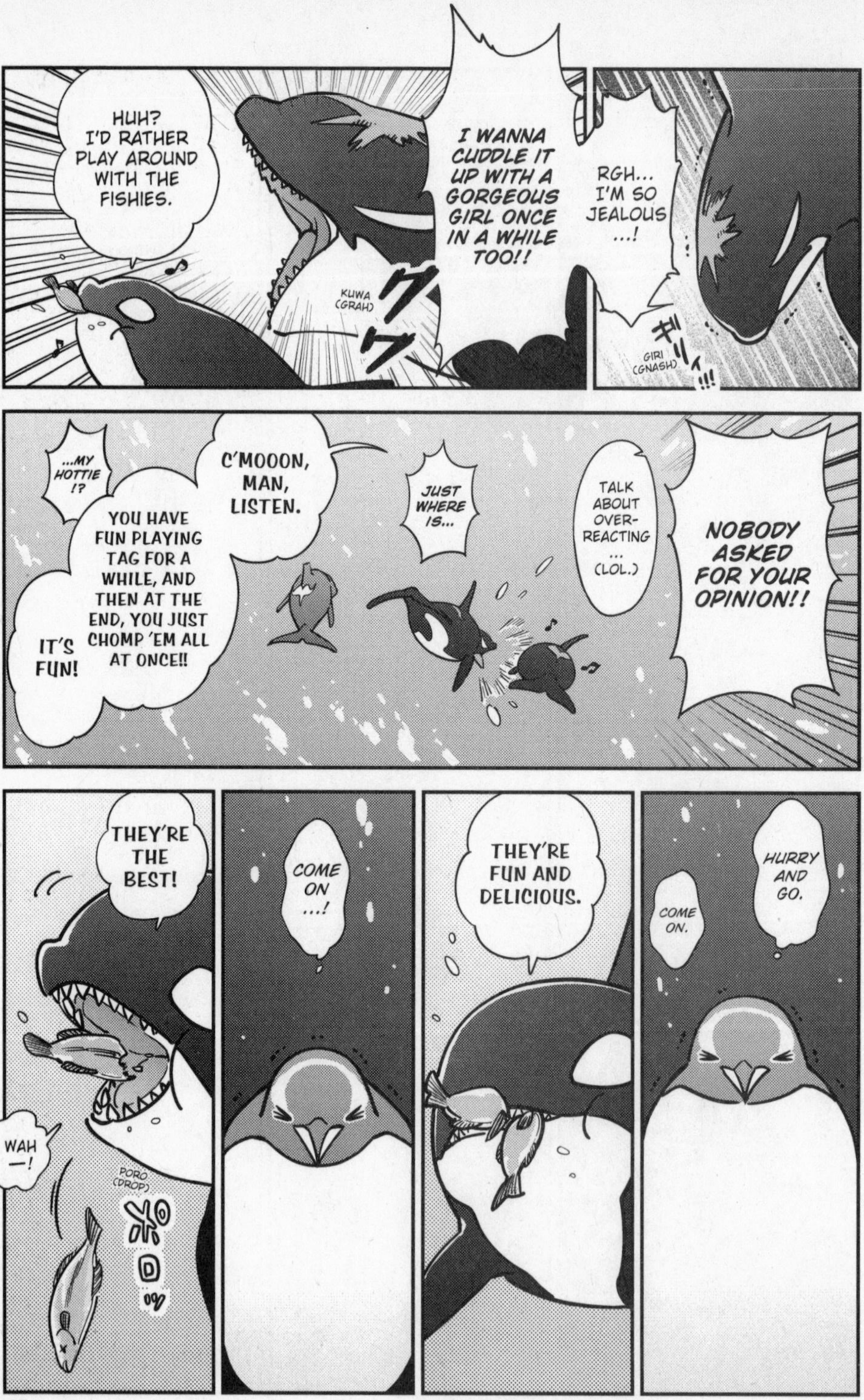
RGH... I'M SO JEALOUS ...!
GIRI (GNASH)
I WANNA CUDDLE IT UP WITH A GORGEOUS GIRL ONCE IN A WHILE TOO!!
KUWA (GRAH)
HUH? I'D RATHER PLAY AROUND WITH THE FISHIES.
NOBODY ASKED FOR YOUR OPINION!!
TALK ABOUT OVER-REACTING ... (LOL.)
JUST WHERE IS...
...MY HOTTIE!?
C'MOOON, MAN, LISTEN.
YOU HAVE FUN PLAYING TAG FOR A WHILE, AND THEN AT THE END, YOU JUST CHOMP 'EM ALL AT ONCE!!
IT'S FUN!
HURRY AND GO.
COME ON.
THEY'RE FUN AND DELICIOUS.
COME ON ...!
THEY'RE THE BEST!
WAH—!
PORO (DROP)

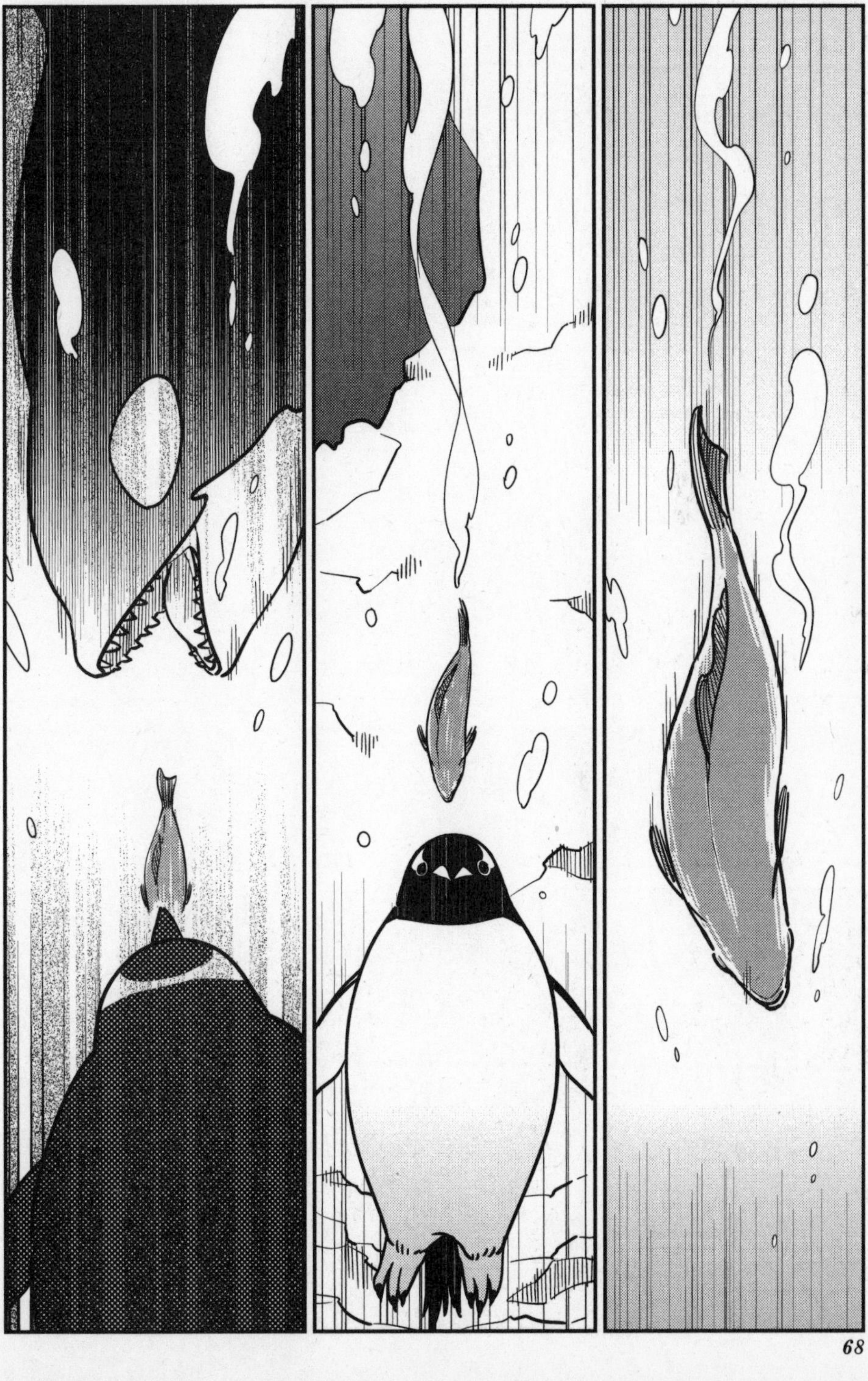

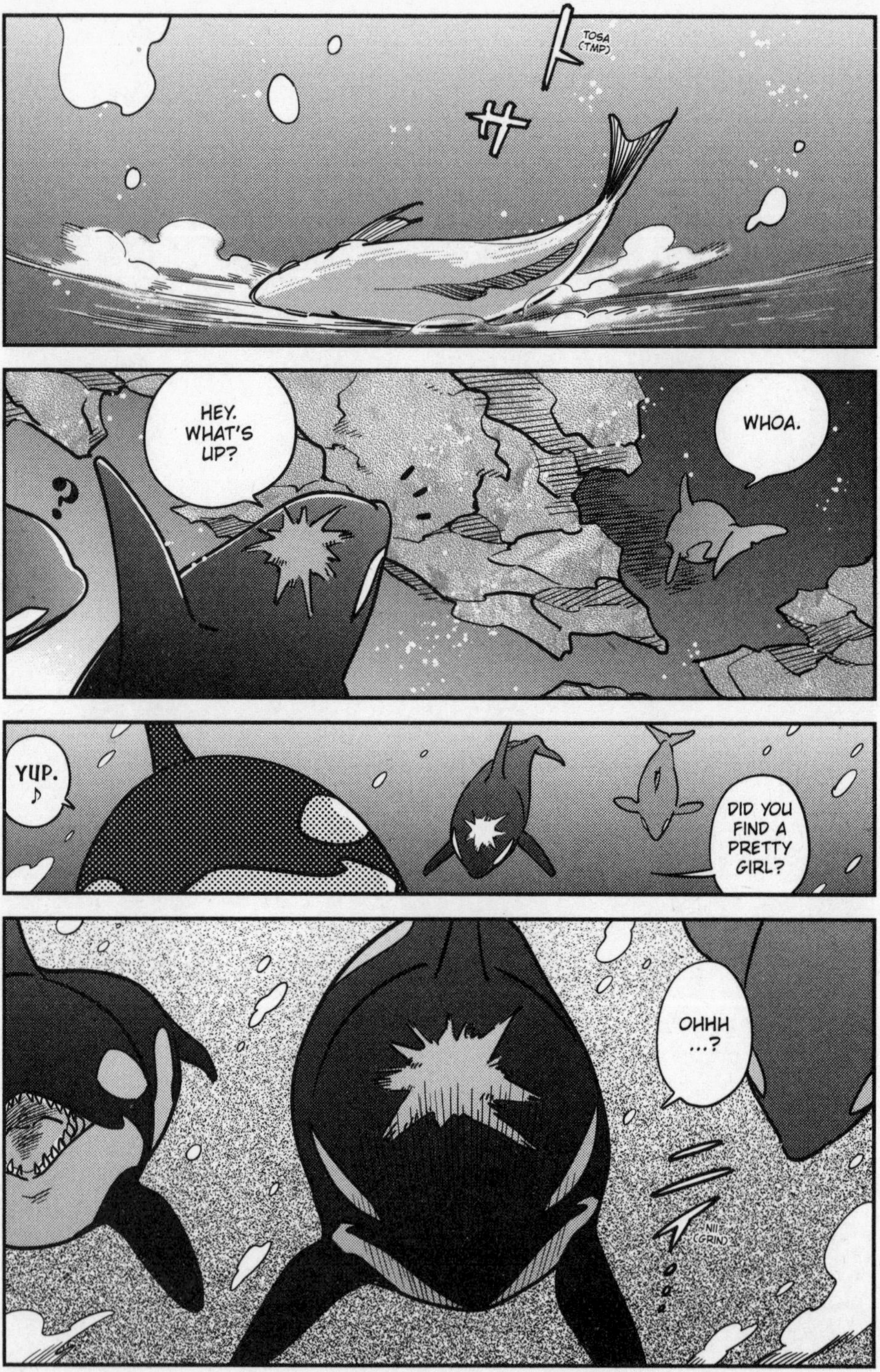
TOSA (TMP)
WHOA.
HEY. WHAT'S UP?
DID YOU FIND A PRETTY GIRL?
YUP. ♪
OHHH ...?
NII (GRIN)

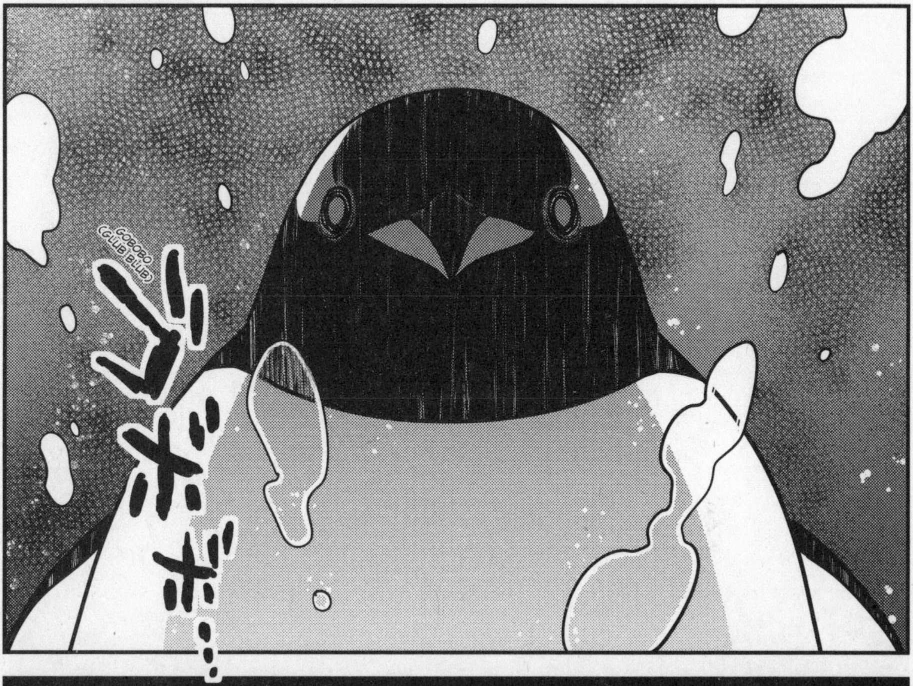
GOBOBO
(GLUB BLUB)

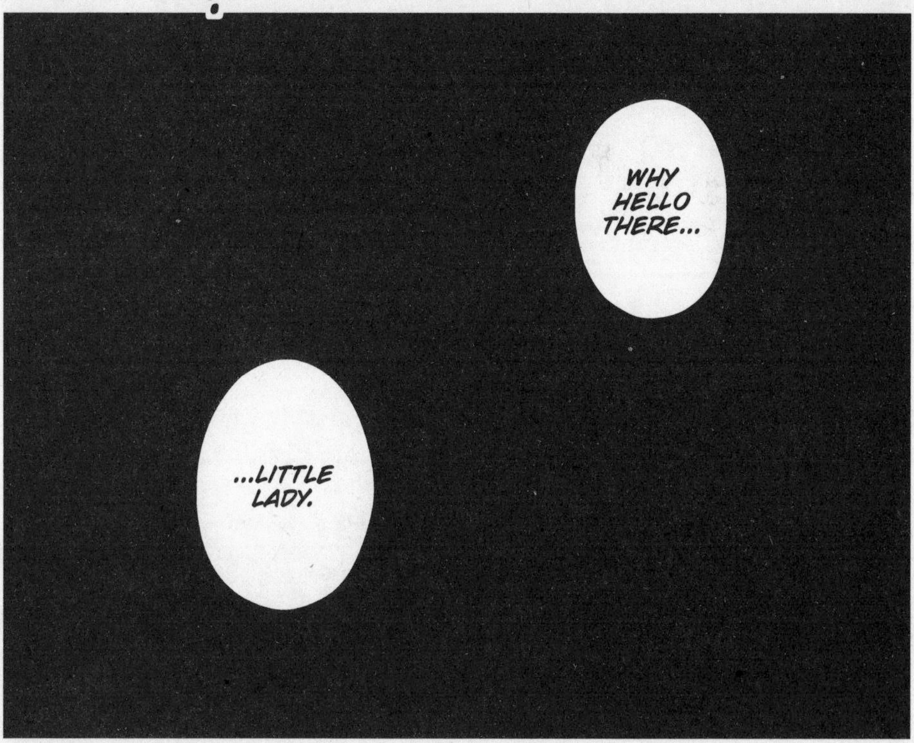
WHY HELLO THERE...
...LITTLE LADY.

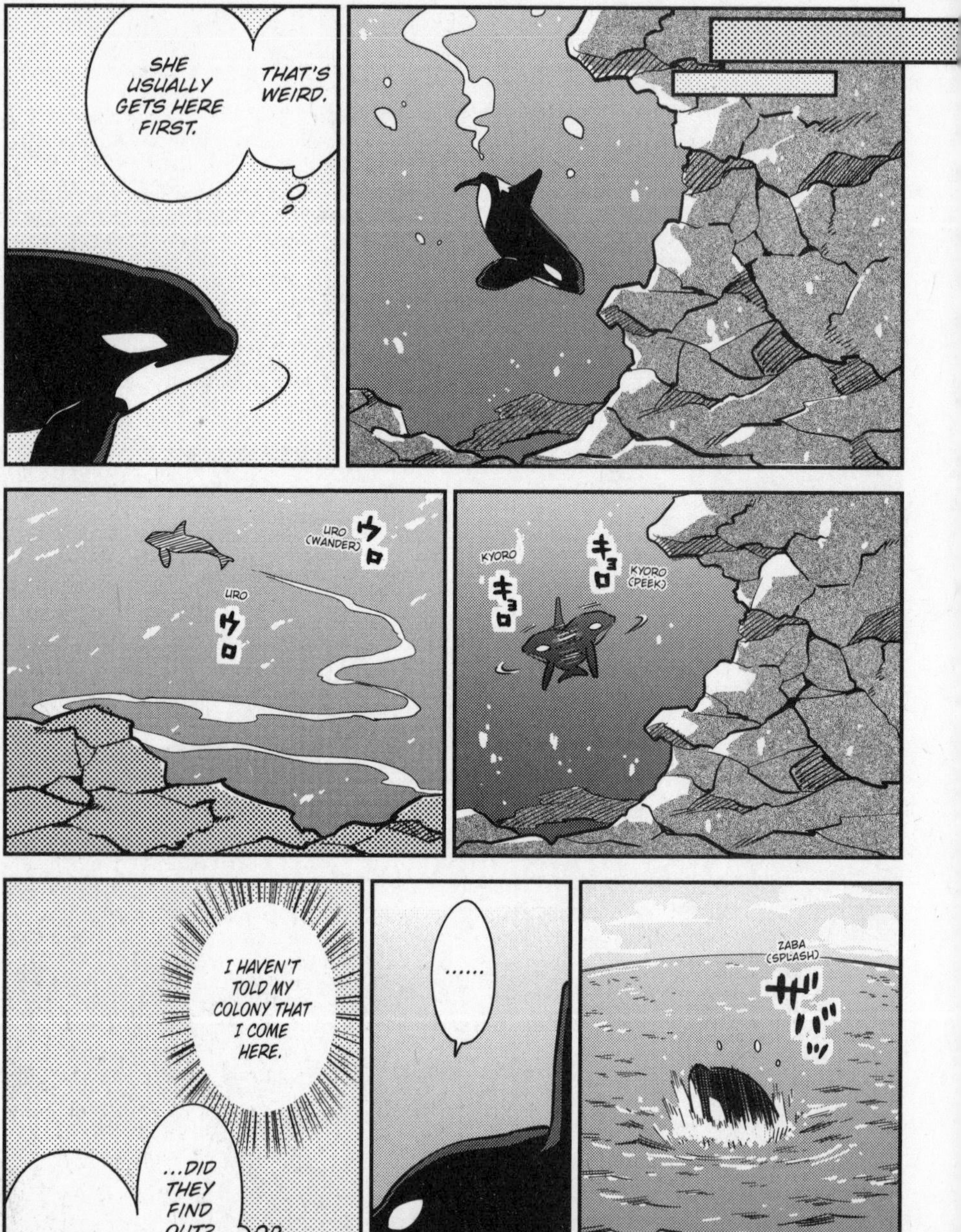
THAT'S WEIRD.
SHE USUALLY GETS HERE FIRST.
KYORO (PEEK)
キョロ
KYORO
キョロ
URO (WANDER)
ウロ
URO
ウロ
ZABA (SPLASH)
ザバッ
......
I HAVEN'T TOLD MY COLONY THAT I COME HERE.
...DID THEY FIND OUT?
...DID SOMETHING HAPPEN?

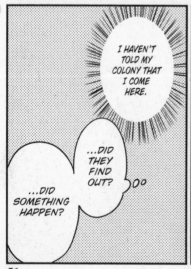

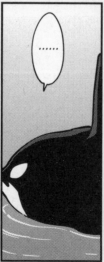

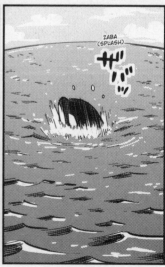

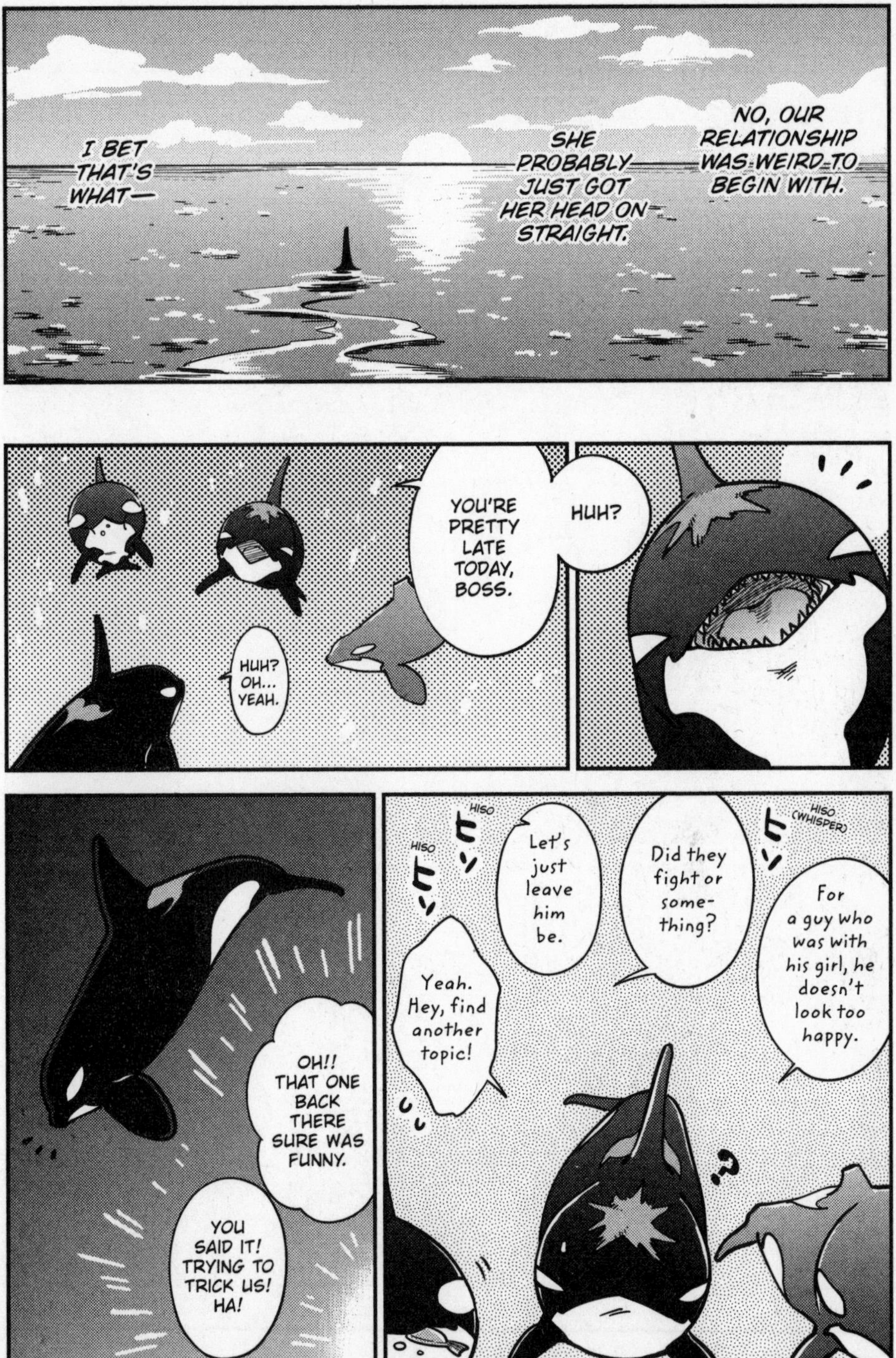
NO, OUR RELATIONSHIP WAS WEIRD TO BEGIN WITH.
SHE PROBABLY JUST GOT HER HEAD ON STRAIGHT.
I BET THAT'S WHAT—
HUH?
YOU'RE PRETTY LATE TODAY, BOSS.
HUH? OH... YEAH.
HISO (WHISPER)
For a guy who was with his girl, he doesn't look too happy.
Did they fight or something?
HISO
Let's just leave him be.
HISO
Yeah. Hey, find another topic!
OH!! THAT ONE BACK THERE SURE WAS FUNNY.
YOU SAID IT! TRYING TO TRICK US! HA!

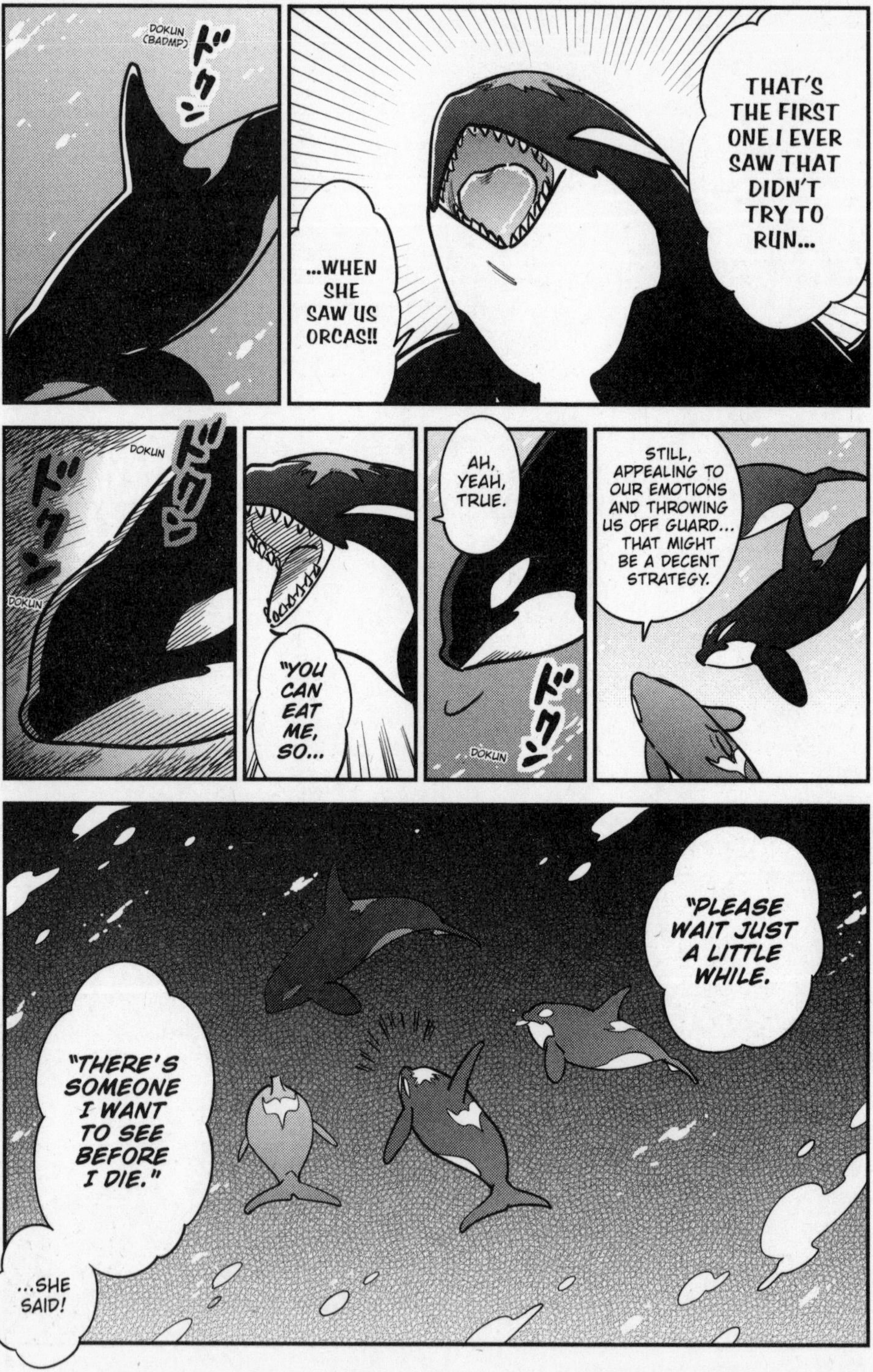
THAT'S THE FIRST ONE I EVER SAW THAT DIDN'T TRY TO RUN...
...WHEN SHE SAW US ORCAS!!
DOKUN (BADMP)
ドクン
STILL, APPEALING TO OUR EMOTIONS AND THROWING US OFF GUARD... THAT MIGHT BE A DECENT STRATEGY.
AH, YEAH, TRUE.
DOKUN
ドクン
"YOU CAN EAT ME, SO...
DOKUN
ドクン
DOKUN
ドクン
"PLEASE WAIT JUST A LITTLE WHILE.
"THERE'S SOMEONE I WANT TO SEE BEFORE I DIE."
...SHE SAID!

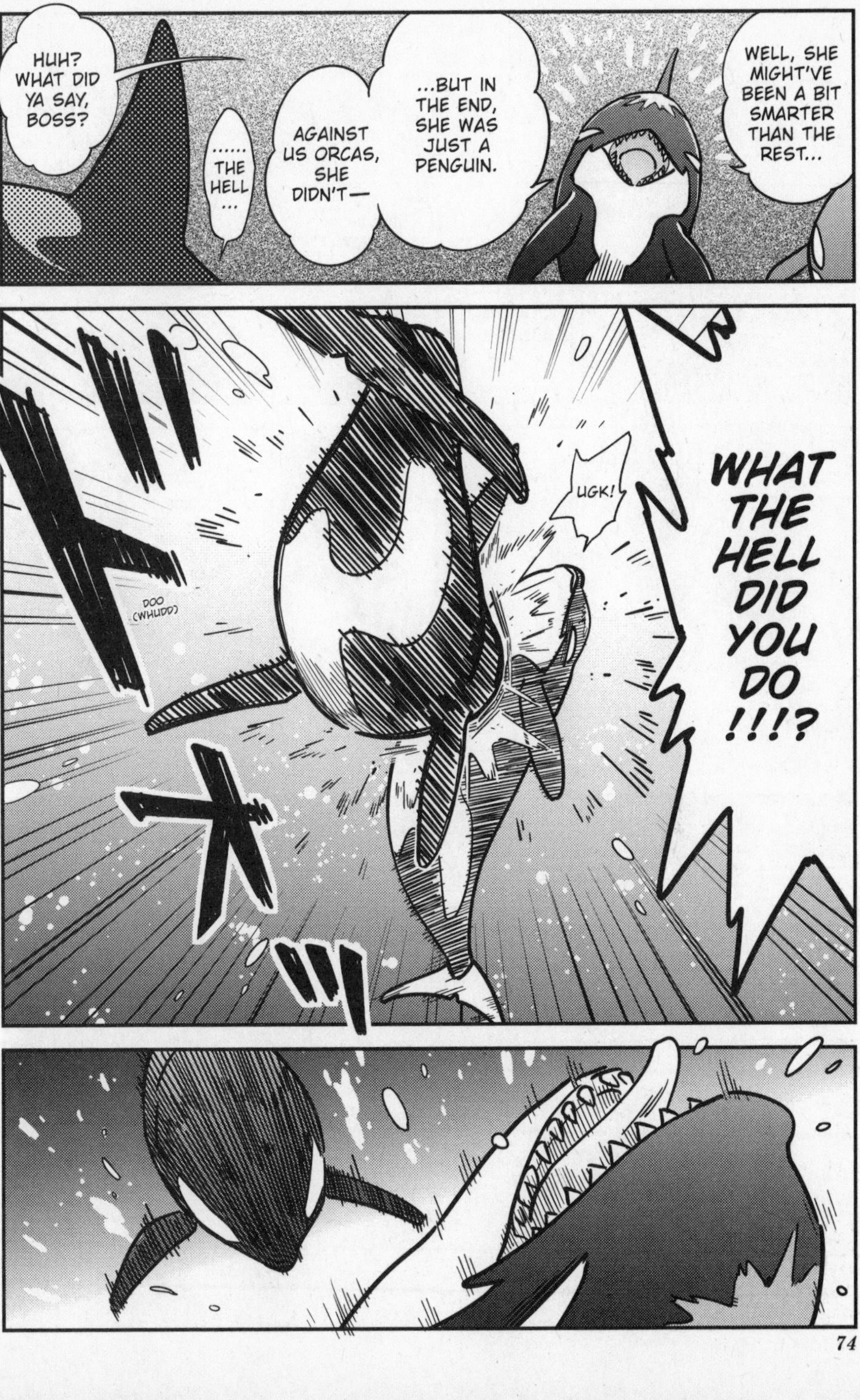
WELL, SHE MIGHT'VE BEEN A BIT SMARTER THAN THE REST...
...BUT IN THE END, SHE WAS JUST A PENGUIN.
AGAINST US ORCAS, SHE DIDN'T—
......THE HELL...
HUH? WHAT DID YA SAY, BOSS?
WHAT THE HELL DID YOU DO !!!?
UGK!
DOO (WHUDD)

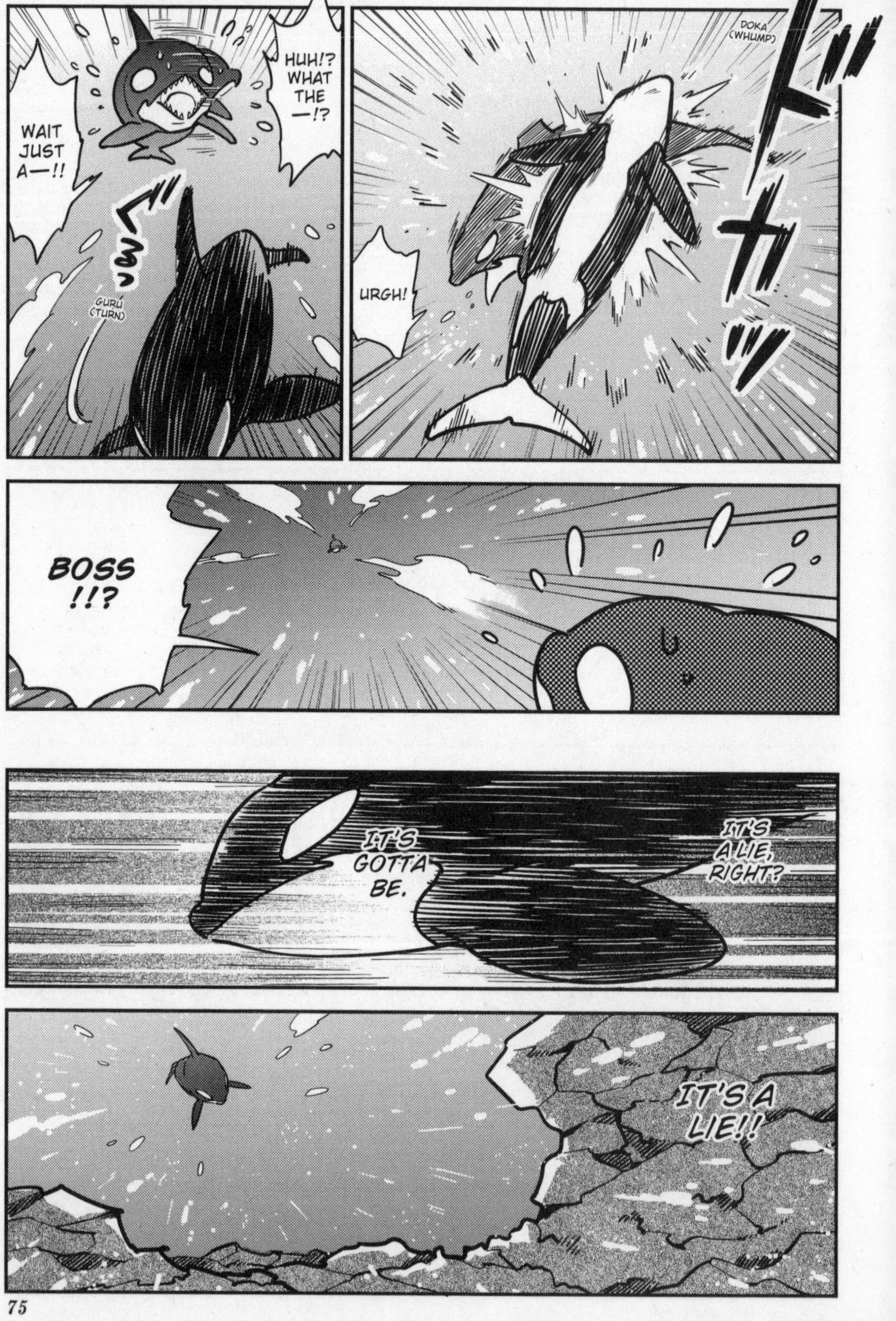

ドガッ
DOKA (WHUMP)
URGH!
HUH!? WHAT THE—!?
WAIT JUST A—!!
ぐるっ
GURU (TURN)
BOSS!!?
IT'S A LIE, RIGHT?
IT'S GOTTA BE.
IT'S A LIE!!

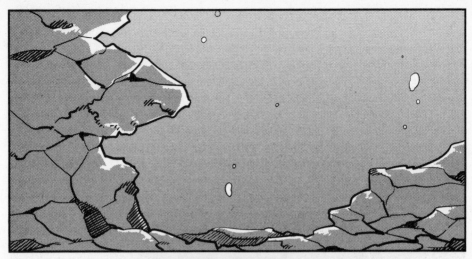

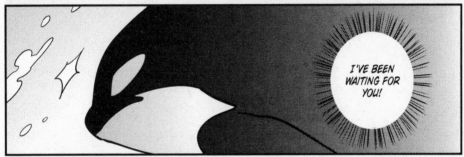

I'VE BEEN WAITING FOR YOU!

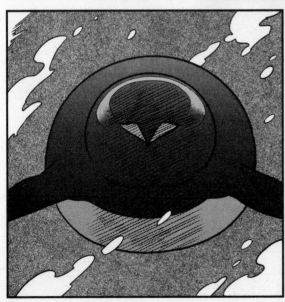

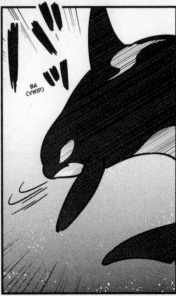

BA
(VWIP)

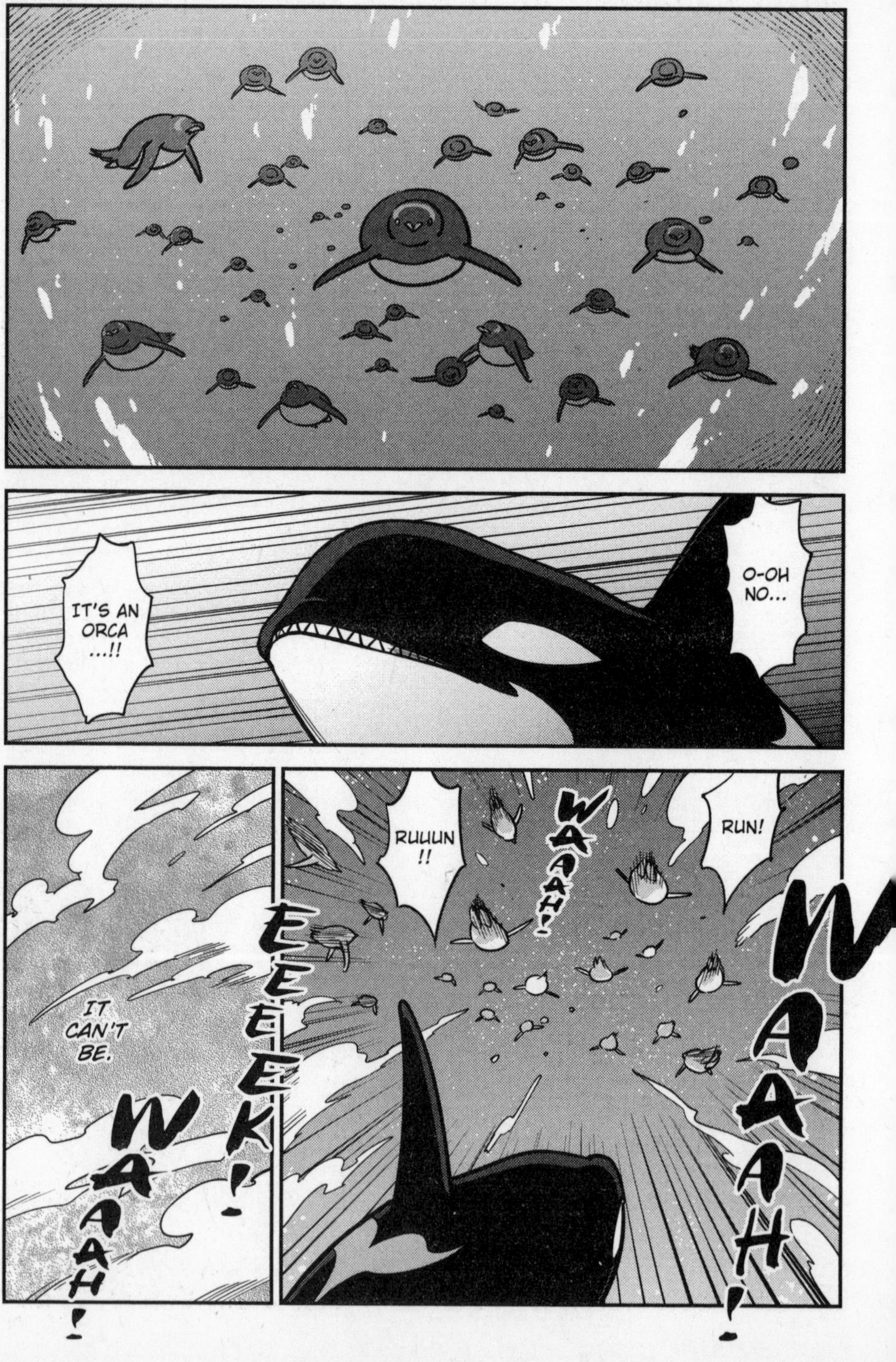
O-OH NO...
IT'S AN ORCA ...!!
WAAAH!
RUN!
WAAAH!
RUUUN !!
EEEEEK!
IT CAN'T BE.
WAAAH!

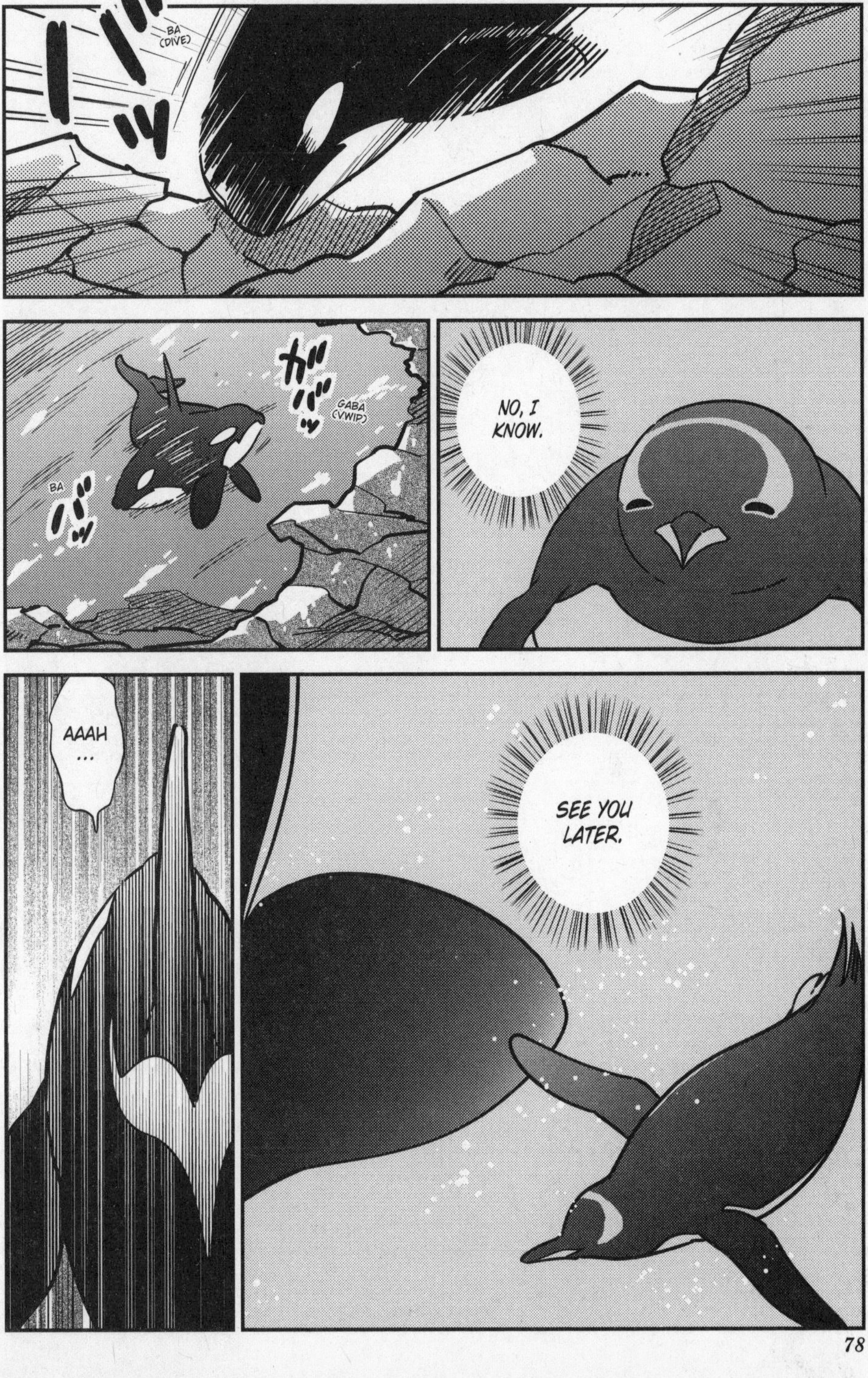
BA
(DIVE)
NO, I KNOW.
GABA
(VWIP)
BA
SEE YOU LATER.
AAAH ...

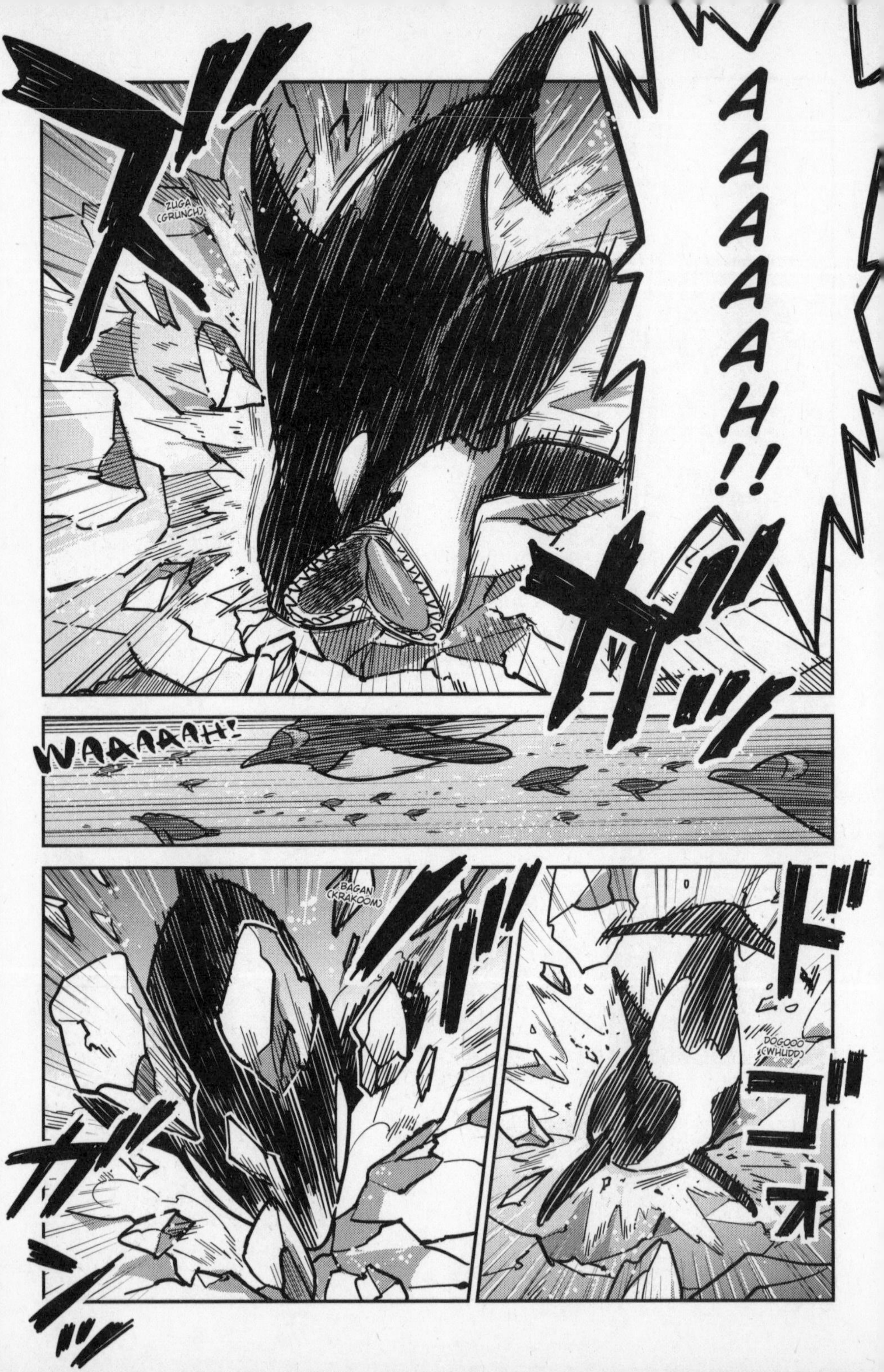
WAAAAAH!!
ZUGA (GRUNCH)
WAAAAAH!
DOGOOO (WHUDD)
BAGAN (KRAKOOM)

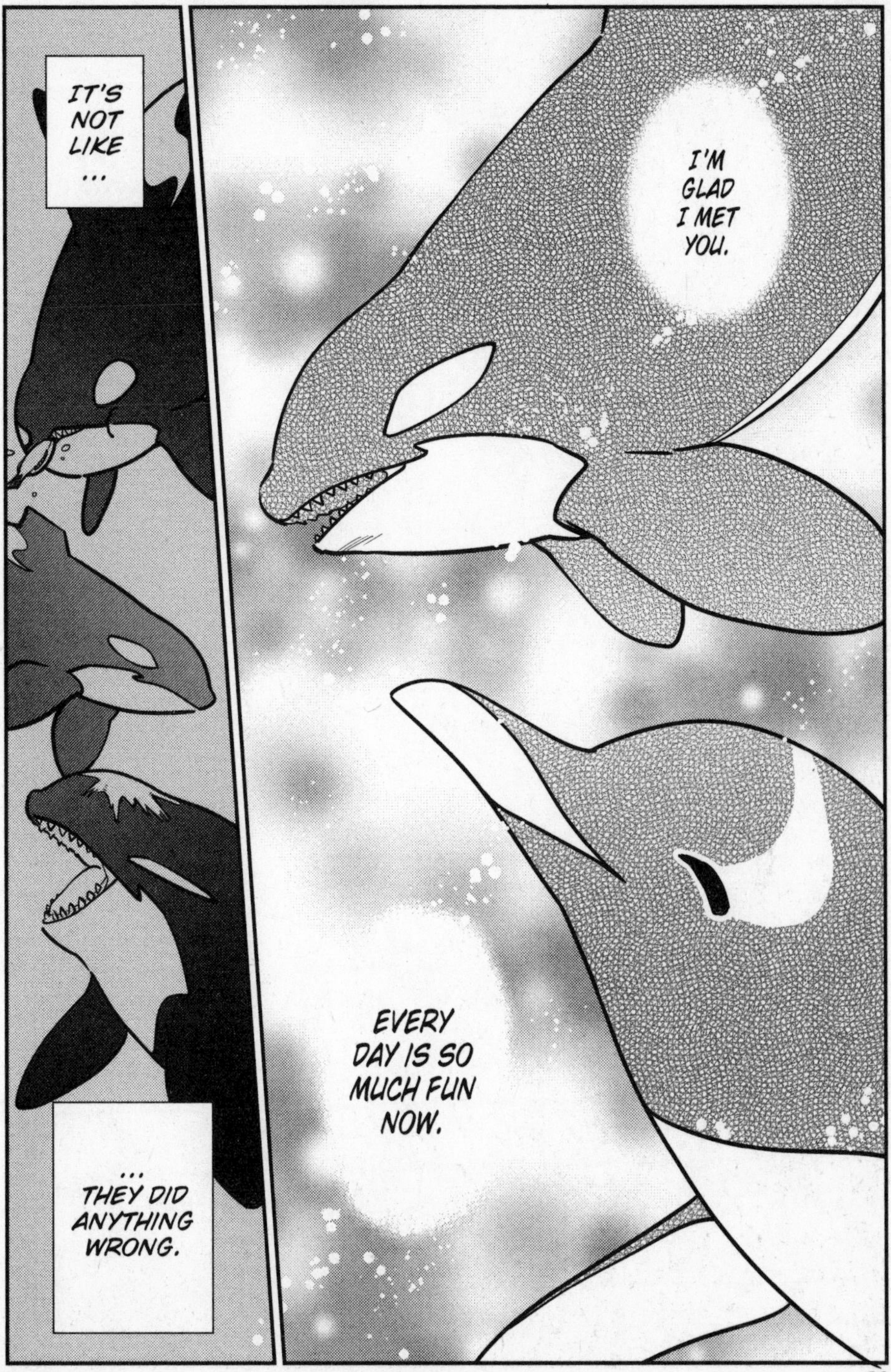
I'M GLAD I MET YOU.
EVERY DAY IS SO MUCH FUN NOW.
IT'S NOT LIKE ...
... THEY DID ANYTHING WRONG.

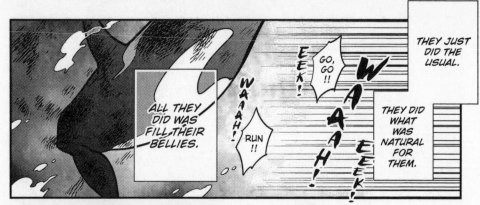

THEY JUST DID THE USUAL.

THEY DID WHAT WAS NATURAL FOR THEM.

ALL THEY DID WAS FILL THEIR BELLIES.

WAAAH!

RUN !!

EEK!

GO, GO !!

WAAAH! EEK!!

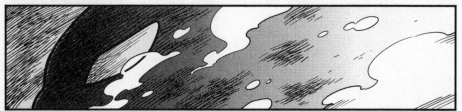

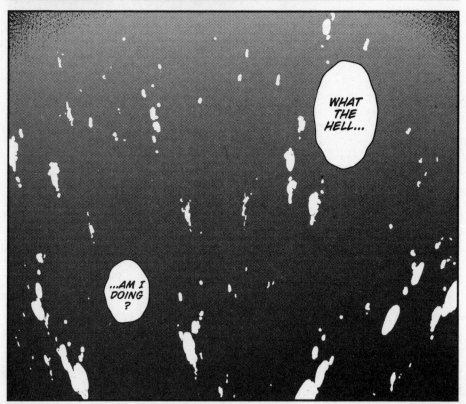

WHAT THE HELL...

...AM I DOING?

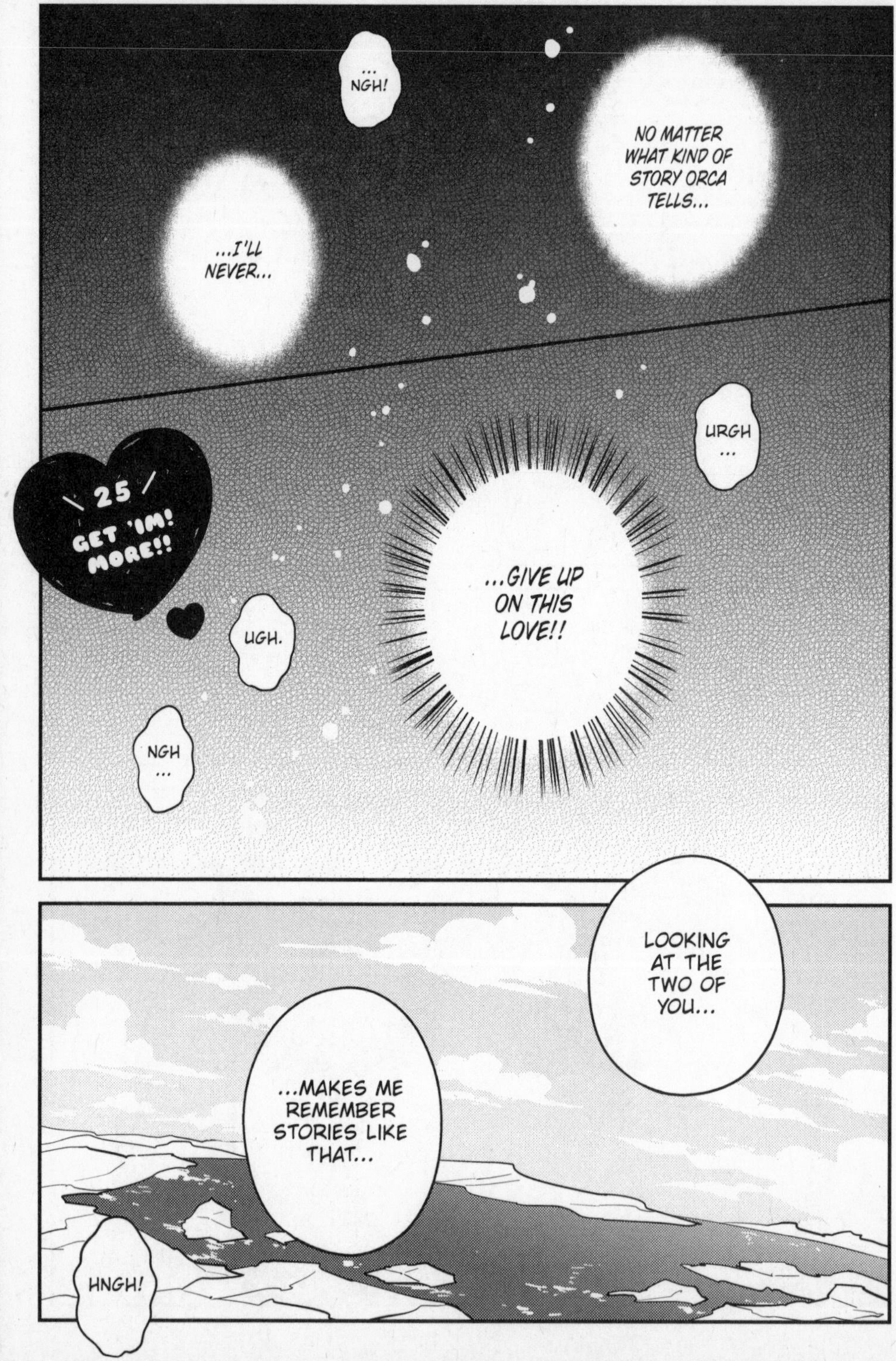
NO MATTER WHAT KIND OF STORY ORCA TELLS...
...NGH!
...I'LL NEVER...
URGH...
...GIVE UP ON THIS LOVE!!
25 GET 'IM! MORE!!
UGH.
NGH...
LOOKING AT THE TWO OF YOU...
...MAKES ME REMEMBER STORIES LIKE THAT...
HNGH!

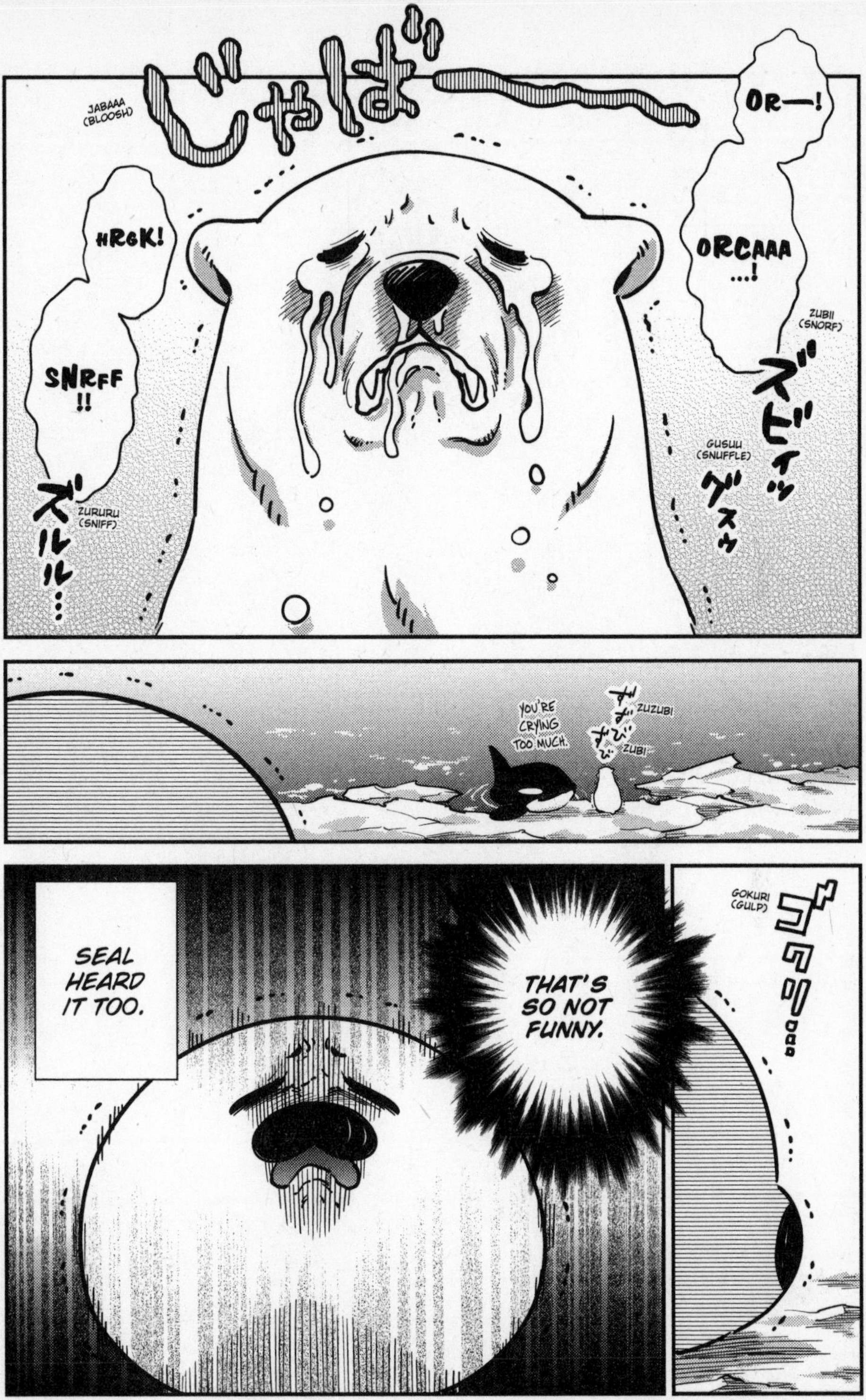
JABAAA (BLOOSH)
OR—!
ORCAAA ...!
ZUBII (SNORF)
GUSUU (SNUFFLE)
HRGK!
SNRFF !!
ZURURU (SNIFF)
ZUZUBI
ZUBI
YOU'RE CRYING TOO MUCH.
GOKURI (GULP)
THAT'S SO NOT FUNNY.
SEAL HEARD IT TOO.

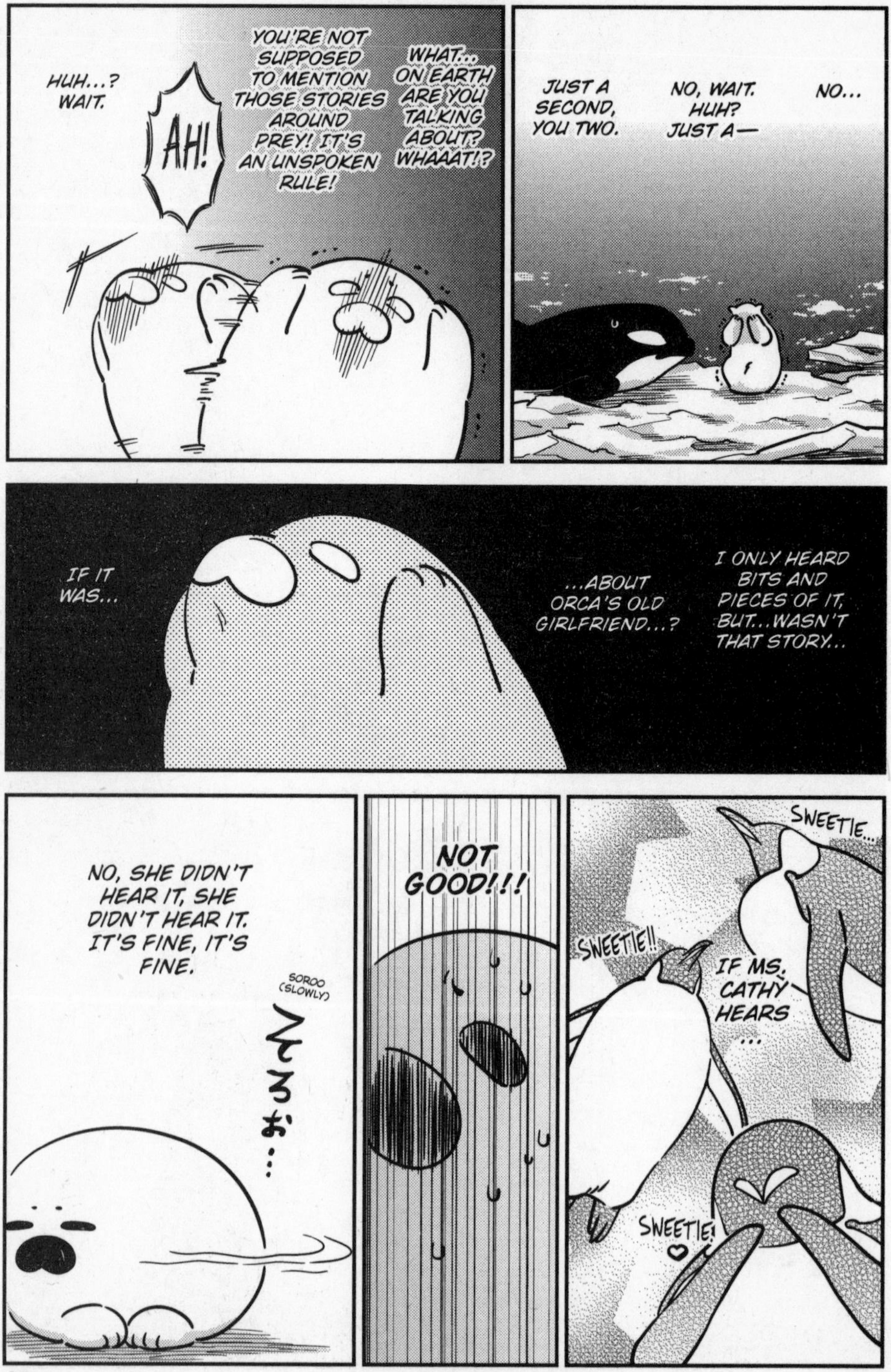
NO...
NO, WAIT. HUH? JUST A—
JUST A SECOND, YOU TWO.
WHAT... ON EARTH ARE YOU TALKING ABOUT? WHAAAT!?
YOU'RE NOT SUPPOSED TO MENTION THOSE STORIES AROUND PREY! IT'S AN UNSPOKEN RULE!
AH!
HUH...? WAIT.
I ONLY HEARD BITS AND PIECES OF IT, BUT...WASN'T THAT STORY...
...ABOUT ORCA'S OLD GIRLFRIEND...?
IF IT WAS...
SWEETIE...
SWEETIE!!
IF MS. CATHY HEARS...
SWEETIE! ♡
NOT GOOD!!!
NO, SHE DIDN'T HEAR IT, SHE DIDN'T HEAR IT. IT'S FINE, IT'S FINE.
SOROO (SLOWLY)
そろぉ…

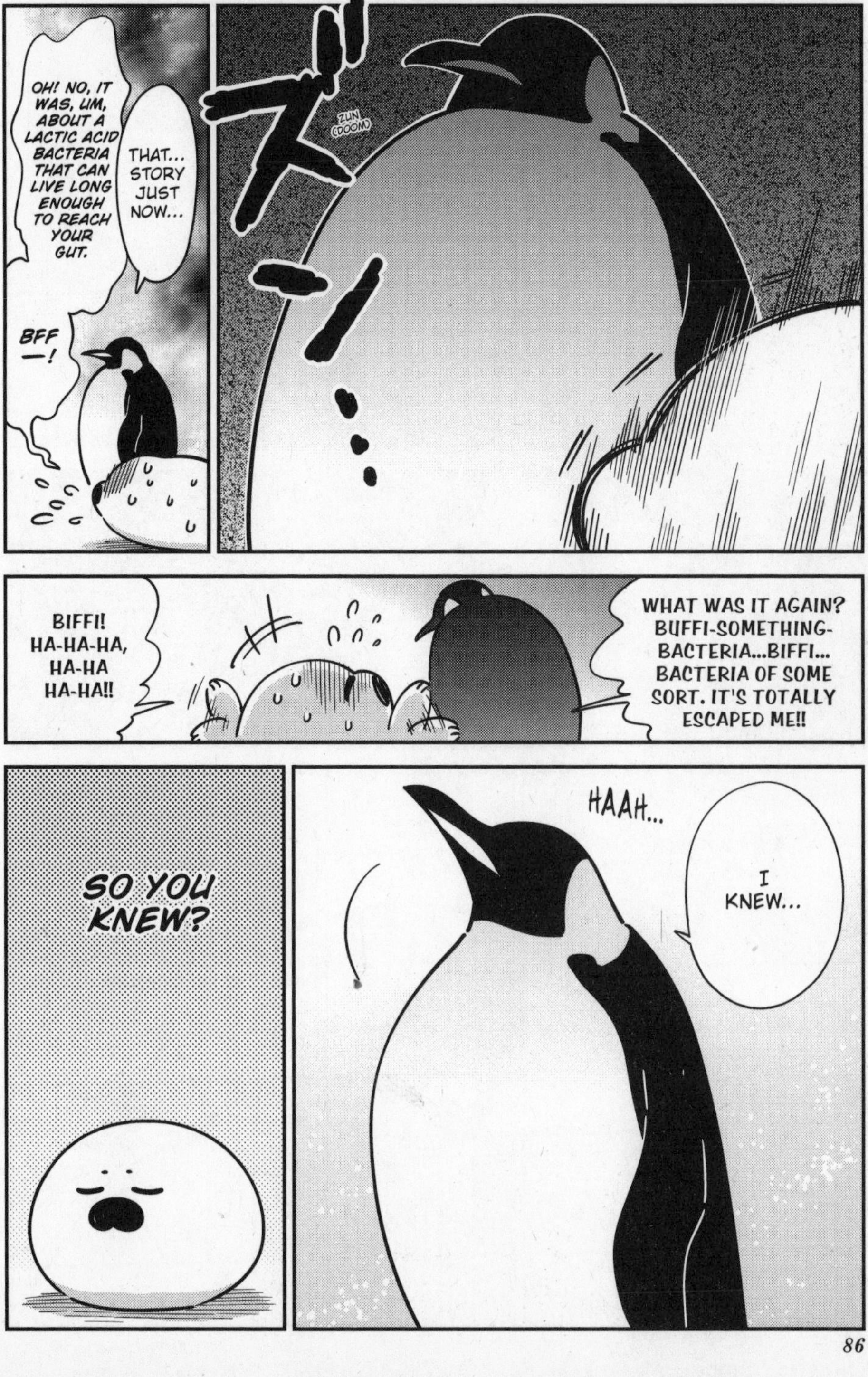
ZUN (DOOM)
THAT... STORY JUST NOW...
OH! NO, IT WAS, UM, ABOUT A LACTIC ACID BACTERIA THAT CAN LIVE LONG ENOUGH TO REACH YOUR GUT.
BFF—!
WHAT WAS IT AGAIN? BUFFI-SOMETHING-BACTERIA...BIFFI... BACTERIA OF SOME SORT. IT'S TOTALLY ESCAPED ME!!
BIFFI! HA-HA-HA, HA-HA HA-HA!!
HAAH...
I KNEW...
SO YOU KNEW?

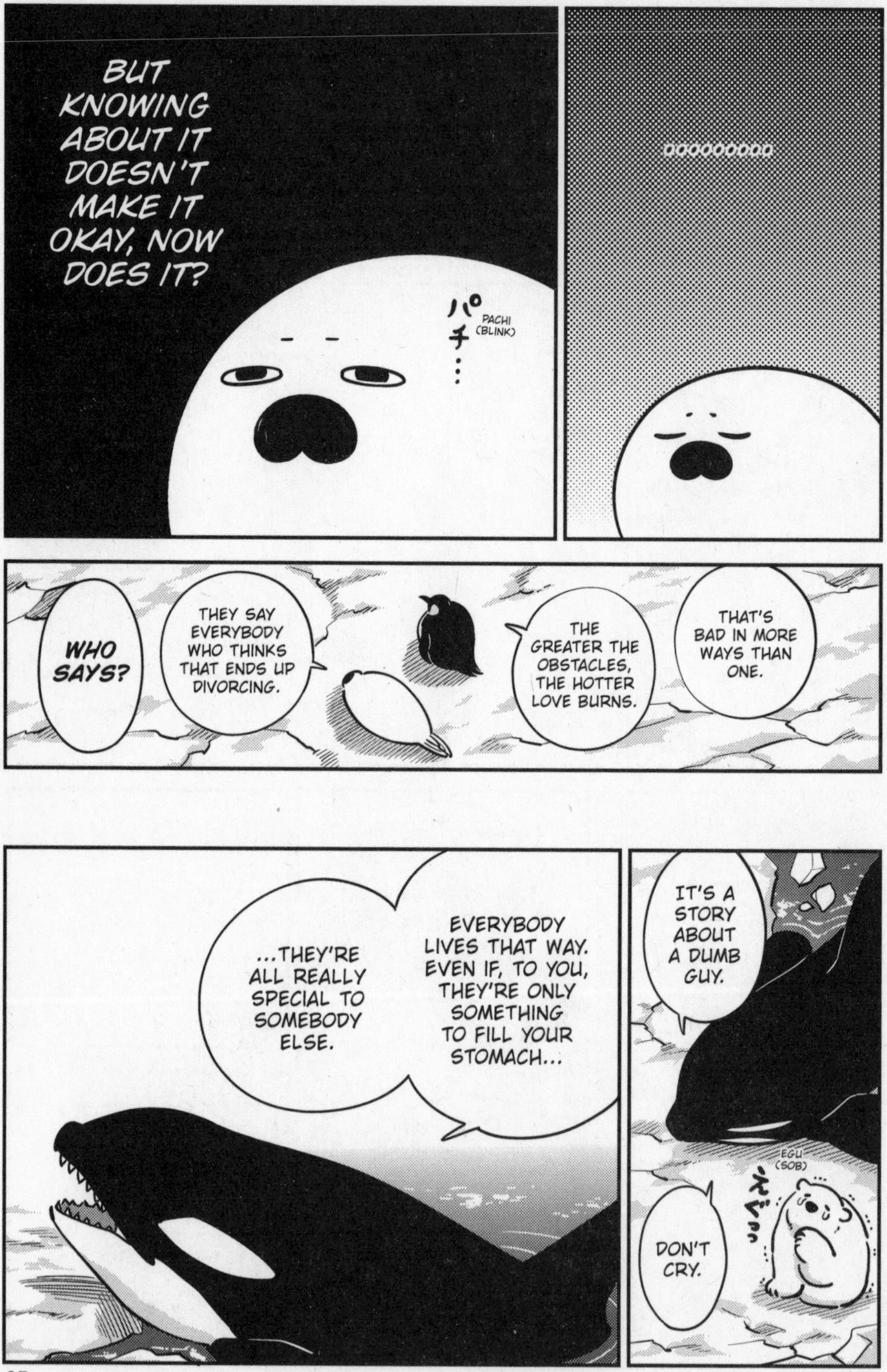
BUT KNOWING ABOUT IT DOESN'T MAKE IT OKAY, NOW DOES IT?
パチ…
PACHI (BLINK)
THAT'S BAD IN MORE WAYS THAN ONE.
THE GREATER THE OBSTACLES, THE HOTTER LOVE BURNS.
THEY SAY EVERYBODY WHO THINKS THAT ENDS UP DIVORCING.
WHO SAYS?
IT'S A STORY ABOUT A DUMB GUY.
EGU (SOB)
DON'T CRY.
EVERYBODY LIVES THAT WAY. EVEN IF, TO YOU, THEY'RE ONLY SOMETHING TO FILL YOUR STOMACH...
...THEY'RE ALL REALLY SPECIAL TO SOMEBODY ELSE.

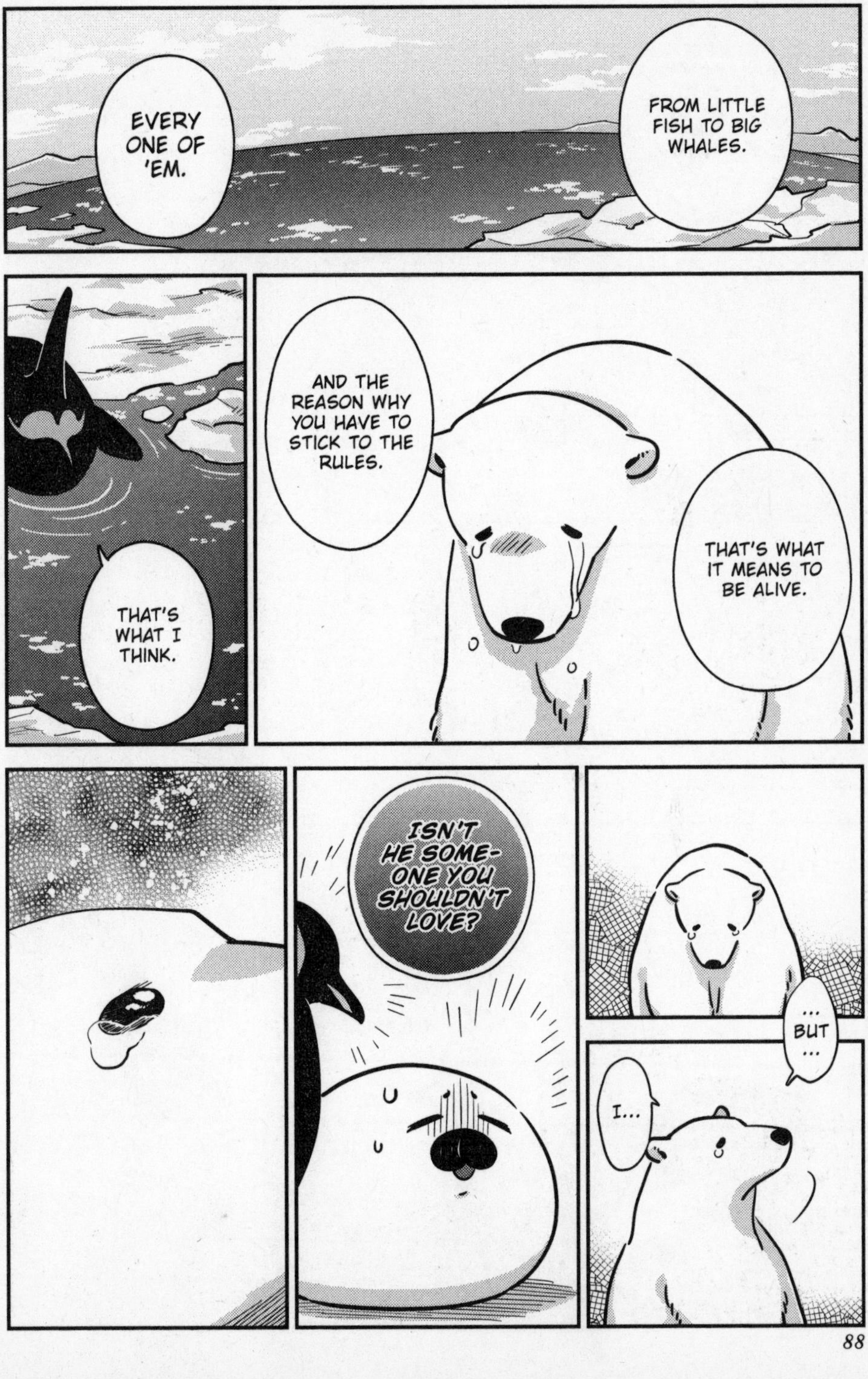
FROM LITTLE FISH TO BIG WHALES.
EVERY ONE OF 'EM.
THAT'S WHAT IT MEANS TO BE ALIVE.
AND THE REASON WHY YOU HAVE TO STICK TO THE RULES.
THAT'S WHAT I THINK.
...BUT...
I...
ISN'T HE SOMEONE YOU SHOULDN'T LOVE?

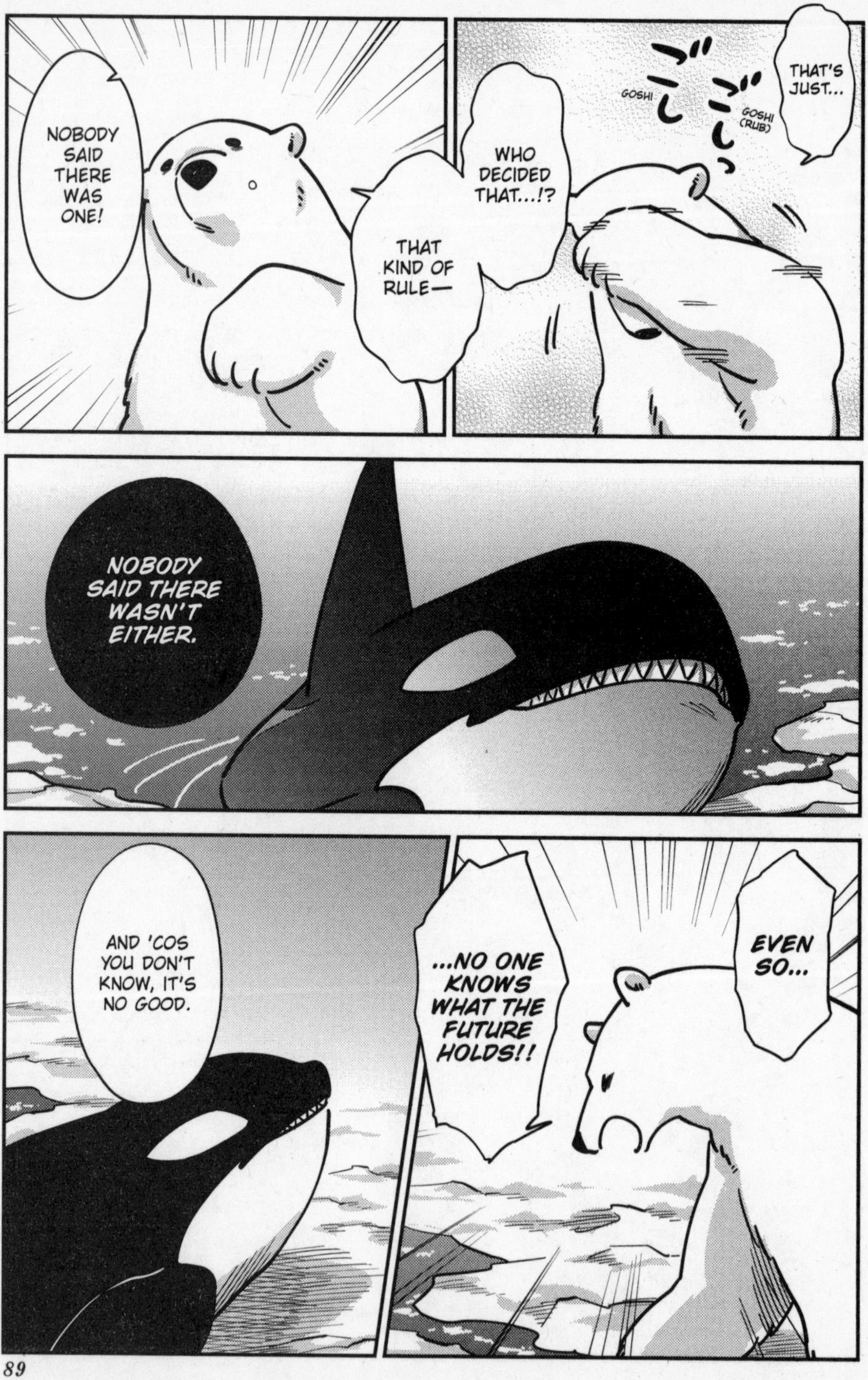
THAT'S JUST...
GOSHI (RUB)
GOSHI
WHO DECIDED THAT...!?
THAT KIND OF RULE—
NOBODY SAID THERE WAS ONE!
NOBODY SAID THERE WASN'T EITHER.
EVEN SO...
...NO ONE KNOWS WHAT THE FUTURE HOLDS!!
AND 'COS YOU DON'T KNOW, IT'S NO GOOD.

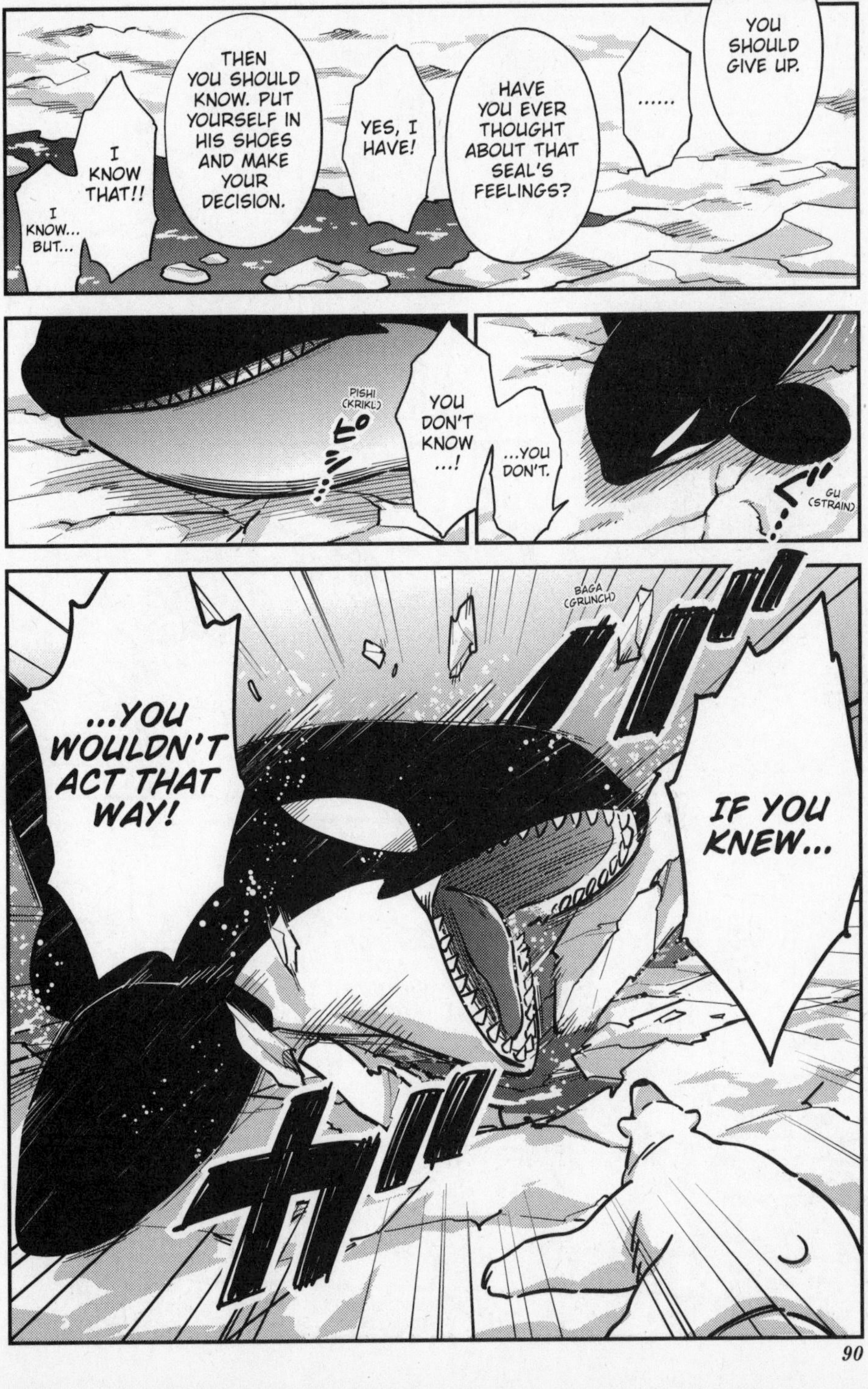
YOU SHOULD GIVE UP.
......
HAVE YOU EVER THOUGHT ABOUT THAT SEAL'S FEELINGS?
YES, I HAVE!
THEN YOU SHOULD KNOW. PUT YOURSELF IN HIS SHOES AND MAKE YOUR DECISION.
I KNOW THAT!!
I KNOW... BUT...
GU (STRAIN)
...YOU DON'T.
YOU DON'T KNOW ...!
PISHI (KRIKL)
BAGA (GRUNCH)
IF YOU KNEW...
...YOU WOULDN'T ACT THAT WAY!

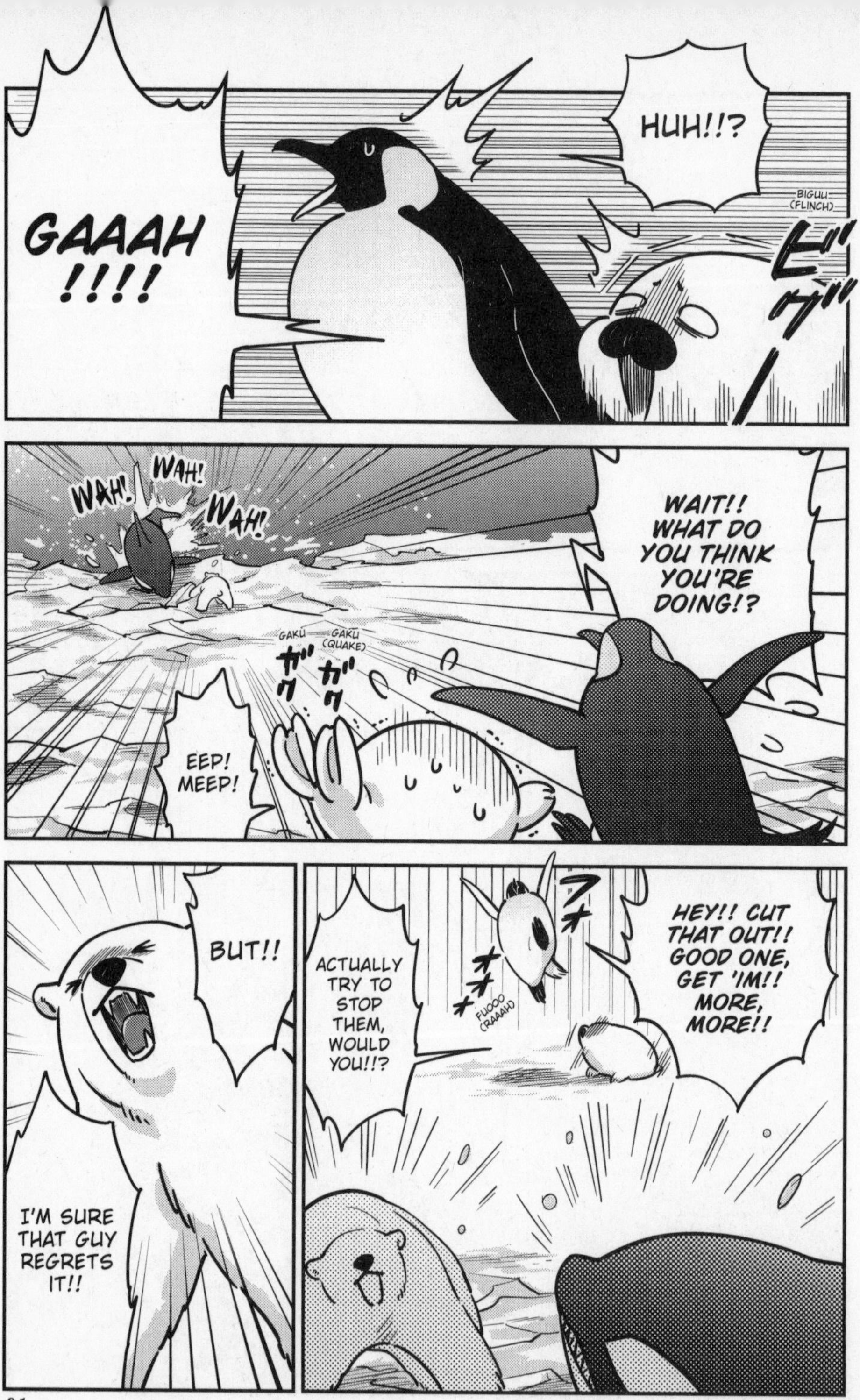

HUH!!?
BIGUU (FLINCH)
GAAAH !!!!
WAIT!! WHAT DO YOU THINK YOU'RE DOING!?
WAH! WAH! WAH!
GAKU GAKU (QUAKE)
EEP! MEEP!
HEY!! CUT THAT OUT!! GOOD ONE, GET 'IM!! MORE, MORE!!
FUOOO (RAAAH)
ACTUALLY TRY TO STOP THEM, WOULD YOU!!?
BUT!!
I'M SURE THAT GUY REGRETS IT!!

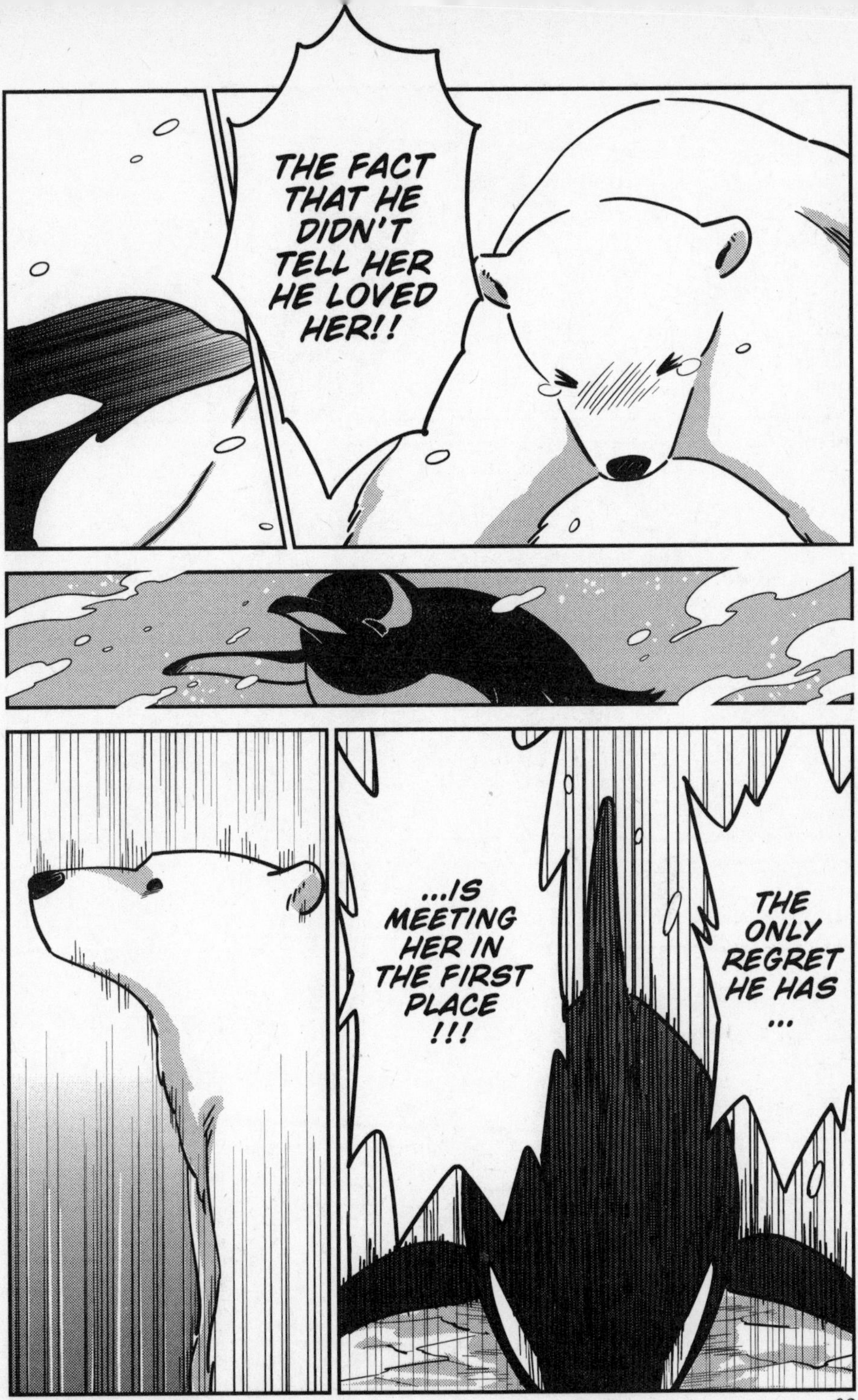
THE FACT THAT HE DIDN'T TELL HER HE LOVED HER!!
THE ONLY REGRET HE HAS ...
...IS MEETING HER IN THE FIRST PLACE !!!

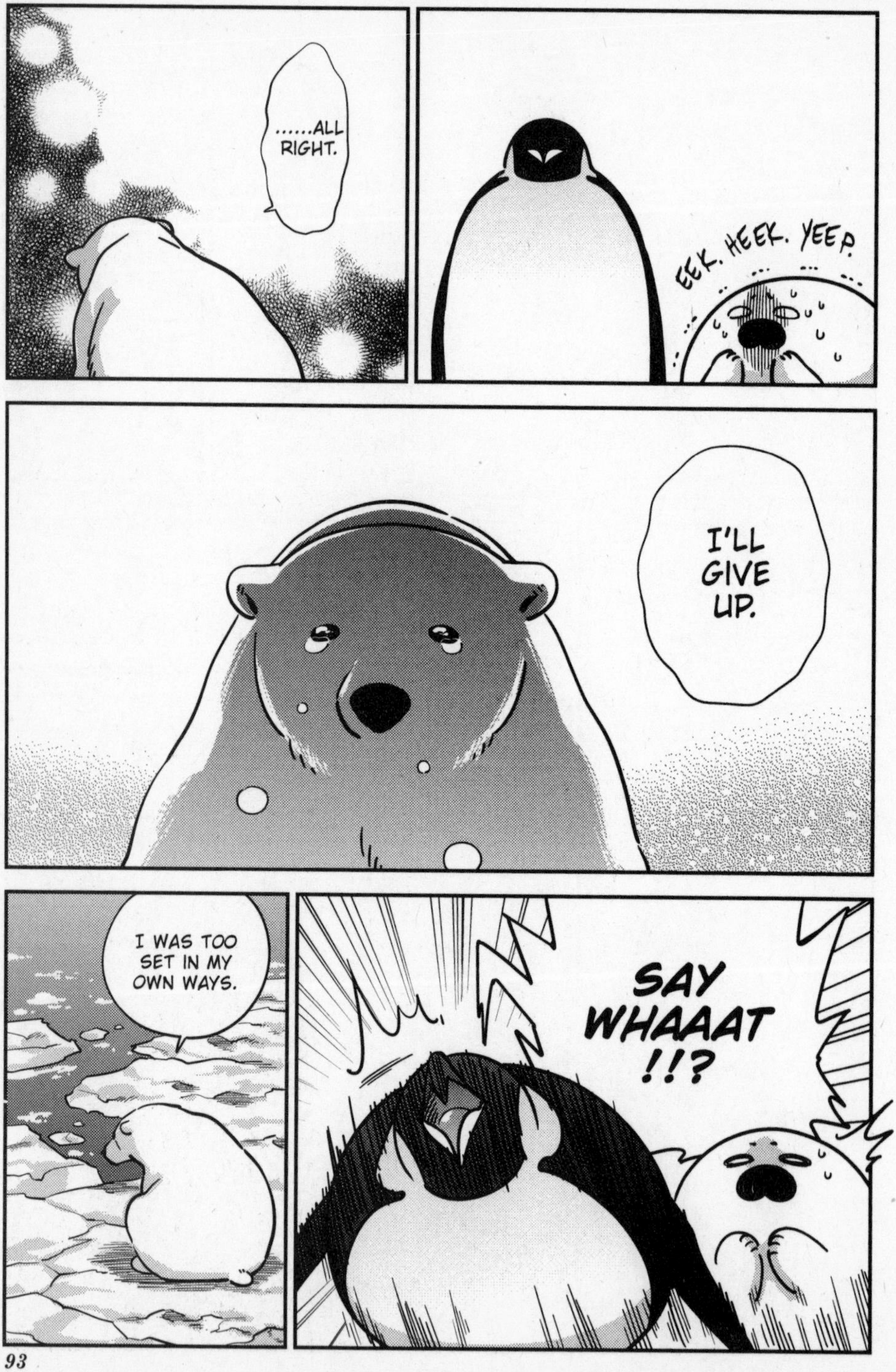
EEK. HEEK. YEEP.
......ALL RIGHT.
I'LL GIVE UP.
SAY WHAAAT !!?
I WAS TOO SET IN MY OWN WAYS.

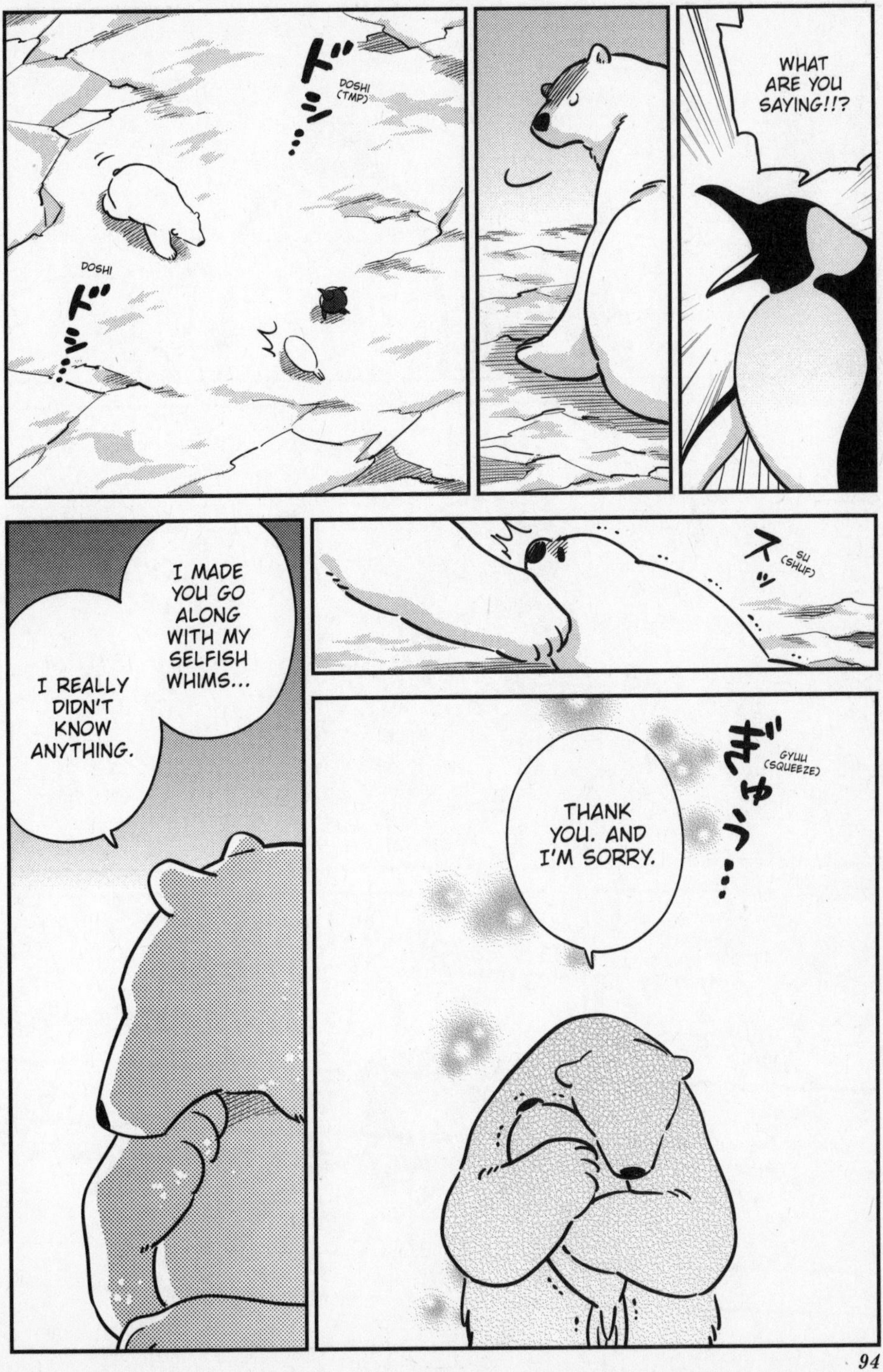
WHAT ARE YOU SAYING!!?
ドシッ…
DOSHI (TMP)
ドシッ…
DOSHI
スッ
SU (SHUF)
ぎゅう…
GYUU (SQUEEZE)
THANK YOU. AND I'M SORRY.
I MADE YOU GO ALONG WITH MY SELFISH WHIMS…
I REALLY DIDN'T KNOW ANYTHING.

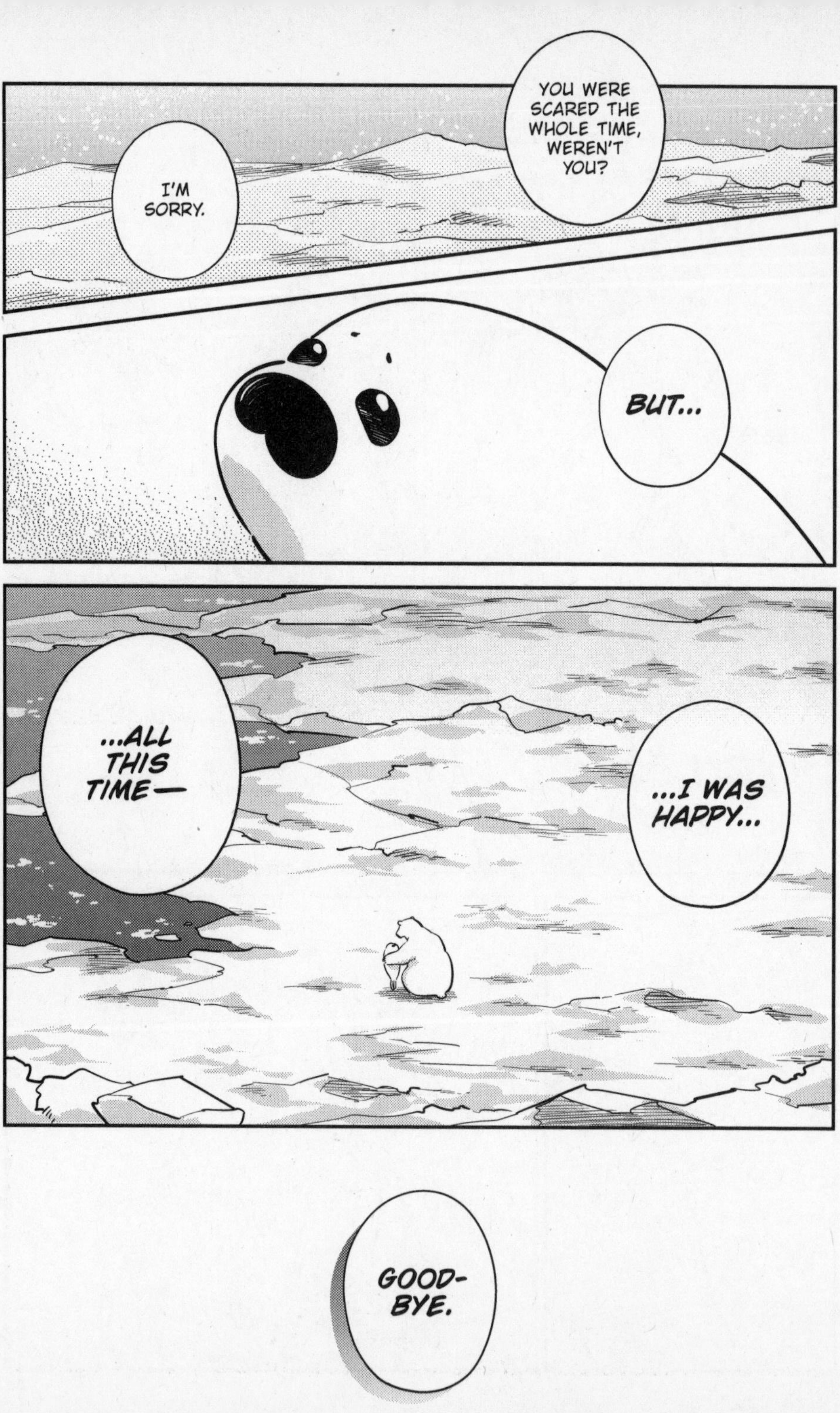
YOU WERE SCARED THE WHOLE TIME, WEREN'T YOU?
I'M SORRY.
BUT...
...I WAS HAPPY...
...ALL THIS TIME—
GOOD-BYE.

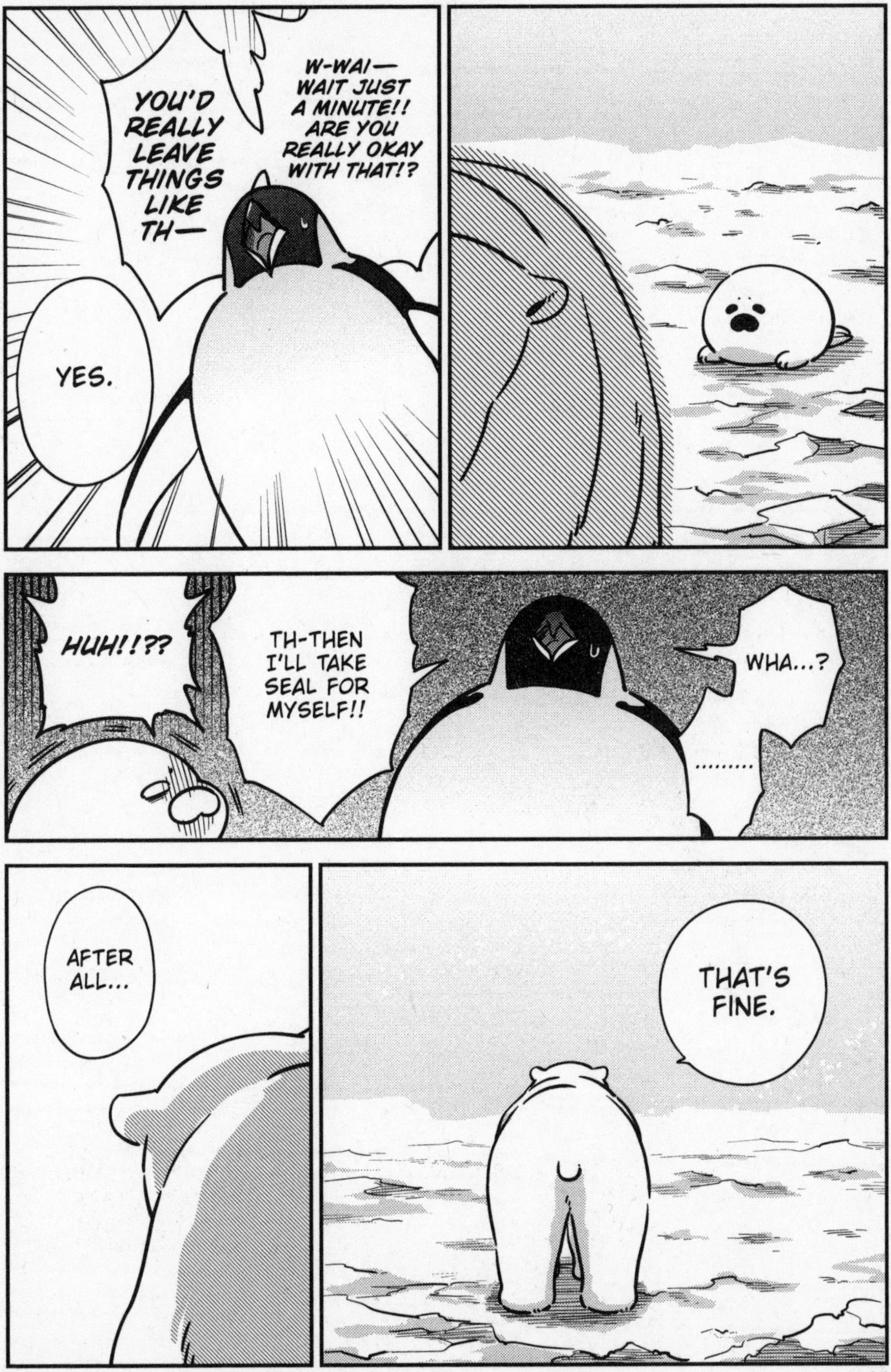
W-WAI— WAIT JUST A MINUTE!! ARE YOU REALLY OKAY WITH THAT!?
YOU'D REALLY LEAVE THINGS LIKE TH—
YES.
WHA...?
....
TH-THEN I'LL TAKE SEAL FOR MYSELF!!
HUH!!??
THAT'S FINE.
AFTER ALL...

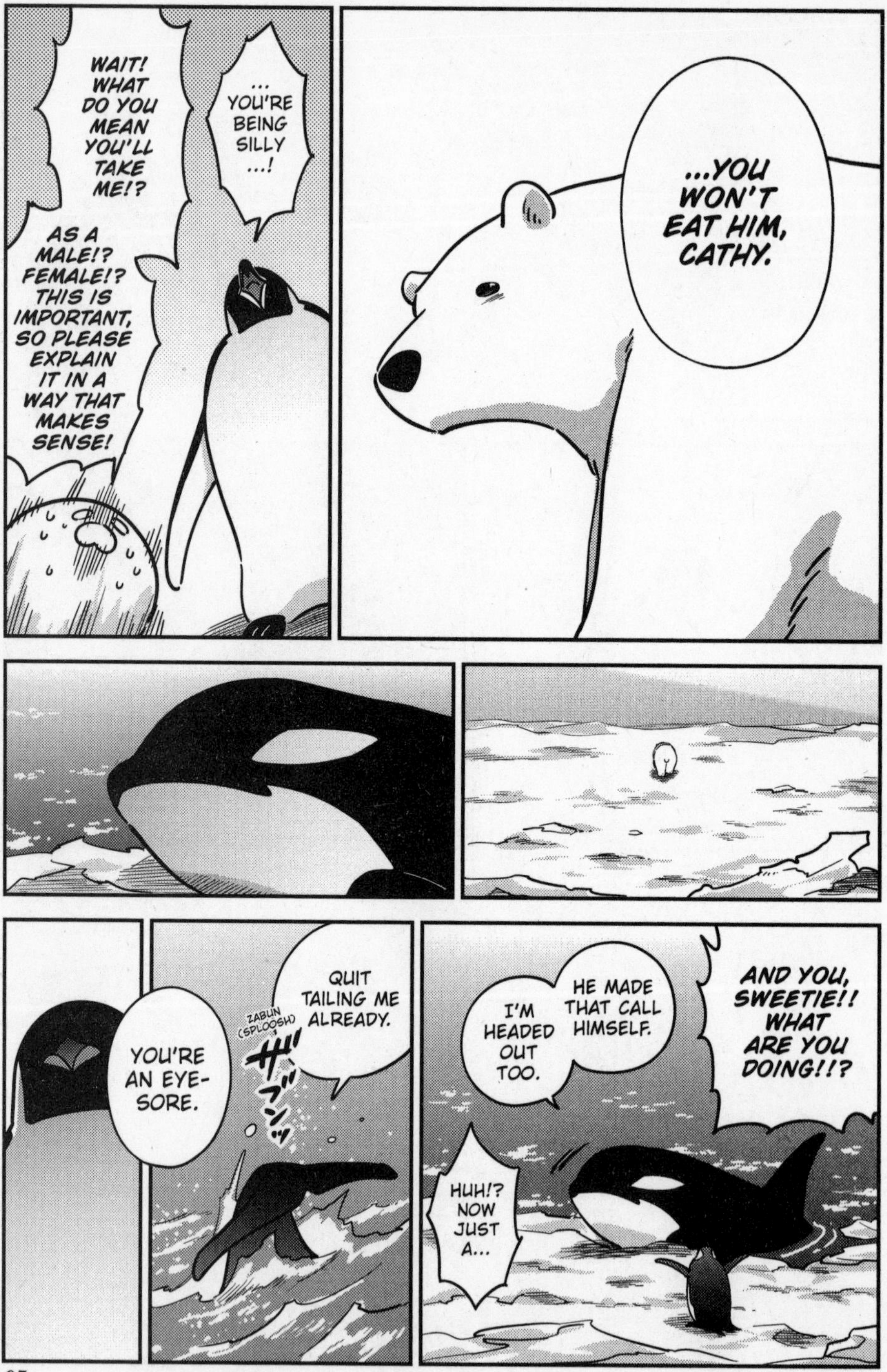
...YOU WON'T EAT HIM, CATHY.
... YOU'RE BEING SILLY ...!
WAIT! WHAT DO YOU MEAN YOU'LL TAKE ME!?
AS A MALE!? FEMALE!? THIS IS IMPORTANT, SO PLEASE EXPLAIN IT IN A WAY THAT MAKES SENSE!
AND YOU, SWEETIE!! WHAT ARE YOU DOING!!?
HE MADE THAT CALL HIMSELF.
I'M HEADED OUT TOO.
HUH!? NOW JUST A...
QUIT TAILING ME ALREADY.
ZABUN (SPLOOSH)
YOU'RE AN EYE-SORE.

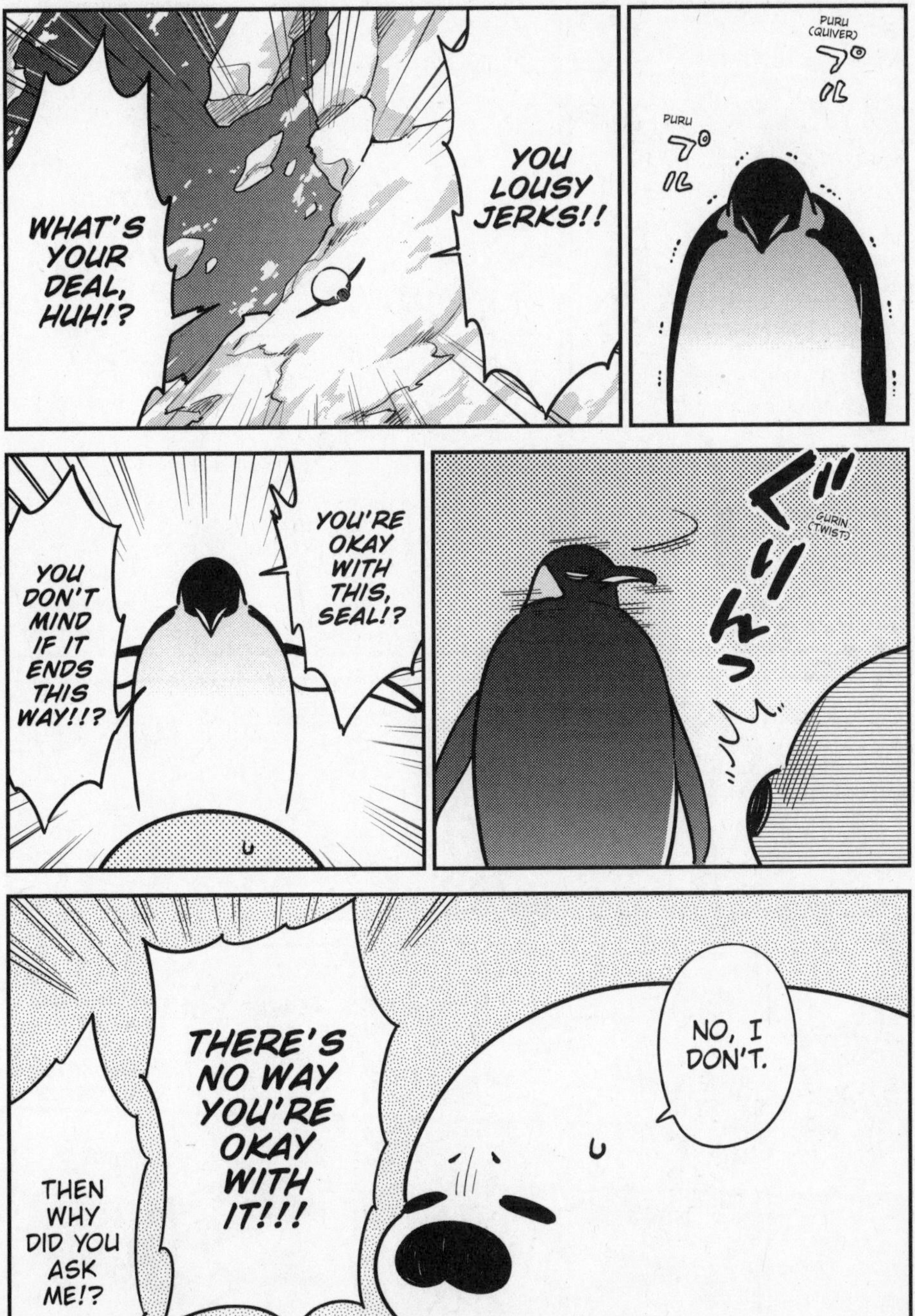
PURU (QUIVER)
プル
PURU
プル
YOU LOUSY JERKS!!
WHAT'S YOUR DEAL, HUH!?
GURIN (TWIST)
ぐりんっ
YOU'RE OKAY WITH THIS, SEAL!?
YOU DON'T MIND IF IT ENDS THIS WAY!!?
NO, I DON'T.
THERE'S NO WAY YOU'RE OKAY WITH IT!!!
THEN WHY DID YOU ASK ME!?

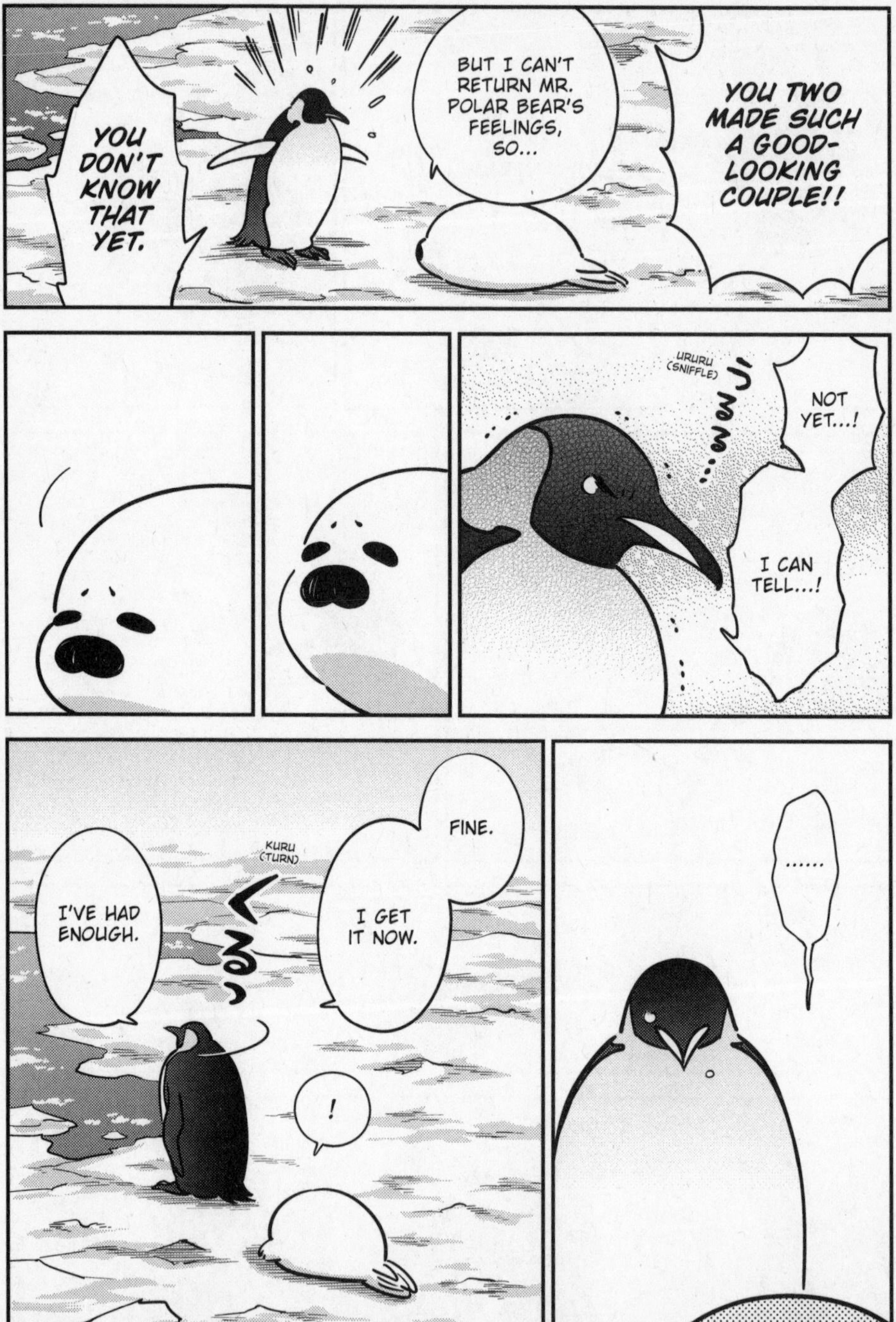
YOU TWO MADE SUCH A GOOD-LOOKING COUPLE!!
BUT I CAN'T RETURN MR. POLAR BEAR'S FEELINGS, SO...
YOU DON'T KNOW THAT YET.
NOT YET...!
URURU (SNIFFLE)
うるる…
I CAN TELL...!
......
FINE.
I GET IT NOW.
KURU (TURN)
くるっ
I'VE HAD ENOUGH.
!

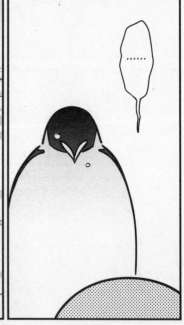

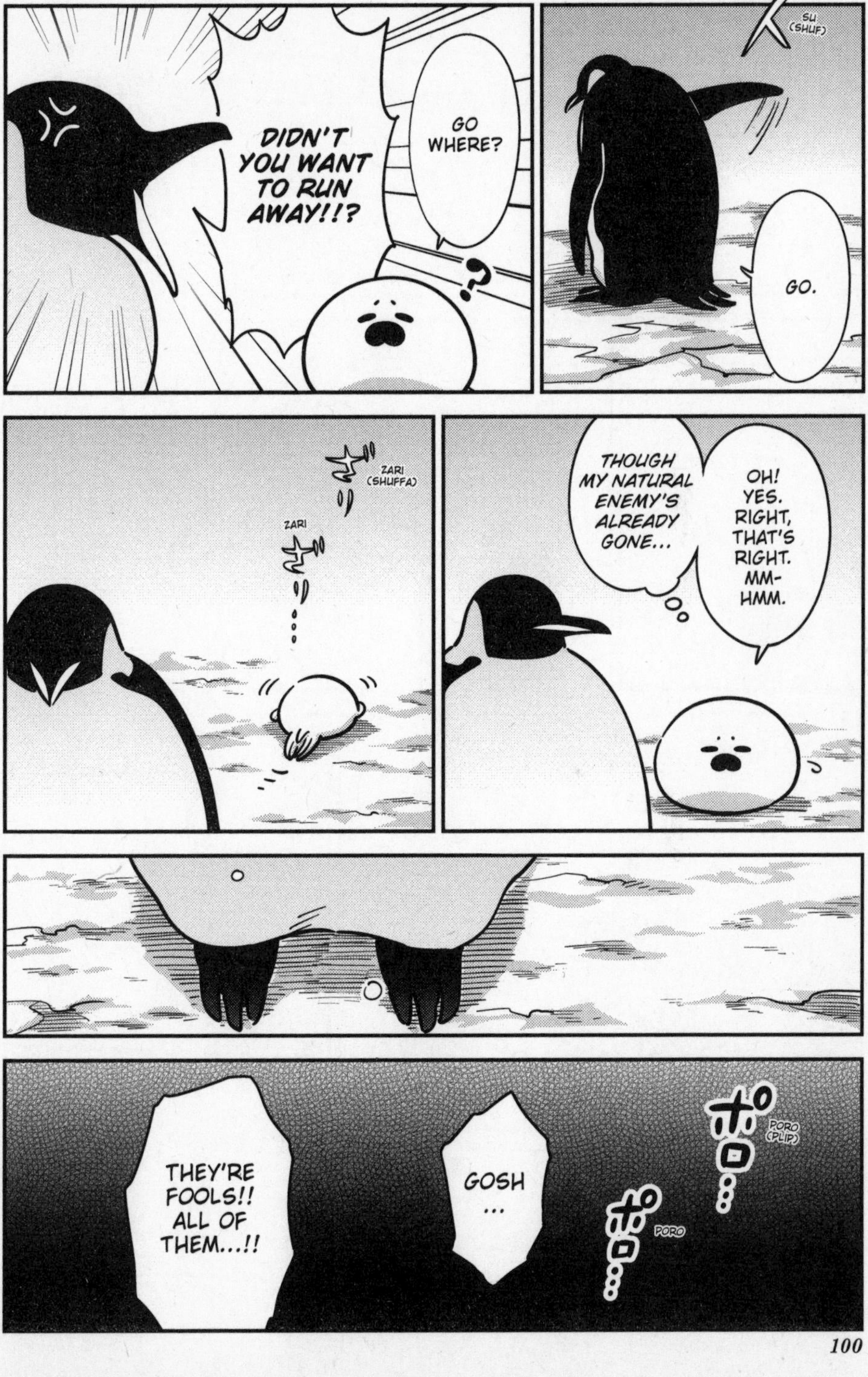

ス
SU (SHUF)
GO.
GO WHERE?
DIDN'T YOU WANT TO RUN AWAY!!?
?
OH! YES. RIGHT, THAT'S RIGHT. MM-HMM.
THOUGH MY NATURAL ENEMY'S ALREADY GONE...
ZARI (SHUFFA)
ZARI
ポロ…
PORO (PLIP)
ポロ…
PORO
GOSH ...
THEY'RE FOOLS!! ALL OF THEM...!!

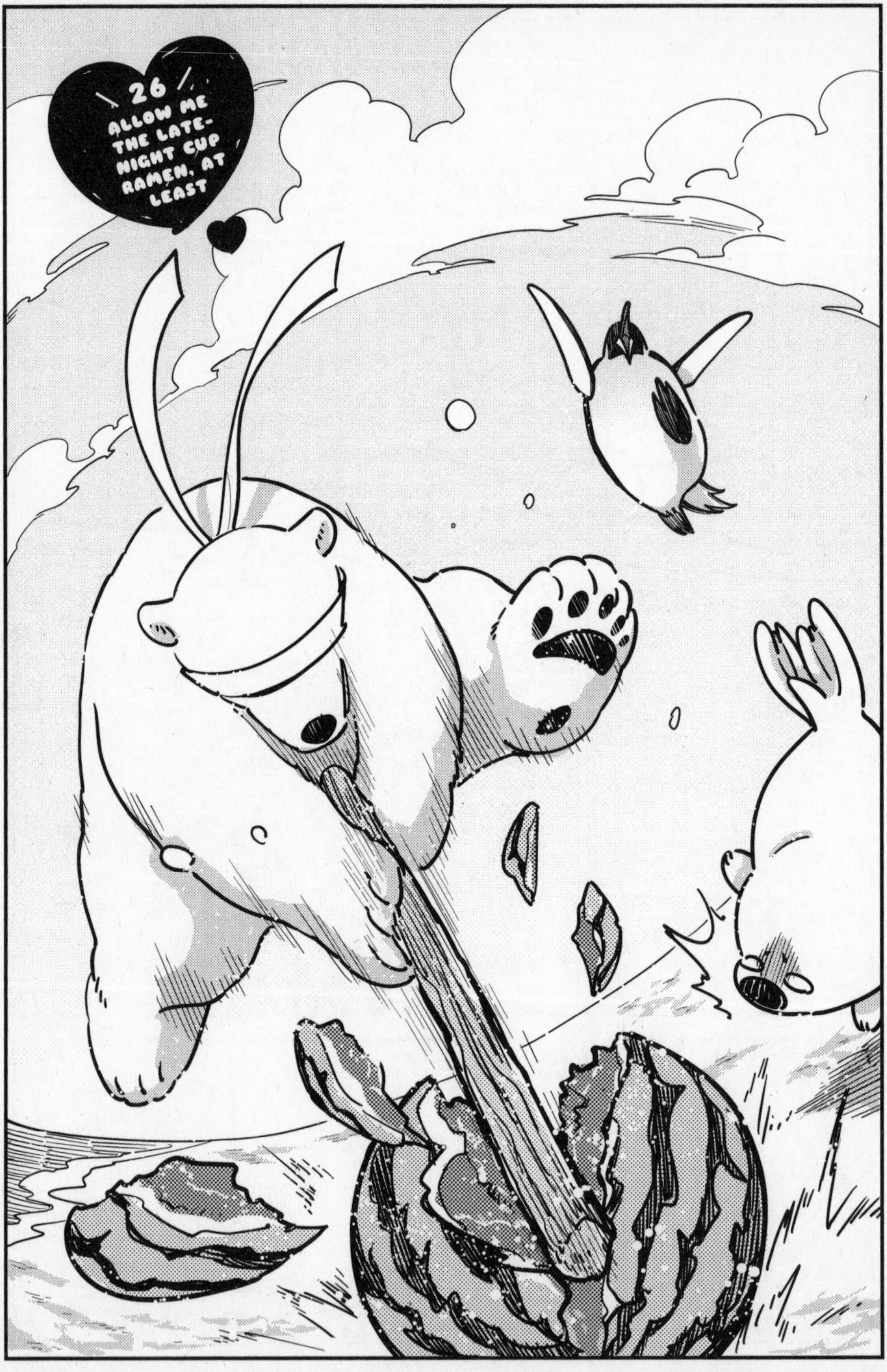
26
ALLOW ME THE LATE-NIGHT CUP RAMEN, AT LEAST

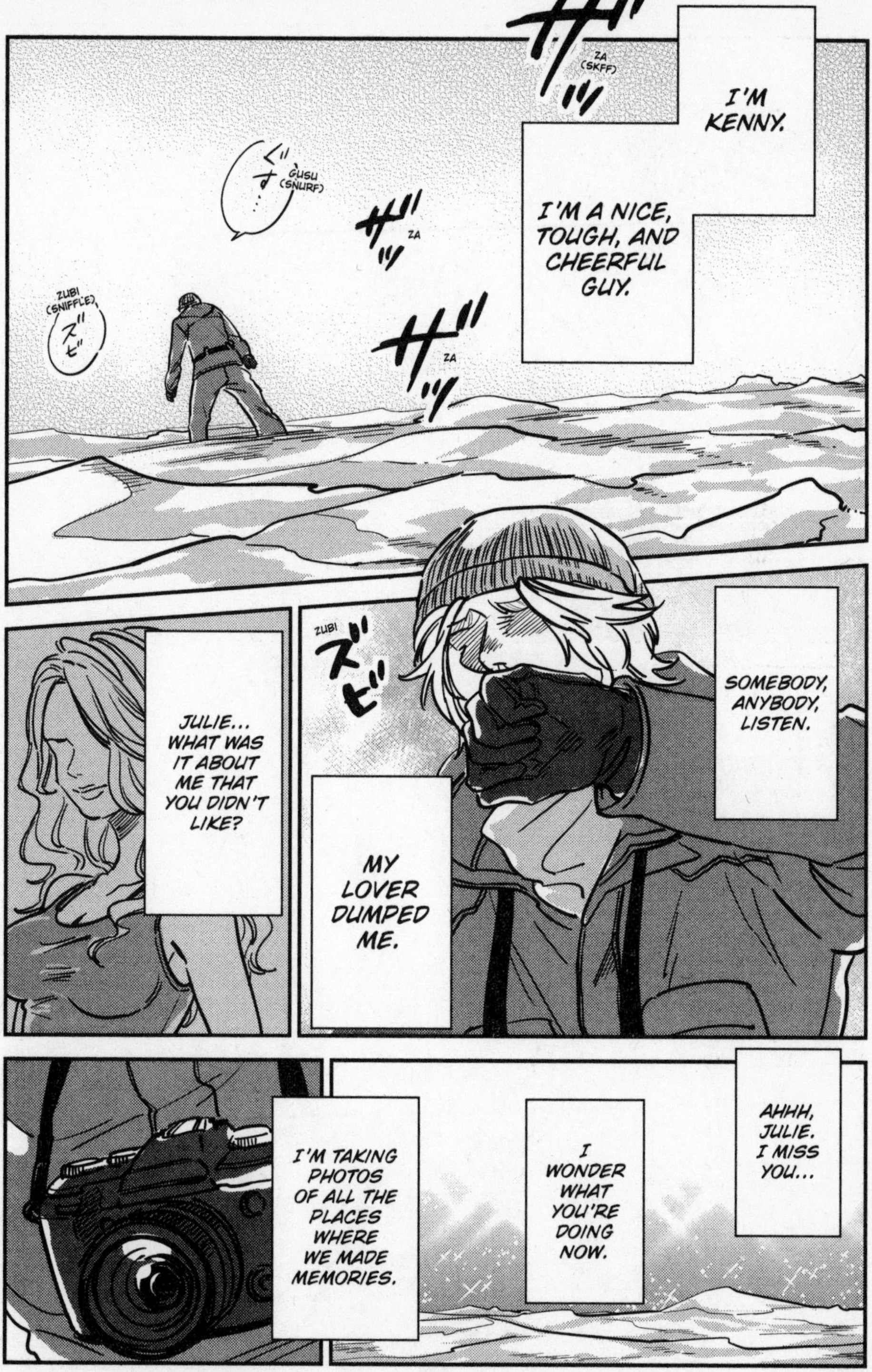
ザッ
ZA (SKFF)
I'M KENNY.
I'M A NICE, TOUGH, AND CHEERFUL GUY.
ザッ
ZA
ぐす…
GUSU (SNURF)
ザッ
ZA
ズビ
ZUBI (SNIFFLE)
SOMEBODY, ANYBODY, LISTEN.
ズビ
ZUBI
MY LOVER DUMPED ME.
JULIE... WHAT WAS IT ABOUT ME THAT YOU DIDN'T LIKE?
AHHH, JULIE. I MISS YOU...
I WONDER WHAT YOU'RE DOING NOW.
I'M TAKING PHOTOS OF ALL THE PLACES WHERE WE MADE MEMORIES.

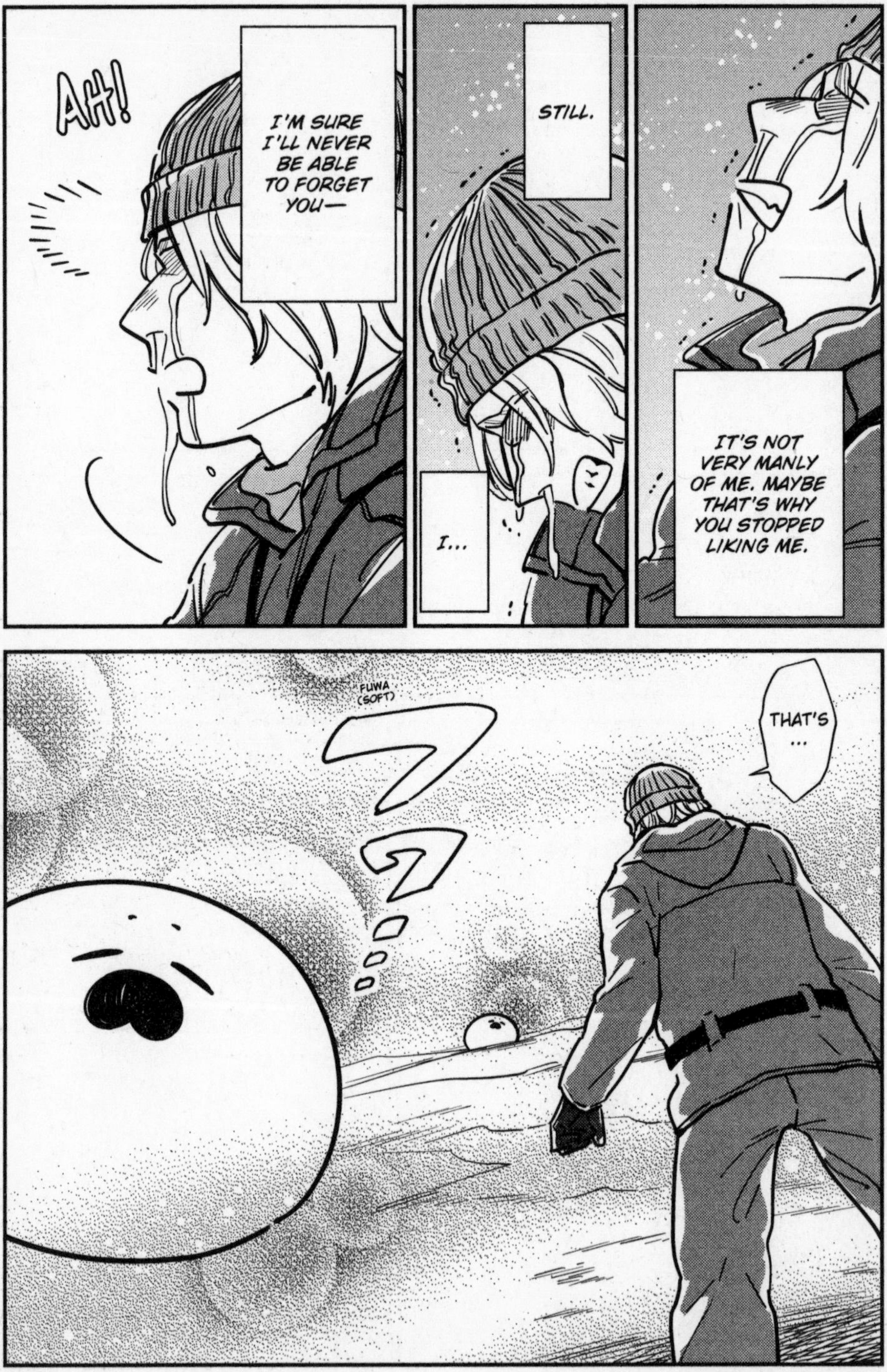
IT'S NOT VERY MANLY OF ME. MAYBE THAT'S WHY YOU STOPPED LIKING ME.
STILL.
I...
I'M SURE I'LL NEVER BE ABLE TO FORGET YOU—
AH!
THAT'S ...
FUWA (SOFT)

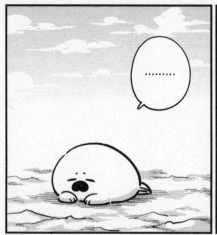

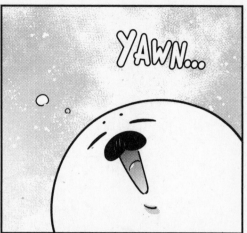

YAWN...
....
GOOD-BYE.
IT'S BETTER THIS WAY.
NOT JUST FOR ME—NOW MR. POLAR BEAR WILL BE ABLE TO FIND HAPPINESS AS WELL.
ALL SORTS OF RIDICULOUS THINGS HAVE BEEN HAPPENING LATELY, BUT...
THE FOOD CHAIN
...FOR A BALANCED WORLD, THIS WAY IS BEST.
THE STRONG EAT THE WEAK.
? ? ? ?

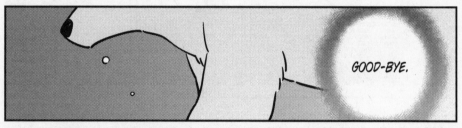

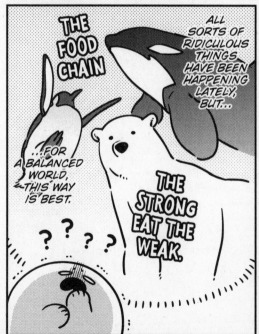

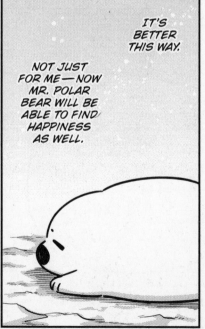

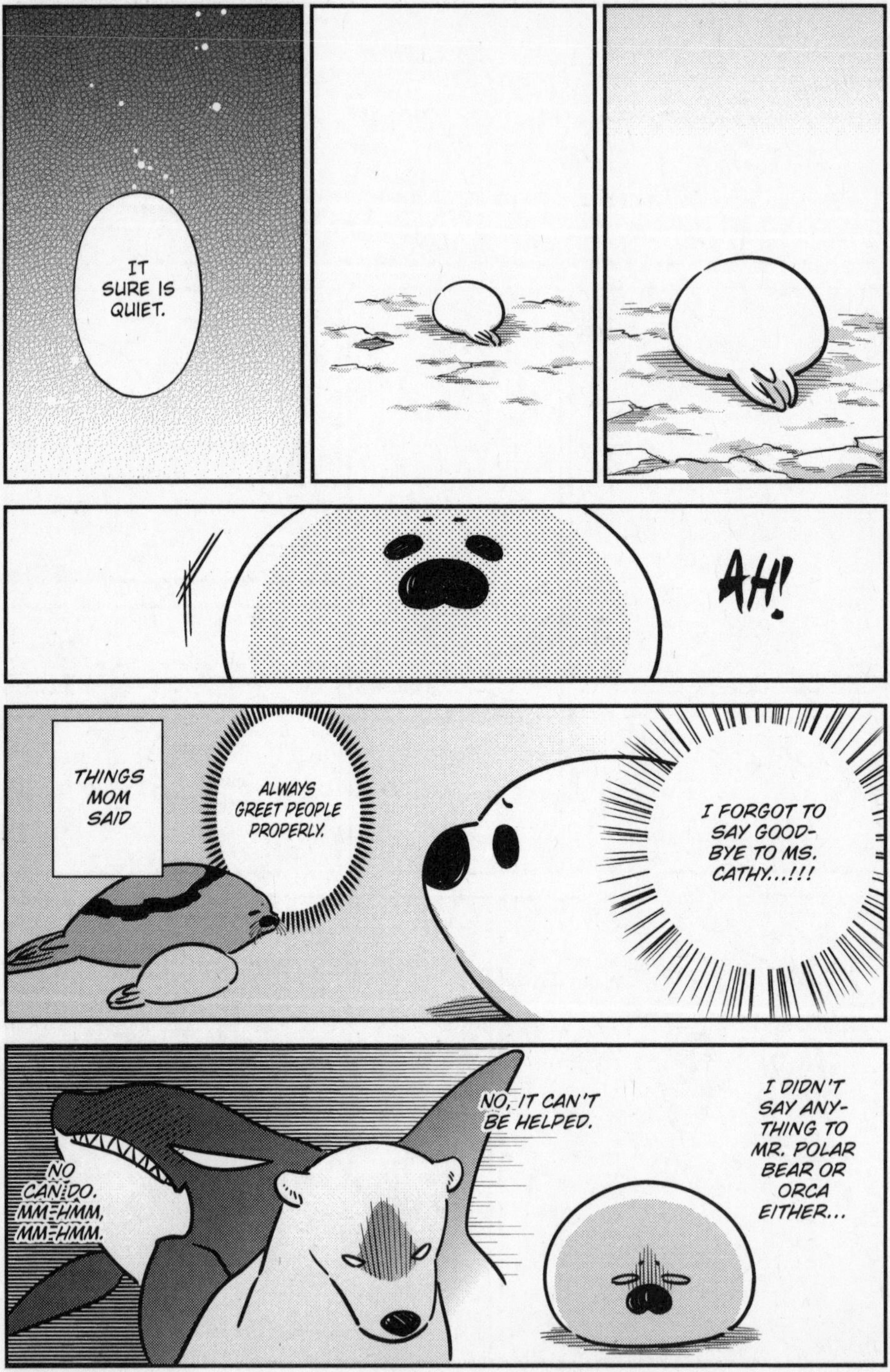
IT SURE IS QUIET.
AH!
I FORGOT TO SAY GOOD-BYE TO MS. CATHY...!!!
THINGS MOM SAID
ALWAYS GREET PEOPLE PROPERLY.
I DIDN'T SAY ANY-THING TO MR. POLAR BEAR OR ORCA EITHER...
NO, IT CAN'T BE HELPED.
NO CAN DO. MM-HMM, MM-HMM.

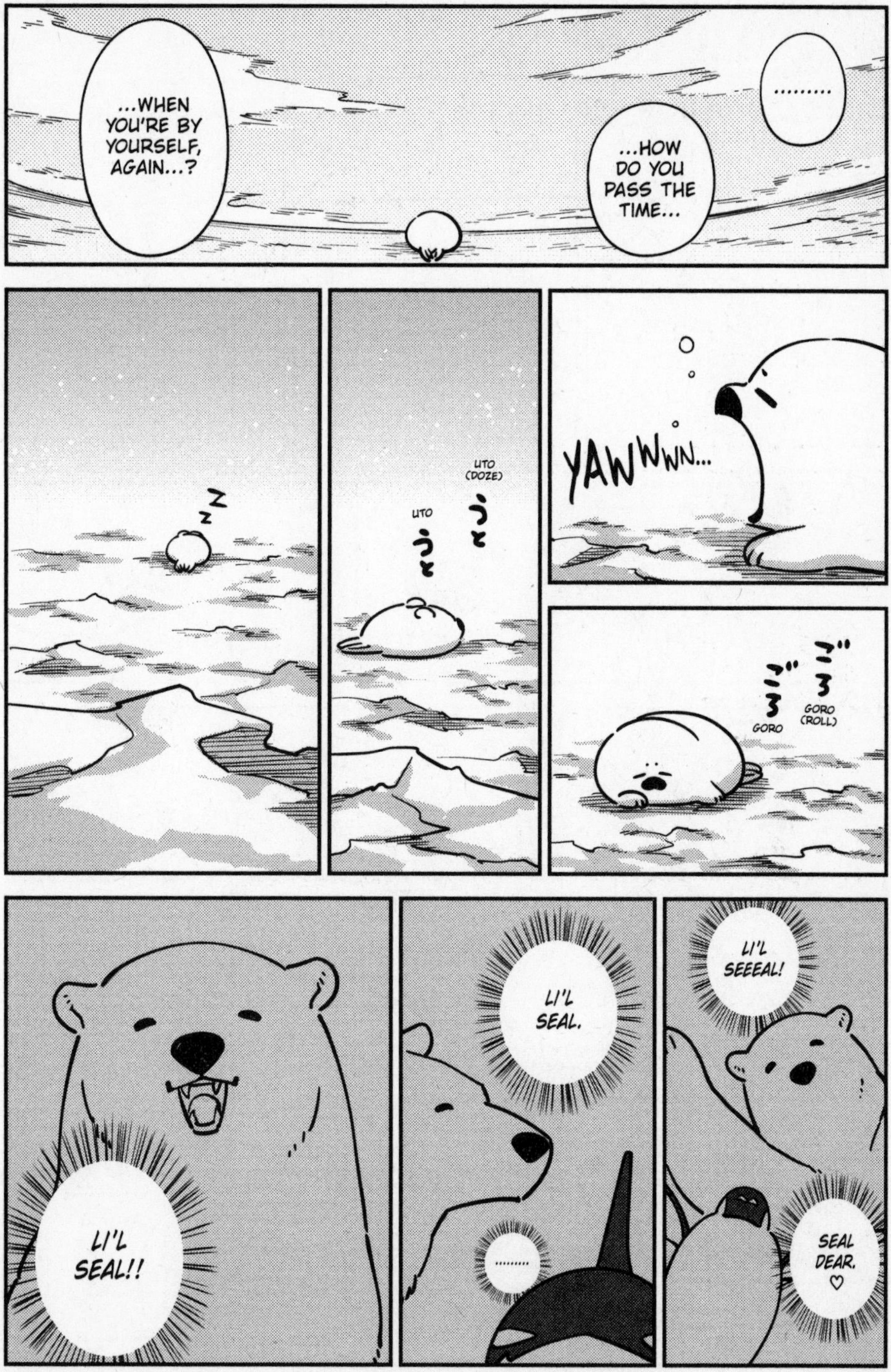
....
...HOW DO YOU PASS THE TIME...
...WHEN YOU'RE BY YOURSELF, AGAIN...?
YAWWWN...
ごろ
GORO (ROLL)
ごろ
GORO
うと
UTO (DOZE)
うと
UTO
Z Z
LI'L SEEEAL!
SEAL DEAR. ♡
LI'L SEAL.
....
LI'L SEAL!!

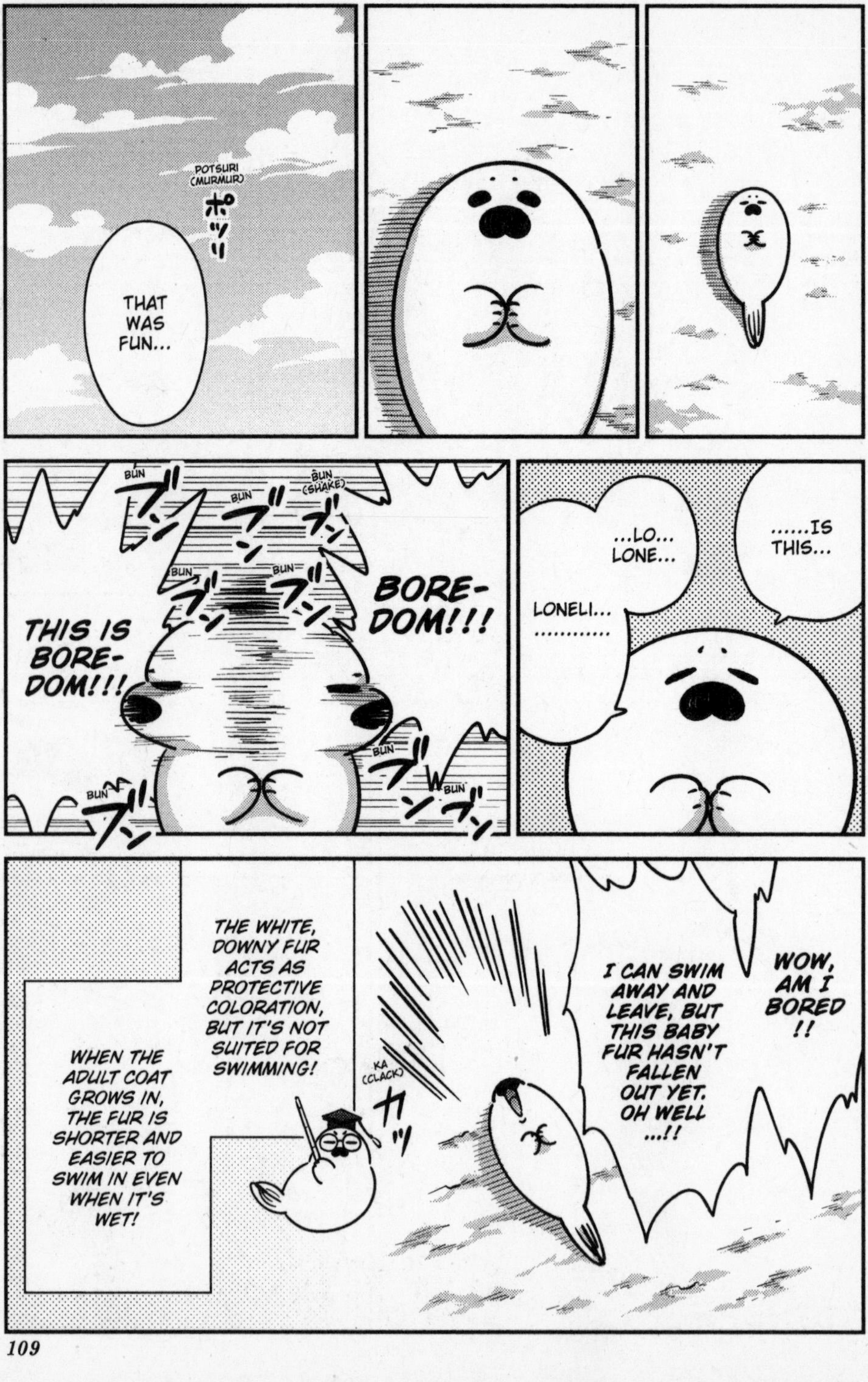
POTSURI (MURMUR)
ポツリ
THAT WAS FUN...
......IS THIS...
...LO... LONE...
LONELI... ....
BUN (SHAKE)
ブン
BUN
ブン
BUN
ブン
BUN
ブン
BORE-DOM!!!
BUN
ブン
THIS IS BORE-DOM!!!
BUN
ブン
BUN
ブン
BUN
ブン
WOW, AM I BORED!!
I CAN SWIM AWAY AND LEAVE, BUT THIS BABY FUR HASN'T FALLEN OUT YET. OH WELL ...!!
KA (CLACK)
カッ
THE WHITE, DOWNY FUR ACTS AS PROTECTIVE COLORATION, BUT IT'S NOT SUITED FOR SWIMMING!
WHEN THE ADULT COAT GROWS IN, THE FUR IS SHORTER AND EASIER TO SWIM IN EVEN WHEN IT'S WET!

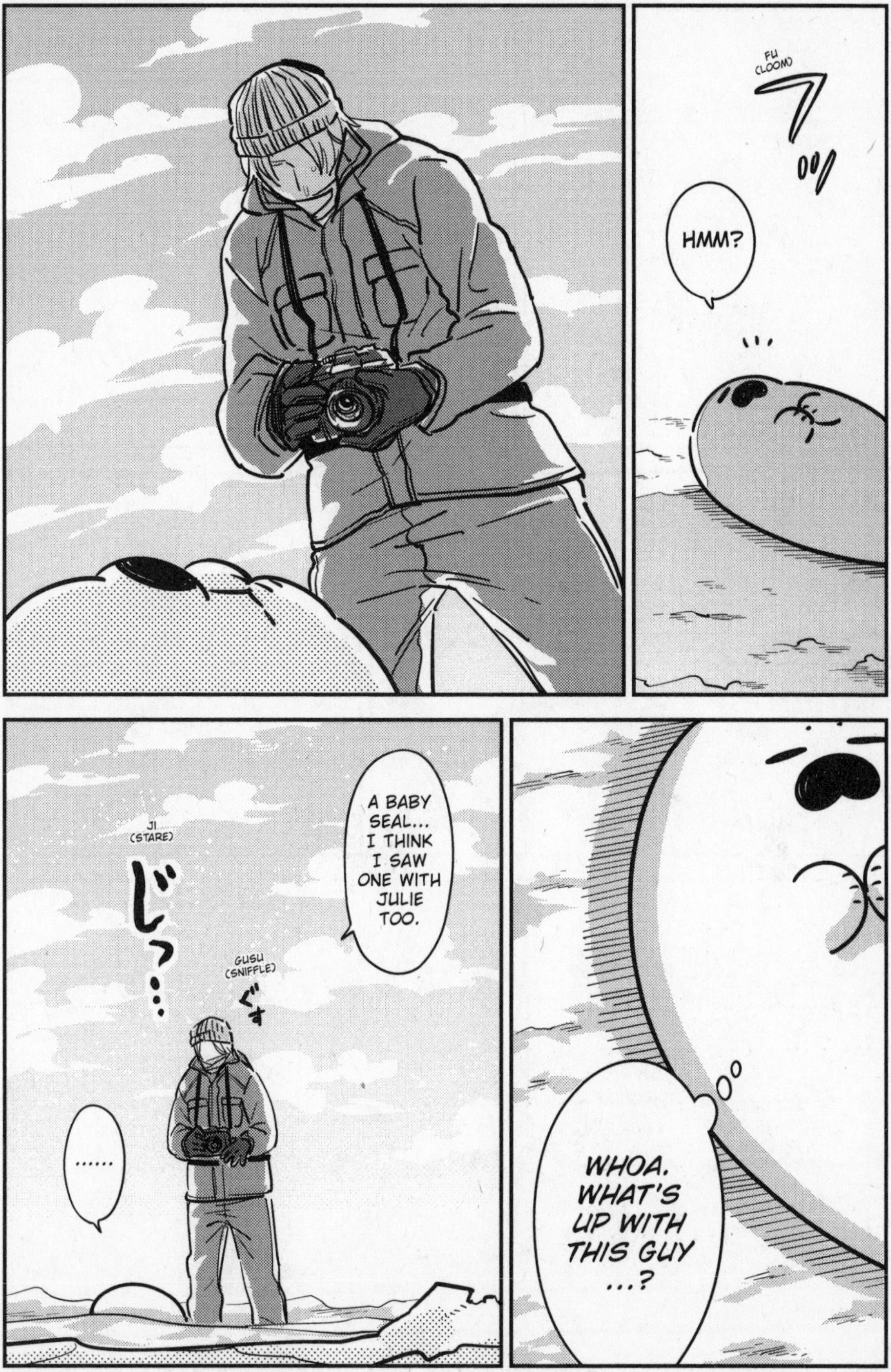
FU (LOOM)
HMM?
WHOA. WHAT'S UP WITH THIS GUY ...?
JI (STARE)
じっ…
A BABY SEAL... I THINK I SAW ONE WITH JULIE TOO.
GUSU (SNIFFLE)
ぐす
......

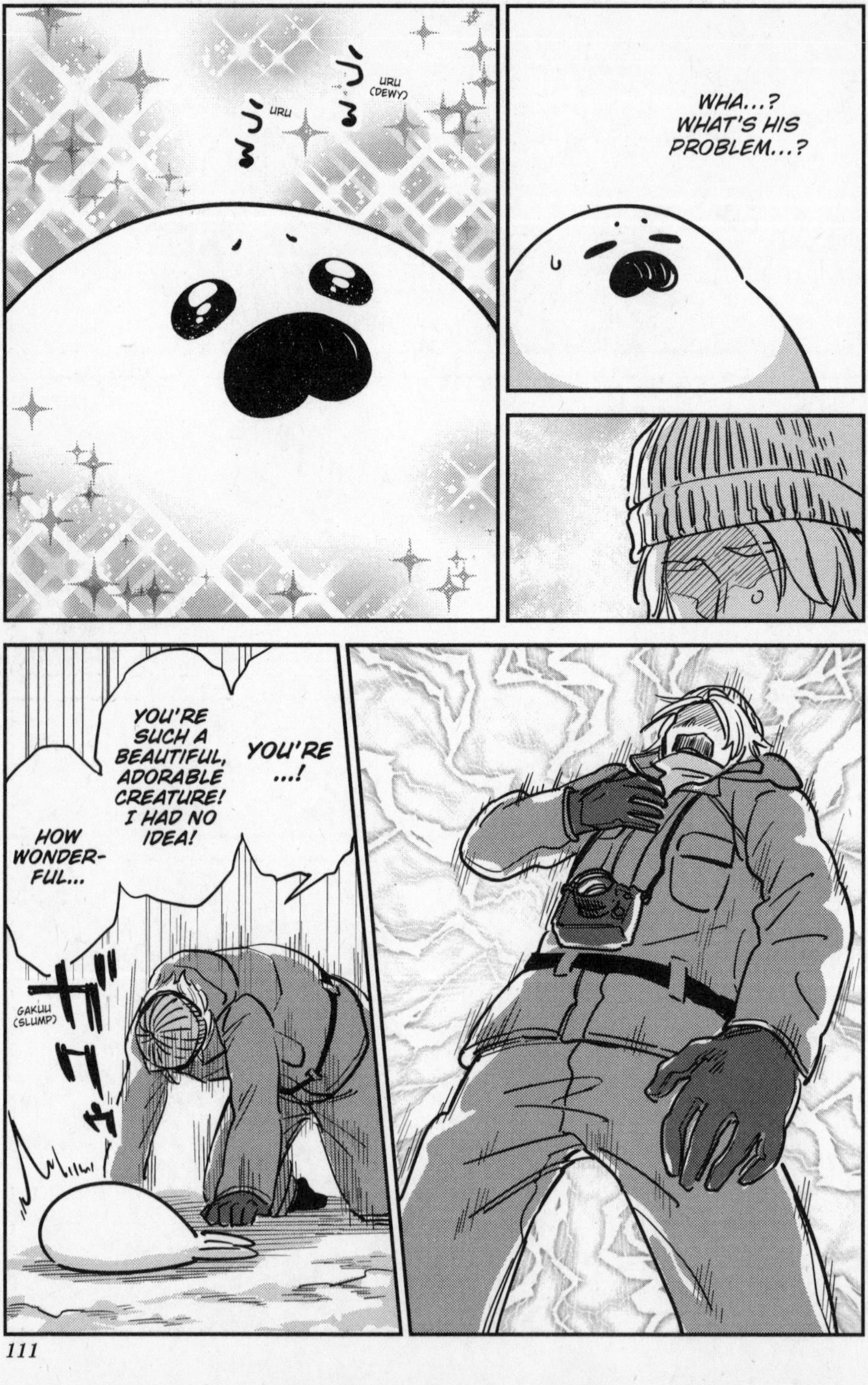
WHA...? WHAT'S HIS PROBLEM...?
うる
URU (DEWY)
うる
URU
YOU'RE ...!
YOU'RE SUCH A BEAUTIFUL, ADORABLE CREATURE! I HAD NO IDEA!
HOW WONDER-FUL...
GAKUU (SLUMP)

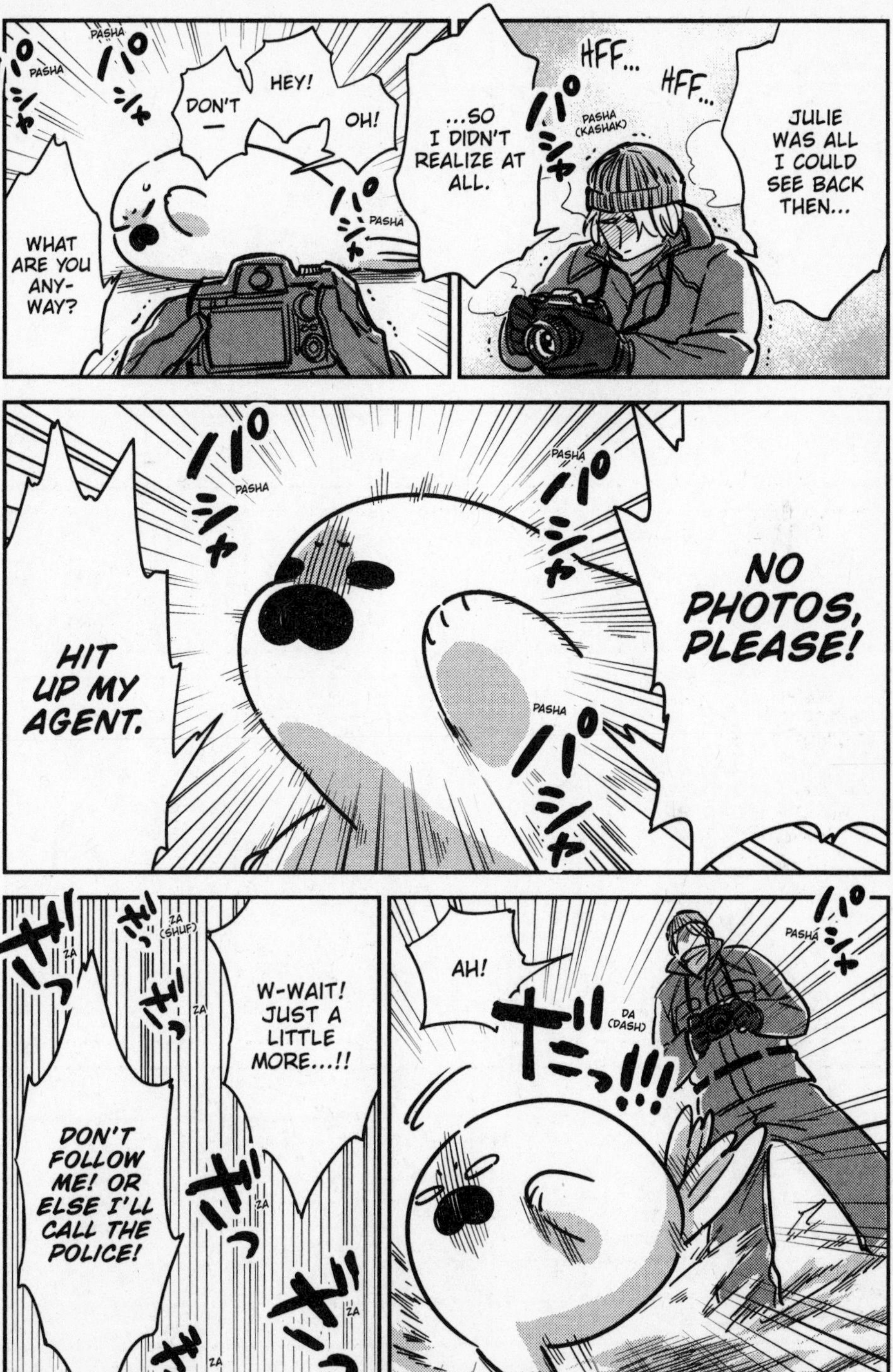
JULIE WAS ALL I COULD SEE BACK THEN...
HFF... HFF...
...SO I DIDN'T REALIZE AT ALL.
PASHA (KASHAK)
OH!
HEY!
DON'T —
PASHA
PASHA
PASHA
WHAT ARE YOU ANYWAY?
NO PHOTOS, PLEASE!
PASHA
PASHA
PASHA
HIT UP MY AGENT.
PASHA
AH!
DA (DASH)
W-WAIT! JUST A LITTLE MORE...!!
ZA (SHUF)
ZA
ZA
ZA
ZA
ZA
DON'T FOLLOW ME! OR ELSE I'LL CALL THE POLICE!

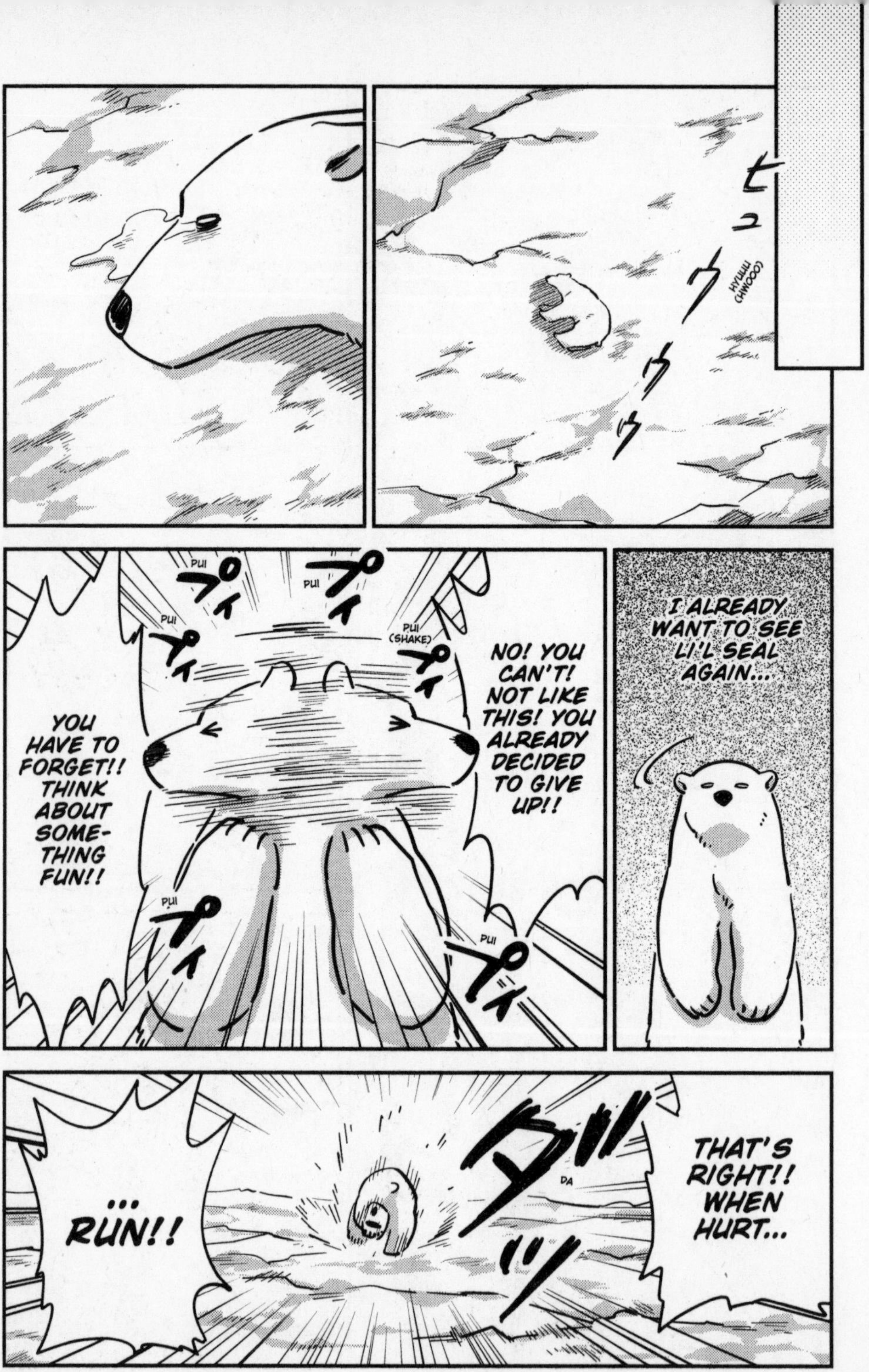
HYUUU CHWOOOO
I ALREADY WANT TO SEE LI'L SEAL AGAIN...
PUI
PUI
PUI (SHAKE)
PUI
NO! YOU CAN'T! NOT LIKE THIS! YOU ALREADY DECIDED TO GIVE UP!!
YOU HAVE TO FORGET!! THINK ABOUT SOME-THING FUN!!
PUI
PUI
THAT'S RIGHT!! WHEN HURT...
DA
... RÜN!!

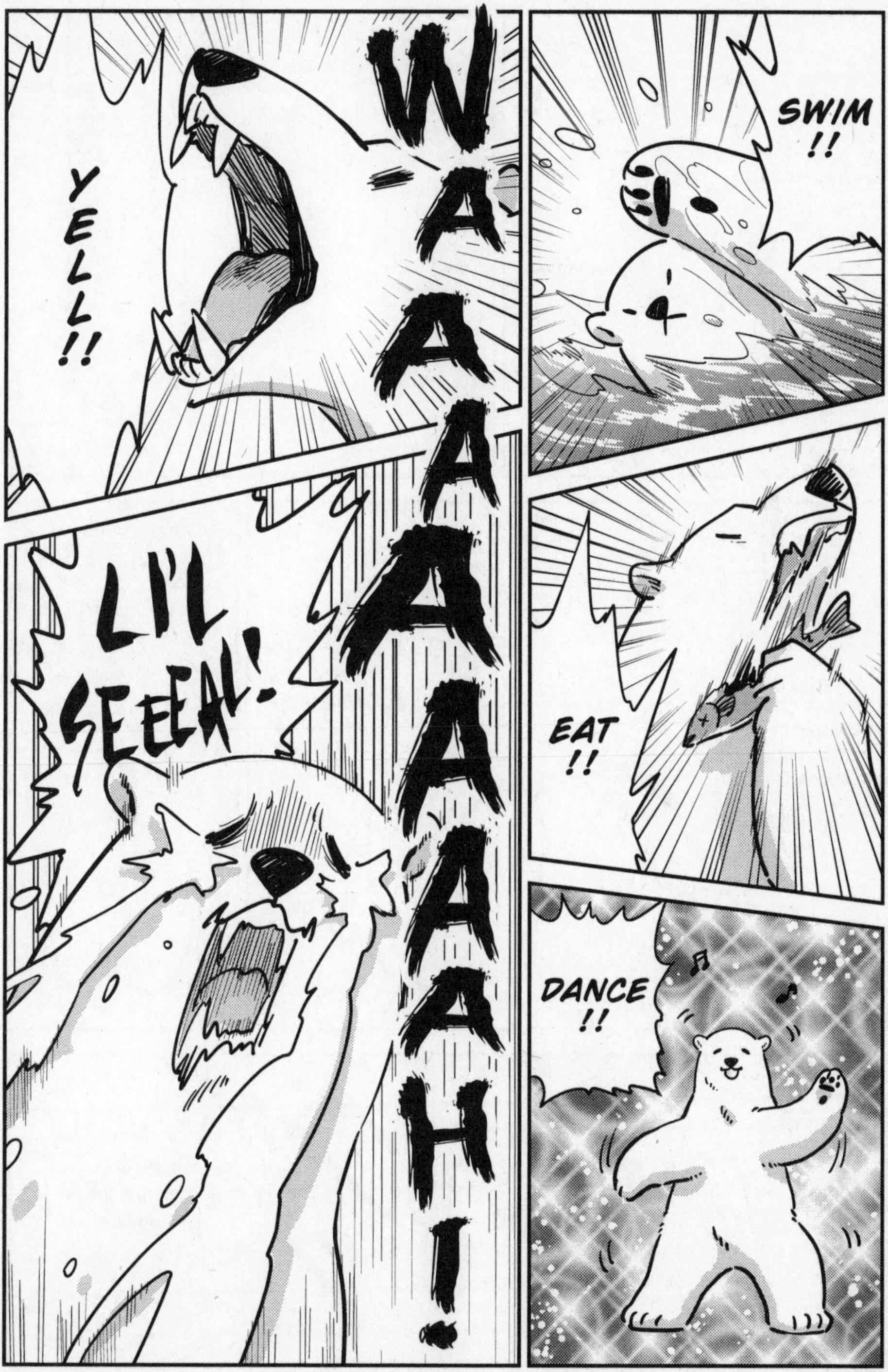
SWIM!!
EAT!!
DANCE!!
YELL!!
WAAAAAAH!
LI'L SEEEAL!

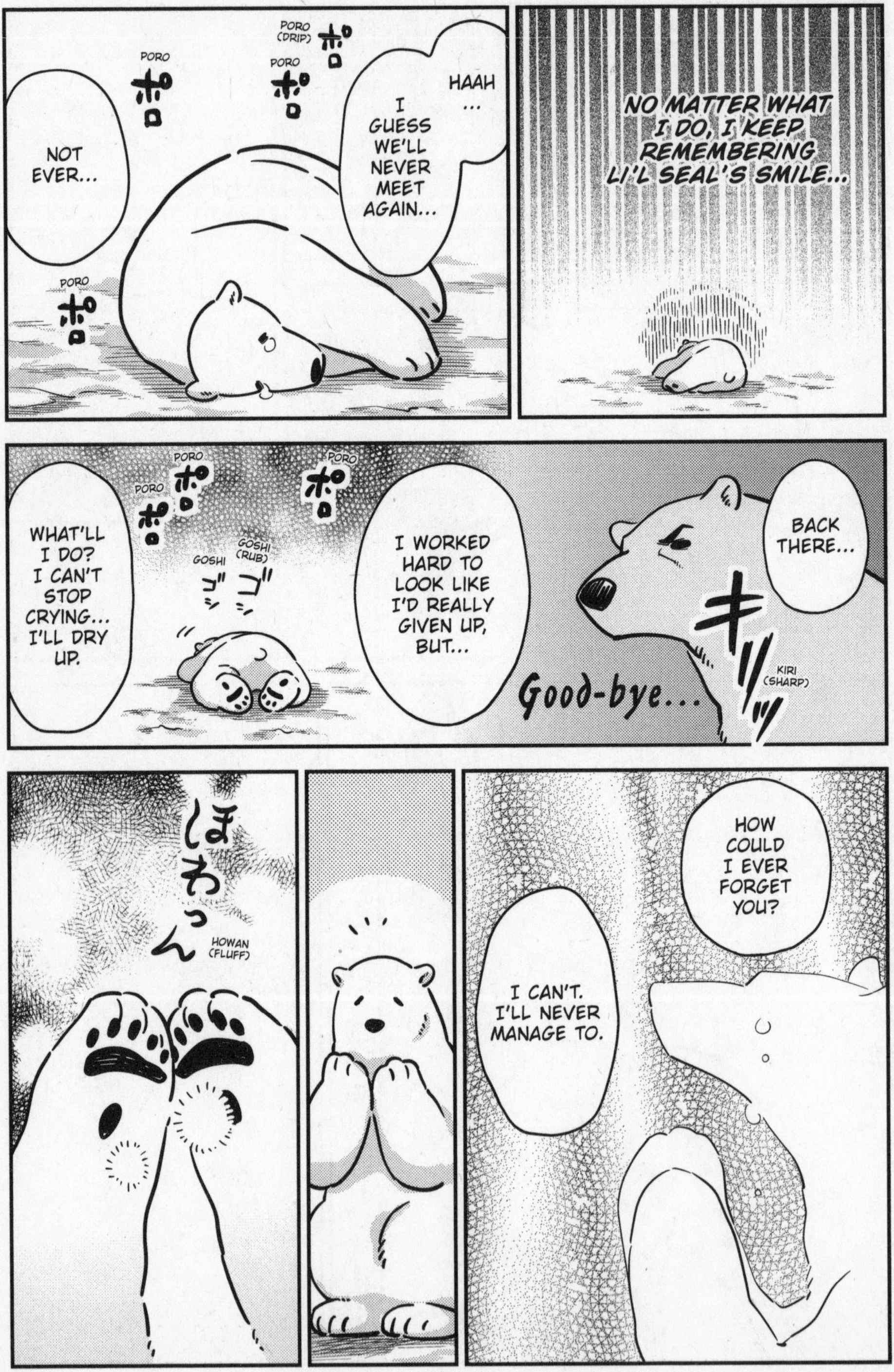
NO MATTER WHAT I DO, I KEEP REMEMBERING LI'L SEAL'S SMILE...
ポロ
PORO (DRIP)
HAAH...
I GUESS WE'LL NEVER MEET AGAIN...
ポロ
PORO
ポロ
PORO
NOT EVER...
ポロ
PORO
BACK THERE...
キッ
KIRI (SHARP)
Good-bye...
I WORKED HARD TO LOOK LIKE I'D REALLY GIVEN UP, BUT...
ポロ
PORO
ポロ
PORO
ポロ
PORO
ゴシ
GOSHI (RUB)
ゴシ
GOSHI
WHAT'LL I DO? I CAN'T STOP CRYING... I'LL DRY UP.
HOW COULD I EVER FORGET YOU?
I CAN'T. I'LL NEVER MANAGE TO.
ほわっん
HOWAN (FLUFF)

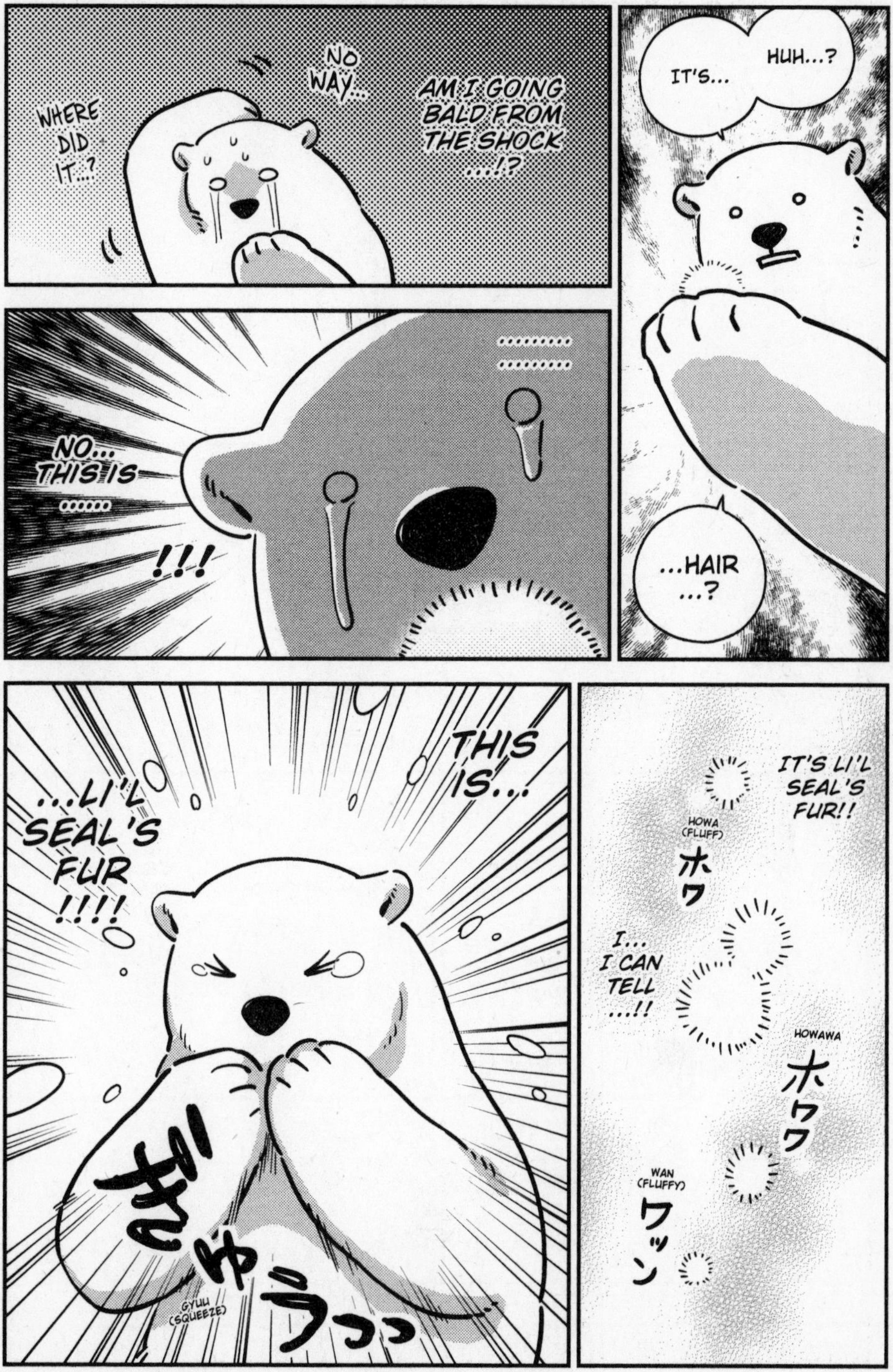

HUH...?
IT'S...
...HAIR ...?
AM I GOING BALD FROM THE SHOCK ...!?
NO WAY..
WHERE DID IT..?
....
....
NO... THIS IS ......
!!!
IT'S LI'L SEAL'S FUR!!
HOWA (FLUFF)
ホワ
I... I CAN TELL ...!!
HOWAWA
ホワワ
WAN (FLUFFY)
ワッン
THIS IS...
...LI'L SEAL'S FUR !!!!
GYUU (SQUEEZE)
ぎゅうっっ

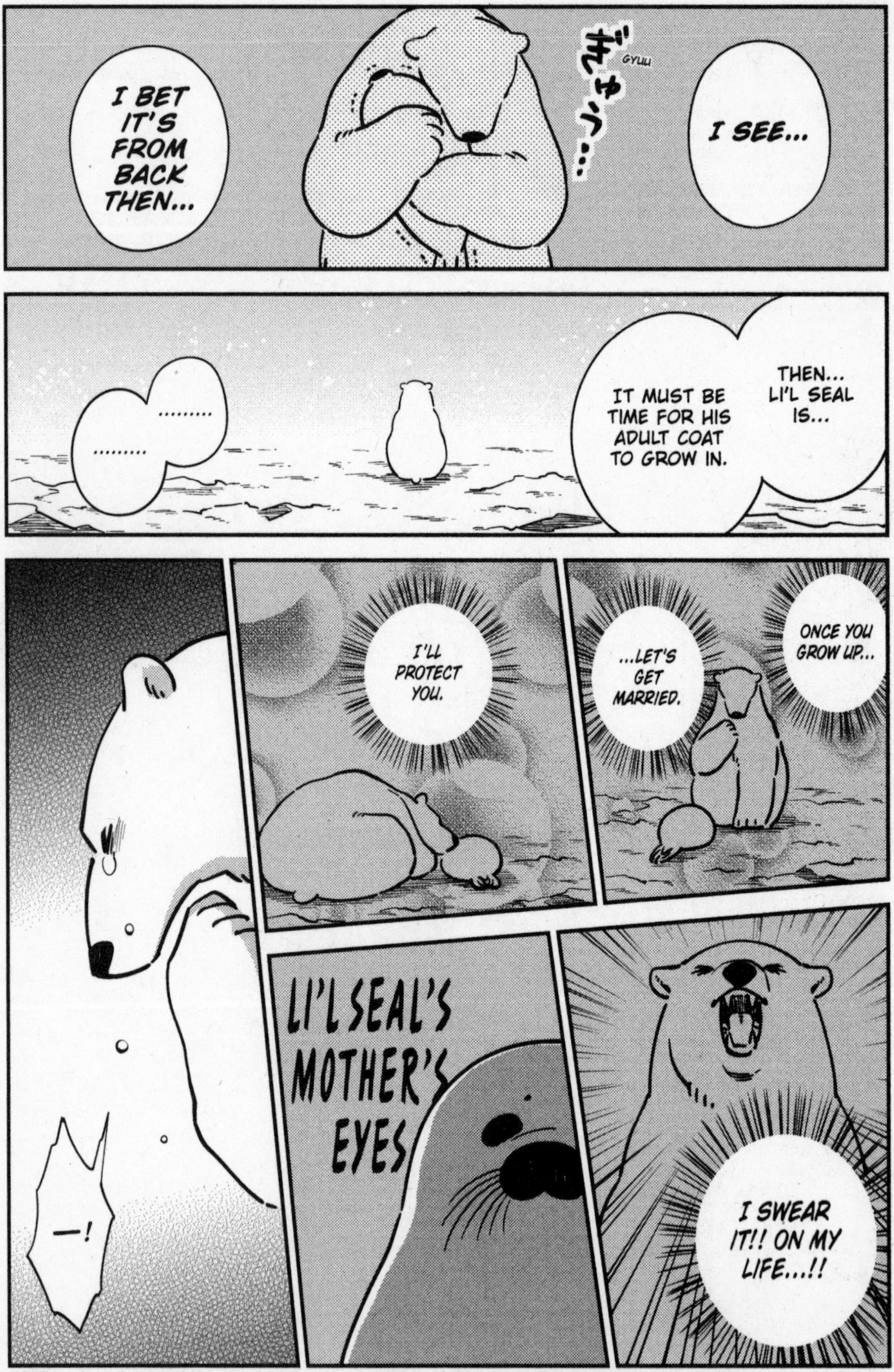
I SEE...
ぎゅう...
GYUU
I BET IT'S FROM BACK THEN...
THEN... LI'L SEAL IS...
IT MUST BE TIME FOR HIS ADULT COAT TO GROW IN.
....
....
ONCE YOU GROW UP...
...LET'S GET MARRIED.
I'LL PROTECT YOU.
I SWEAR IT!! ON MY LIFE...!!
LI'L SEAL'S MOTHER'S EYES
—!

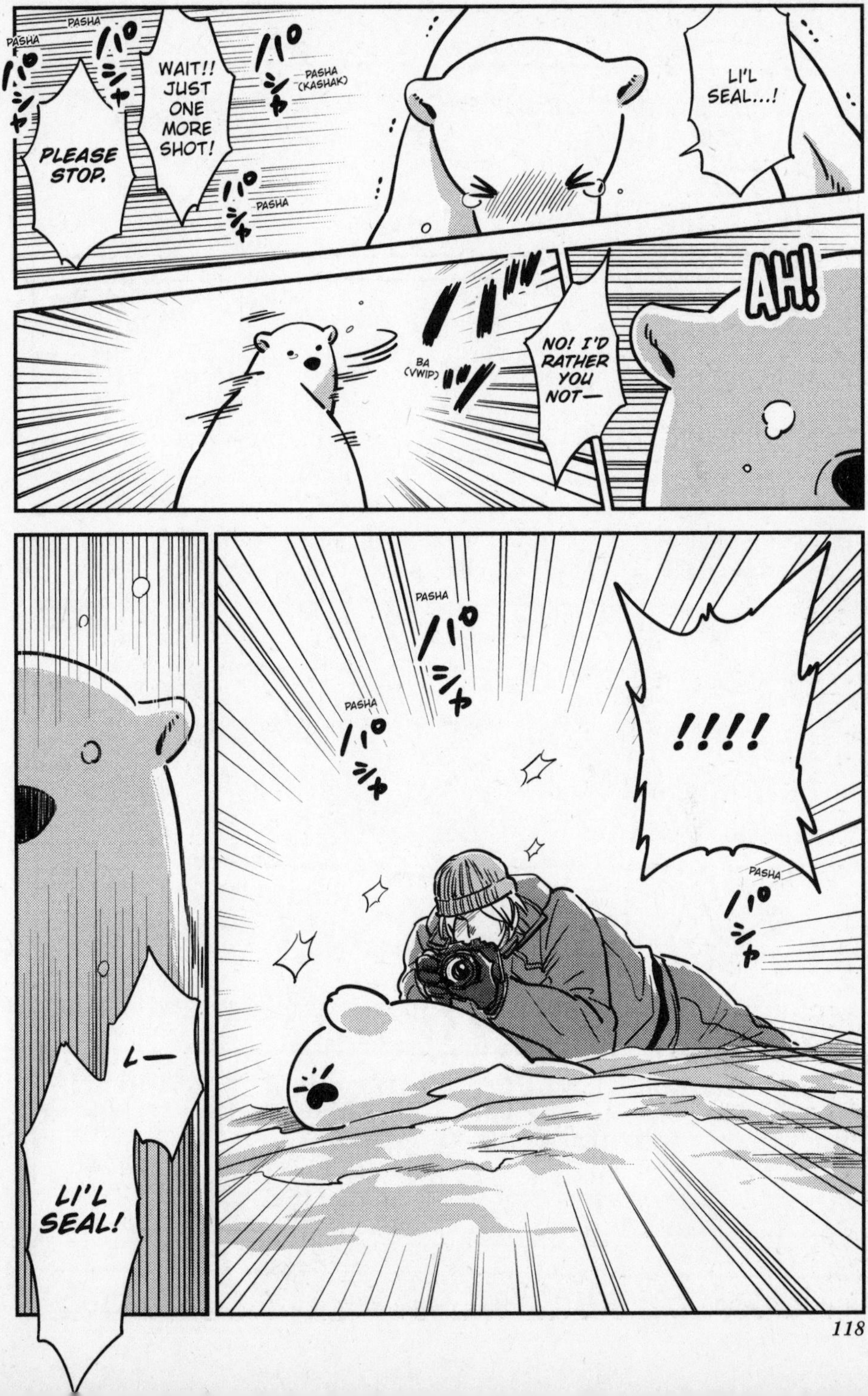
LI'L SEAL...!
PASHA (KASHAK)
WAIT!! JUST ONE MORE SHOT!
PASHA
PASHA
PLEASE STOP.
PASHA
AH!
NO! I'D RATHER YOU NOT—
BA (VWIP)
!!!!
PASHA
PASHA
PASHA
LI'L SEAL!

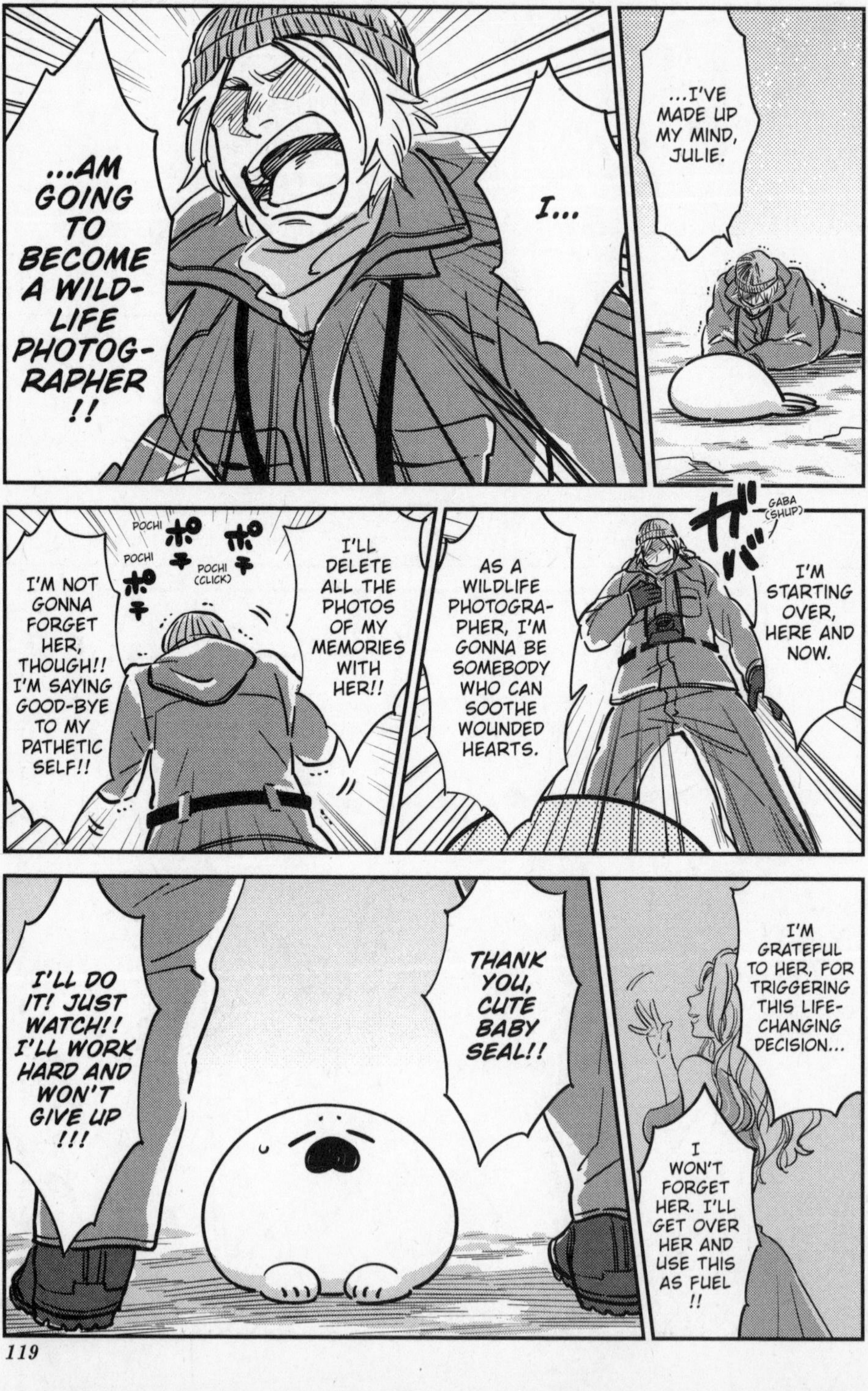
...I'VE MADE UP MY MIND, JULIE.
I...
...AM GOING TO BECOME A WILD-LIFE PHOTOG-RAPHER!!
ガバ
GABA (SHUP)
I'M STARTING OVER, HERE AND NOW.
AS A WILDLIFE PHOTOGRA-PHER, I'M GONNA BE SOMEBODY WHO CAN SOOTHE WOUNDED HEARTS.
I'LL DELETE ALL THE PHOTOS OF MY MEMORIES WITH HER!!
ポチ ポチ ポチ
POCHI POCHI POCHI (CLICK)
I'M NOT GONNA FORGET HER, THOUGH!! I'M SAYING GOOD-BYE TO MY PATHETIC SELF!!
I'M GRATEFUL TO HER, FOR TRIGGERING THIS LIFE-CHANGING DECISION...
I WON'T FORGET HER. I'LL GET OVER HER AND USE THIS AS FUEL!!
THANK YOU, CUTE BABY SEAL!!
I'LL DO IT! JUST WATCH!! I'LL WORK HARD AND WON'T GIVE UP!!!

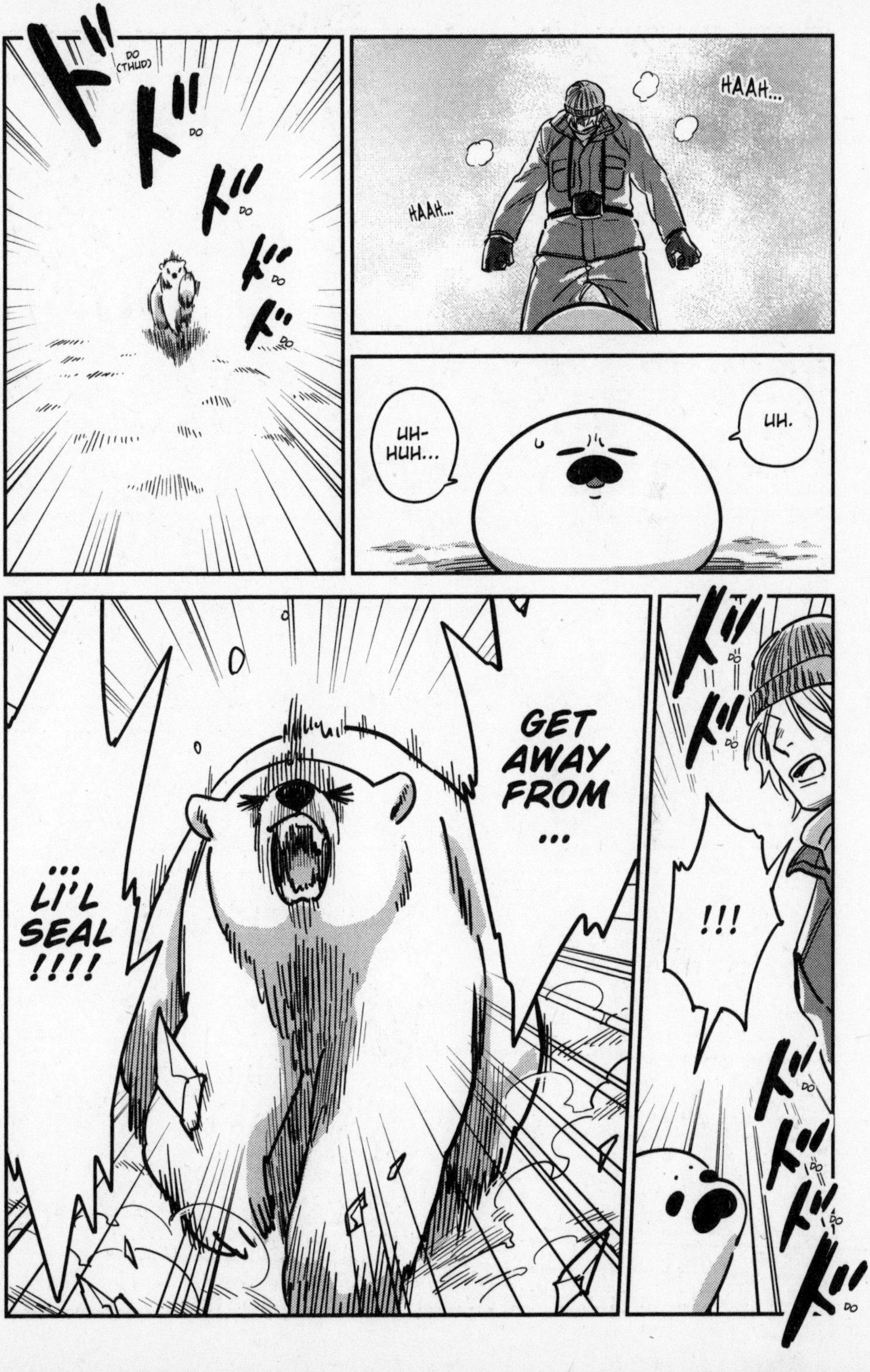
HAAH...
HAAH...
UH.
UH-HUH...
ド
DO (THUD)
ド
DO
ド
DO
ド
DO
ド
DO
ド
DO
ド
DO
!!!
ド
DO
ド
DO
ド
DO
ド
DO
GET AWAY FROM ...
... LI'L SEAL !!!!

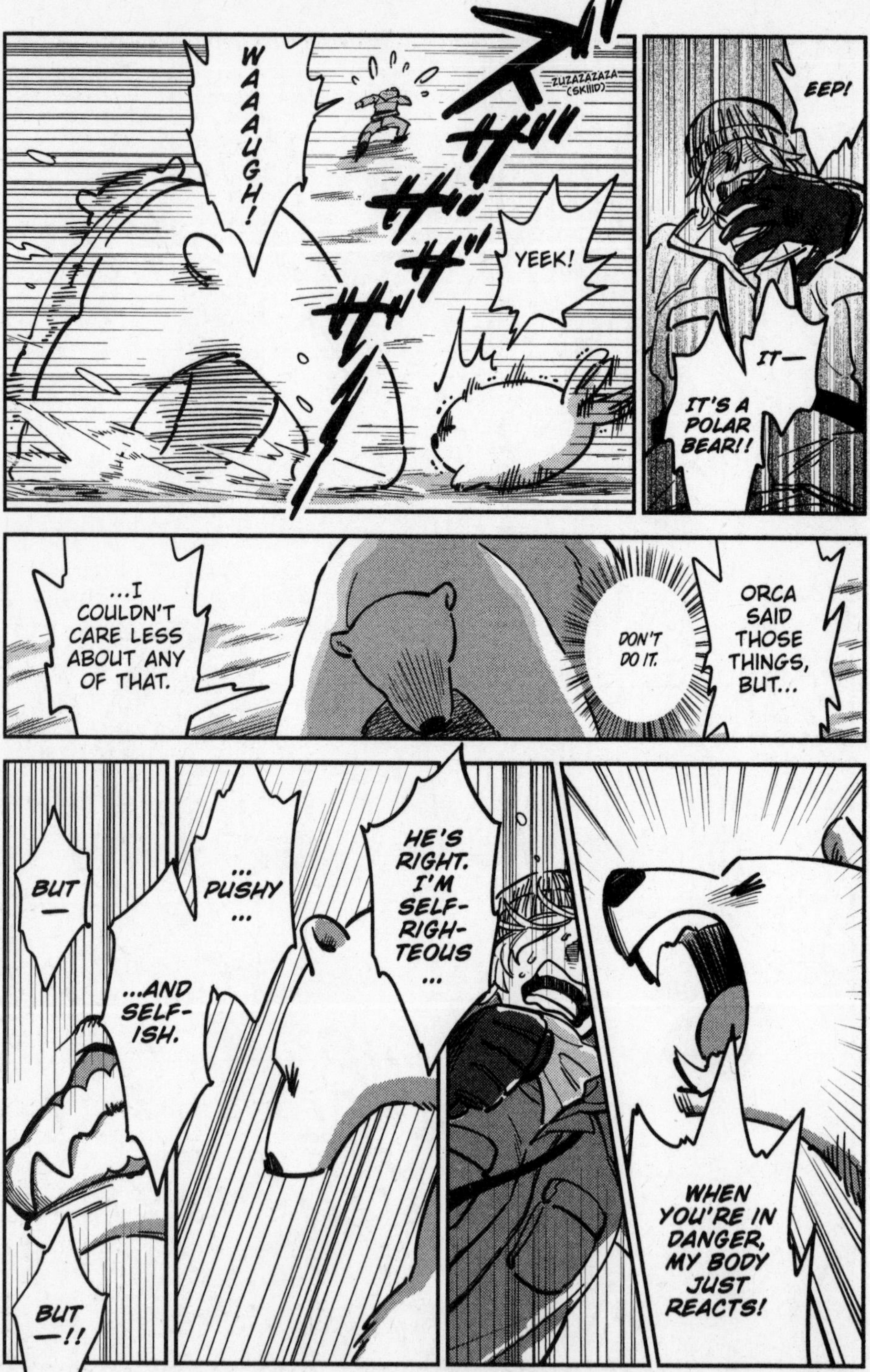
EEP!
IT—
IT'S A POLAR BEAR!!
ZUZAZAZAZA (SKIIID)
YEEK!
WAAAAUGH!
ORCA SAID THOSE THINGS, BUT...
DON'T DO IT.
...I COULDN'T CARE LESS ABOUT ANY OF THAT.
WHEN YOU'RE IN DANGER, MY BODY JUST REACTS!
HE'S RIGHT. I'M SELF-RIGHTEOUS...
...PUSHY...
...AND SELFISH.
BUT—
BUT—!!

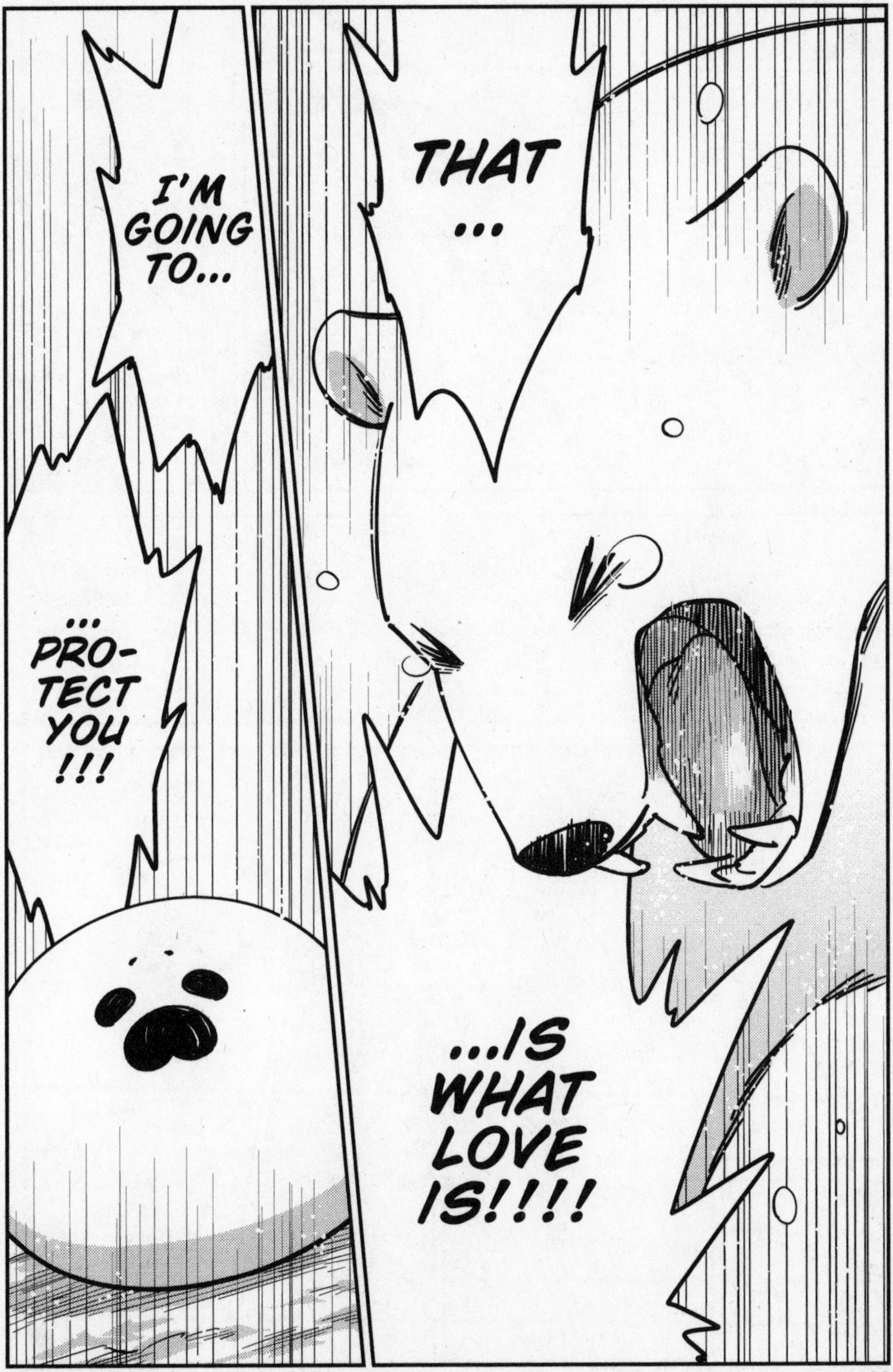
THAT ...
...IS WHAT LOVE IS!!!!
I'M GOING TO...
...PROTECT YOU!!!

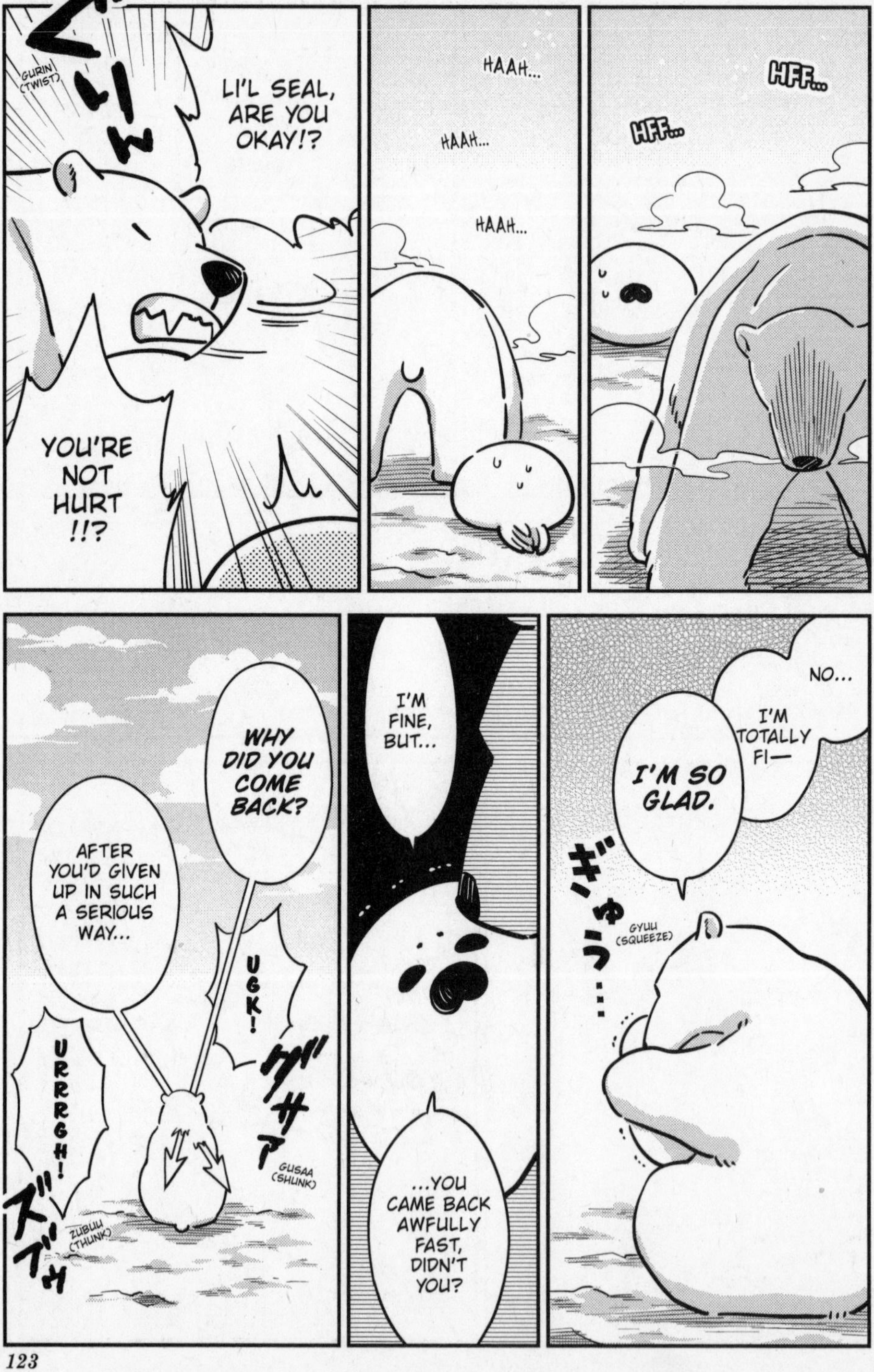
HFF...
HFF...
HAAH...
HAAH...
HAAH...
GURIN (TWIST)
LI'L SEAL, ARE YOU OKAY!?
YOU'RE NOT HURT!!?
NO...
I'M TOTALLY FI—
I'M SO GLAD.
GYUU (SQUEEZE)
I'M FINE, BUT...
...YOU CAME BACK AWFULLY FAST, DIDN'T YOU?
WHY DID YOU COME BACK?
AFTER YOU'D GIVEN UP IN SUCH A SERIOUS WAY...
UGK!
GUSAA (SHUNK)
URRRGH!
ZUBUU (THUNK)

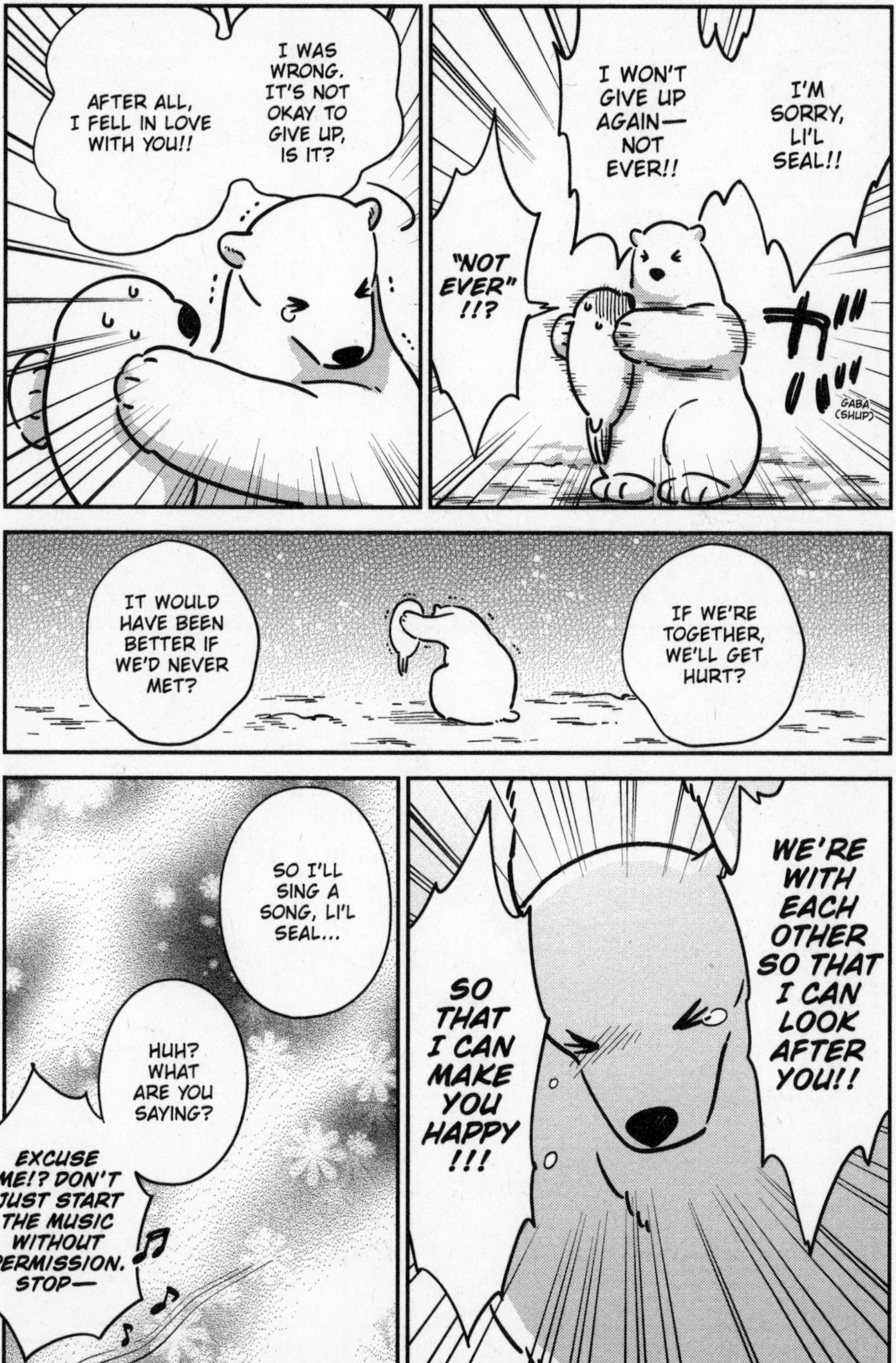
I'M SORRY, LI'L SEAL!!
I WON'T GIVE UP AGAIN—NOT EVER!!
GABA (SHUP)
"NOT EVER"!!?
I WAS WRONG. IT'S NOT OKAY TO GIVE UP, IS IT?
AFTER ALL, I FELL IN LOVE WITH YOU!!
IF WE'RE TOGETHER, WE'LL GET HURT?
IT WOULD HAVE BEEN BETTER IF WE'D NEVER MET?
WE'RE WITH EACH OTHER SO THAT I CAN LOOK AFTER YOU!!
SO THAT I CAN MAKE YOU HAPPY!!!
SO I'LL SING A SONG, LI'L SEAL...
HUH? WHAT ARE YOU SAYING?
EXCUSE ME!? DON'T JUST START THE MUSIC WITHOUT PERMISSION. STOP—

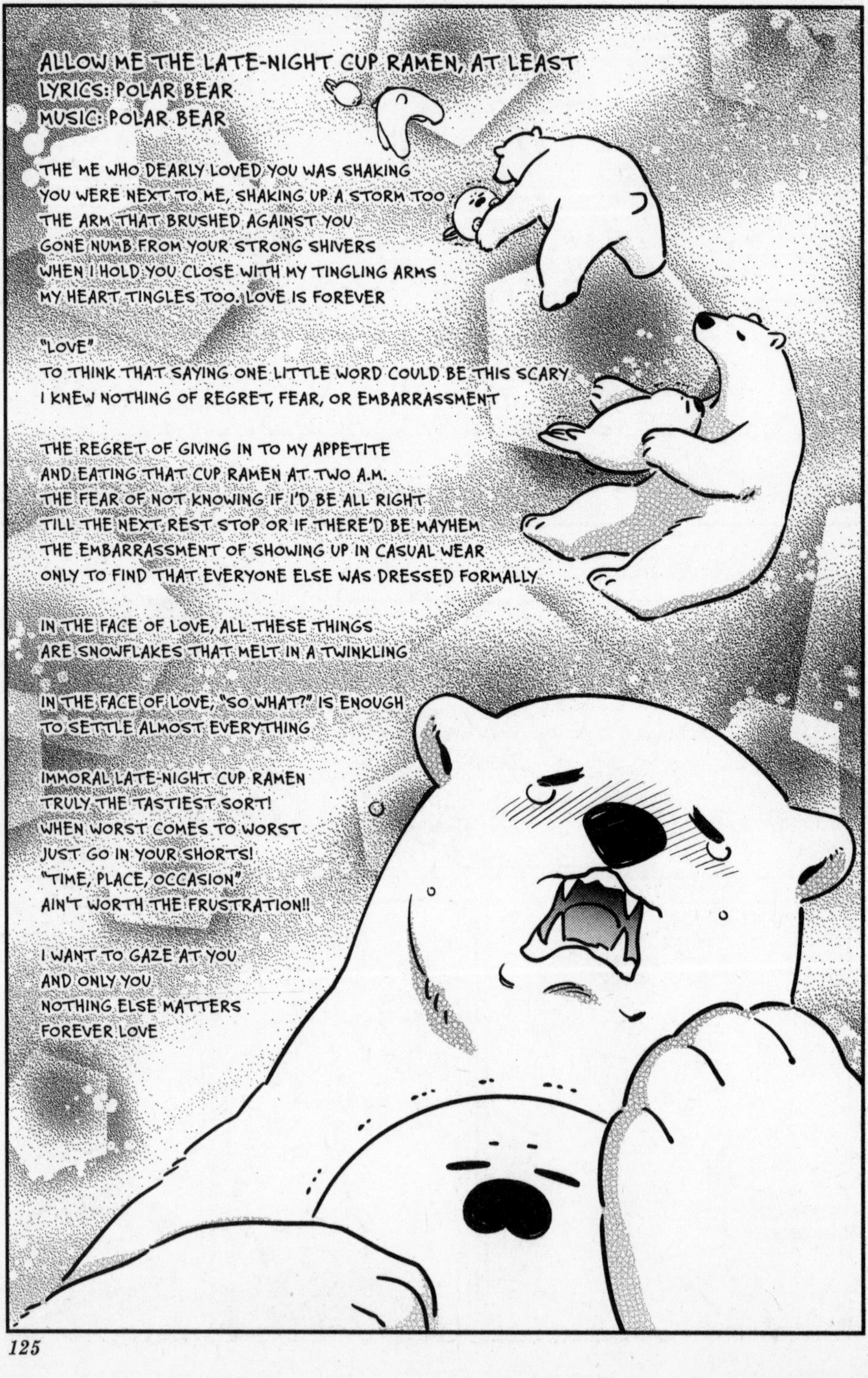
ALLOW ME THE LATE-NIGHT CUP RAMEN, AT LEAST
LYRICS: POLAR BEAR
MUSIC: POLAR BEAR
THE ME WHO DEARLY LOVED YOU WAS SHAKING
YOU WERE NEXT TO ME, SHAKING UP A STORM TOO
THE ARM THAT BRUSHED AGAINST YOU
GONE NUMB FROM YOUR STRONG SHIVERS
WHEN I HOLD YOU CLOSE WITH MY TINGLING ARMS
MY HEART TINGLES TOO. LOVE IS FOREVER
"LOVE"
TO THINK THAT SAYING ONE LITTLE WORD COULD BE THIS SCARY
I KNEW NOTHING OF REGRET, FEAR, OR EMBARRASSMENT
THE REGRET OF GIVING IN TO MY APPETITE
AND EATING THAT CUP RAMEN AT TWO A.M.
THE FEAR OF NOT KNOWING IF I'D BE ALL RIGHT
TILL THE NEXT REST STOP OR IF THERE'D BE MAYHEM
THE EMBARRASSMENT OF SHOWING UP IN CASUAL WEAR
ONLY TO FIND THAT EVERYONE ELSE WAS DRESSED FORMALLY
IN THE FACE OF LOVE, ALL THESE THINGS
ARE SNOWFLAKES THAT MELT IN A TWINKLING
IN THE FACE OF LOVE, "SO WHAT?" IS ENOUGH
TO SETTLE ALMOST EVERYTHING
IMMORAL LATE-NIGHT CUP RAMEN
TRULY THE TASTIEST SORT!
WHEN WORST COMES TO WORST
JUST GO IN YOUR SHORTS!
"TIME, PLACE, OCCASION"
AIN'T WORTH THE FRUSTRATION!!
I WANT TO GAZE AT YOU
AND ONLY YOU
NOTHING ELSE MATTERS
FOREVER LOVE

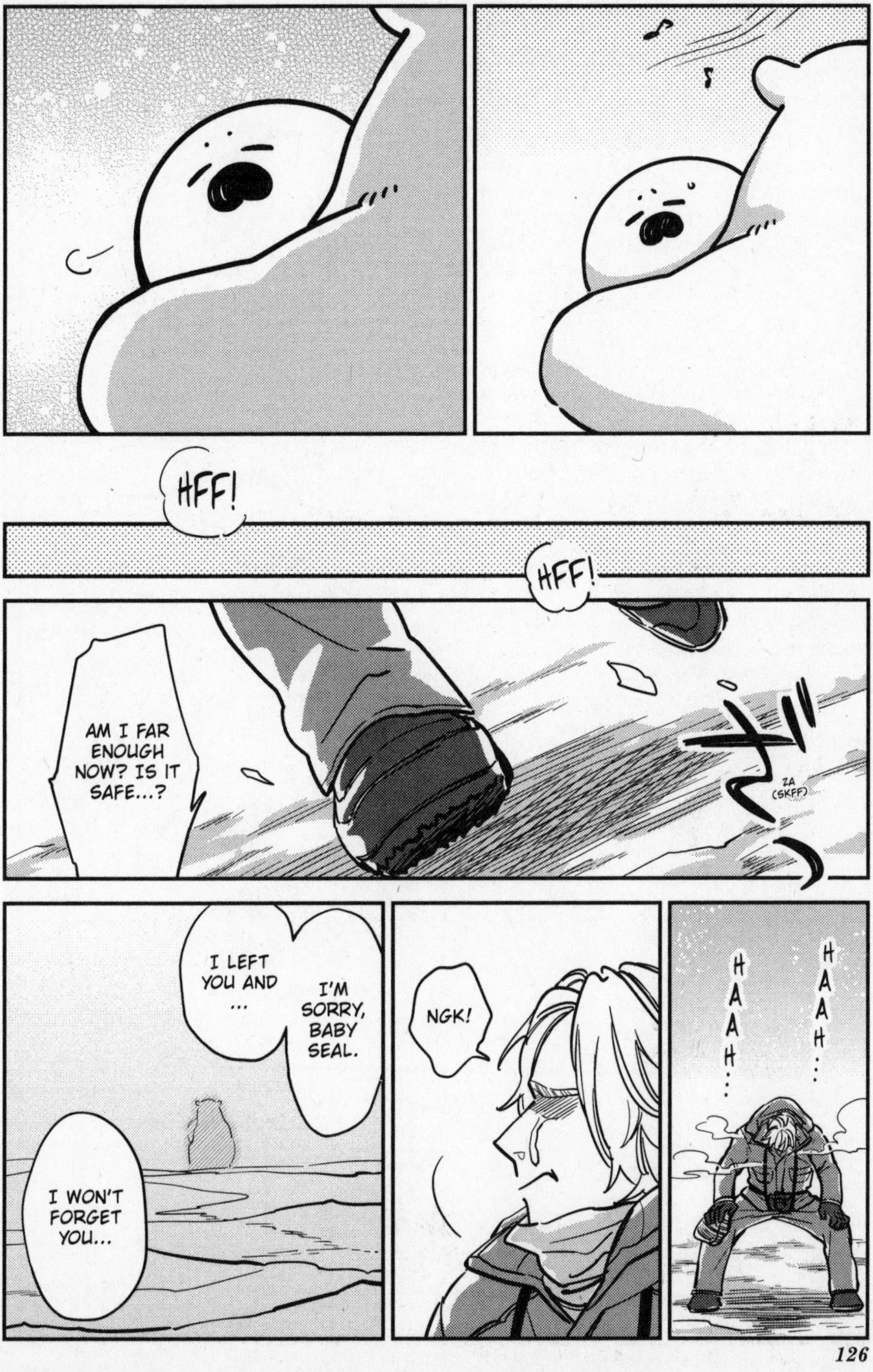
HFF!
HFF!
ZA (SKFF)
AM I FAR ENOUGH NOW? IS IT SAFE...?
HAAH...
HAAH...
NGK!
I'M SORRY, BABY SEAL.
I LEFT YOU AND ...
I WON'T FORGET YOU...

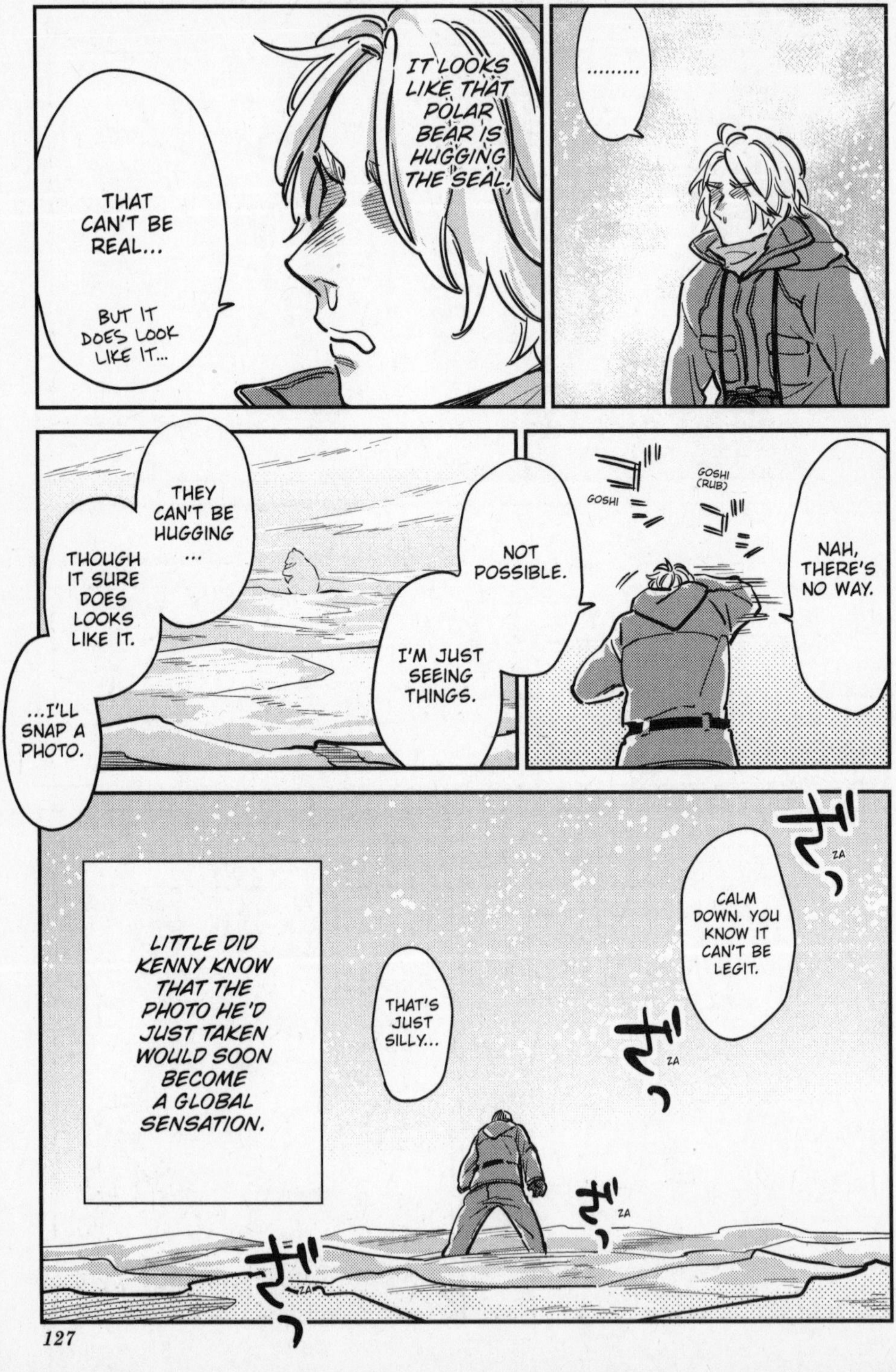
....
IT LOOKS LIKE THAT POLAR BEAR IS HUGGING THE SEAL.
THAT CAN'T BE REAL...
BUT IT DOES LOOK LIKE IT...
NAH, THERE'S NO WAY.
GOSHI (RUB)
GOSHI
NOT POSSIBLE.
I'M JUST SEEING THINGS.
THEY CAN'T BE HUGGING ...
THOUGH IT SURE DOES LOOKS LIKE IT.
...I'LL SNAP A PHOTO.
ZA
CALM DOWN. YOU KNOW IT CAN'T BE LEGIT.
ZA
THAT'S JUST SILLY...
ZA
ZA
LITTLE DID KENNY KNOW THAT THE PHOTO HE'D JUST TAKEN WOULD SOON BECOME A GLOBAL SENSATION.

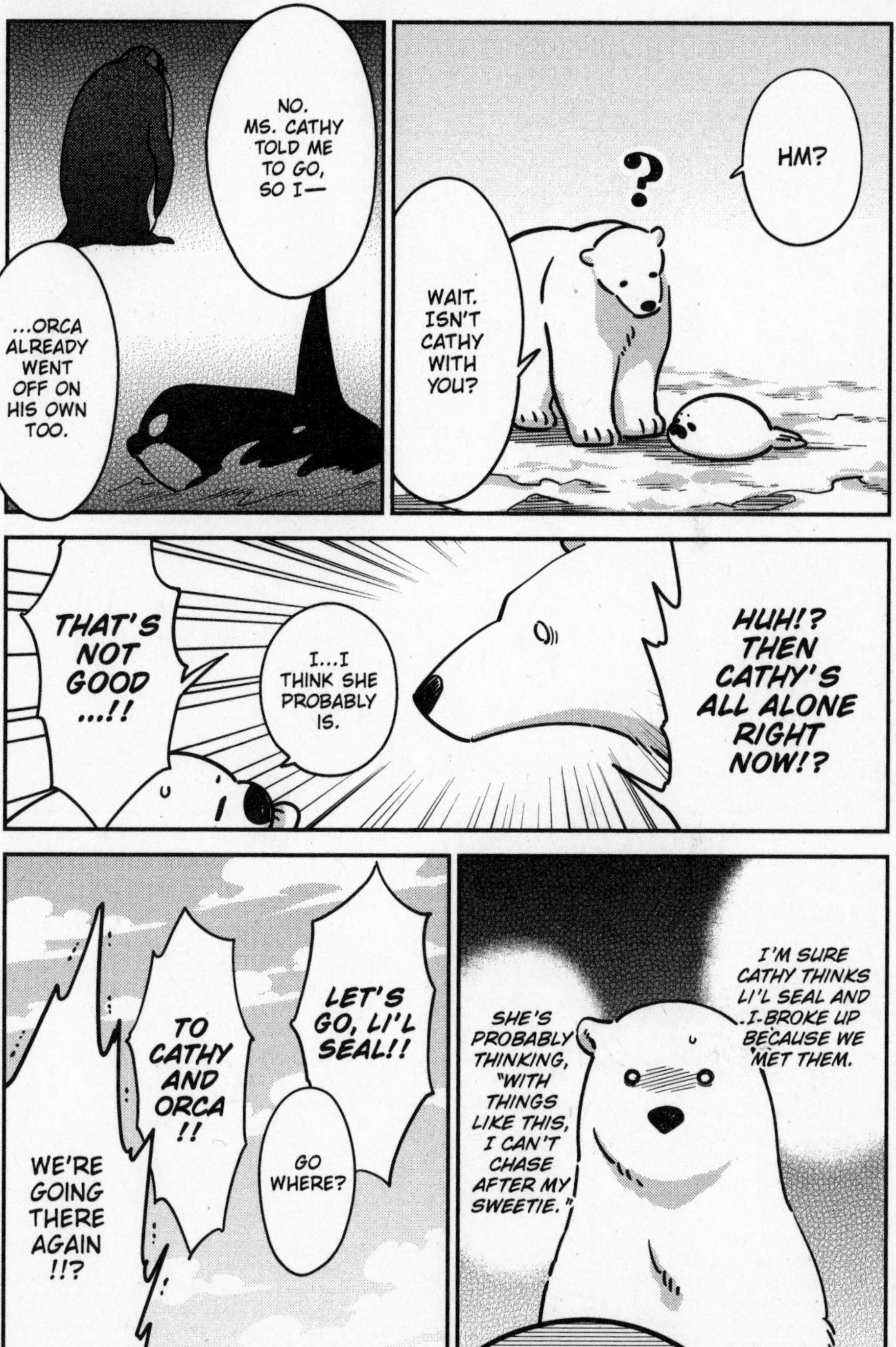
HM?
WAIT. ISN'T CATHY WITH YOU?
NO. MS. CATHY TOLD ME TO GO, SO I—
...ORCA ALREADY WENT OFF ON HIS OWN TOO.
HUH!? THEN CATHY'S ALL ALONE RIGHT NOW!?
I...I THINK SHE PROBABLY IS.
THAT'S NOT GOOD ...!!
I'M SURE CATHY THINKS LI'L SEAL AND I BROKE UP BECAUSE WE MET THEM.
SHE'S PROBABLY THINKING, "WITH THINGS LIKE THIS, I CAN'T CHASE AFTER MY SWEETIE."
LET'S GO, LI'L SEAL!!
GO WHERE?
TO CATHY AND ORCA!!
WE'RE GOING THERE AGAIN!!?

TO BE CONTINUED IN VOLUME 5 ♥

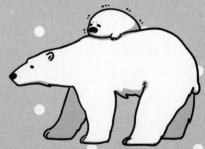

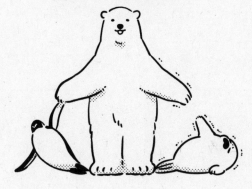

BACKGROUND MANGA FOR THE CHAPTER SPLASH PAGES

FISHING ①

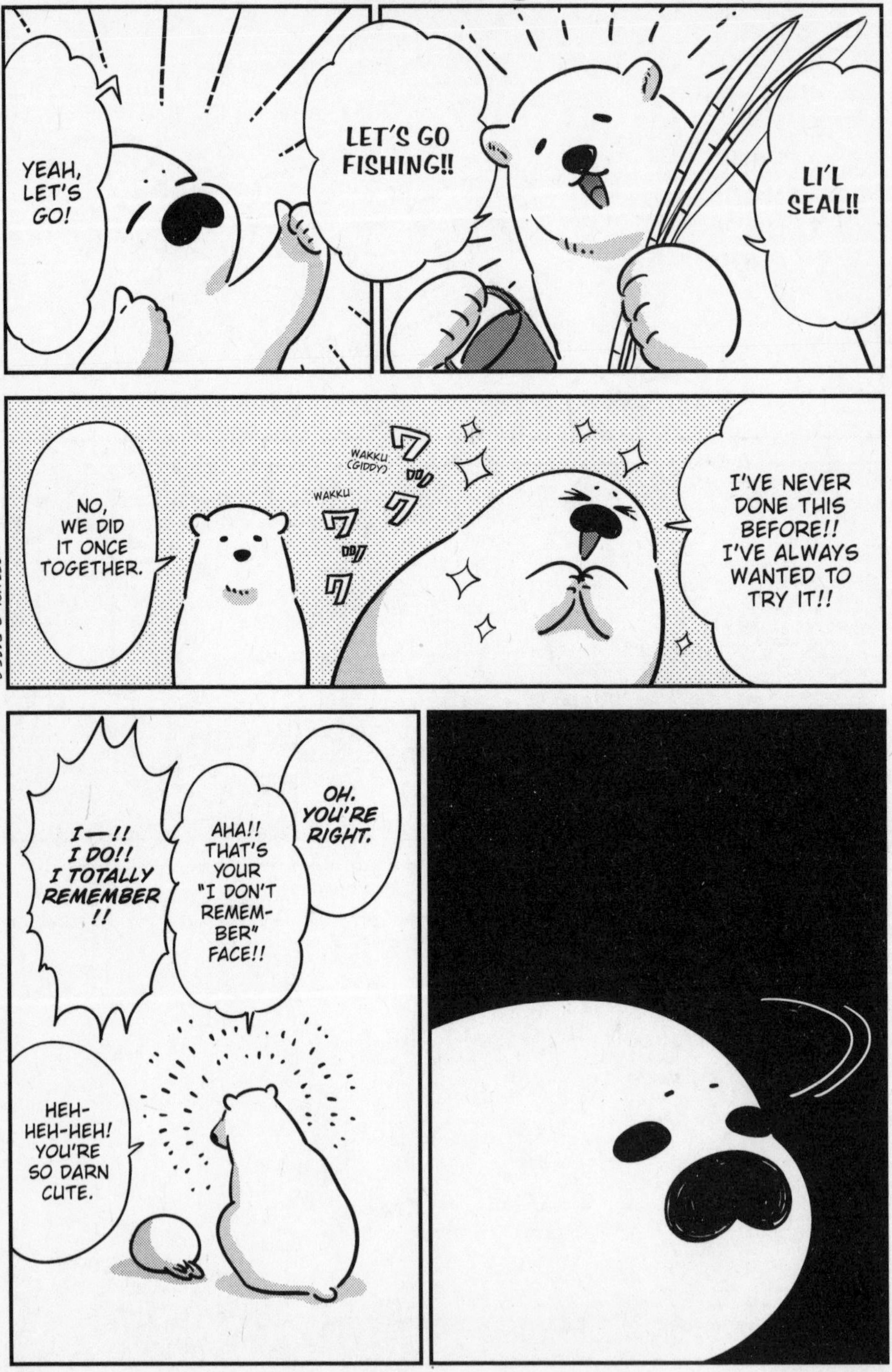

LI'L SEAL!!
LET'S GO FISHING!!
YEAH, LET'S GO!
I'VE NEVER DONE THIS BEFORE!! I'VE ALWAYS WANTED TO TRY IT!!
WAKKU (GIDDY)
WAKKU
NO, WE DID IT ONCE TOGETHER.
OH. YOU'RE RIGHT.
AHA!! THAT'S YOUR "I DON'T REMEMBER" FACE!!
I—!! I DO!! I TOTALLY REMEMBER!!
HEH-HEH-HEH! YOU'RE SO DARN CUTE.

※SEE VOL. 2, PAGE 8.

FISHING ②

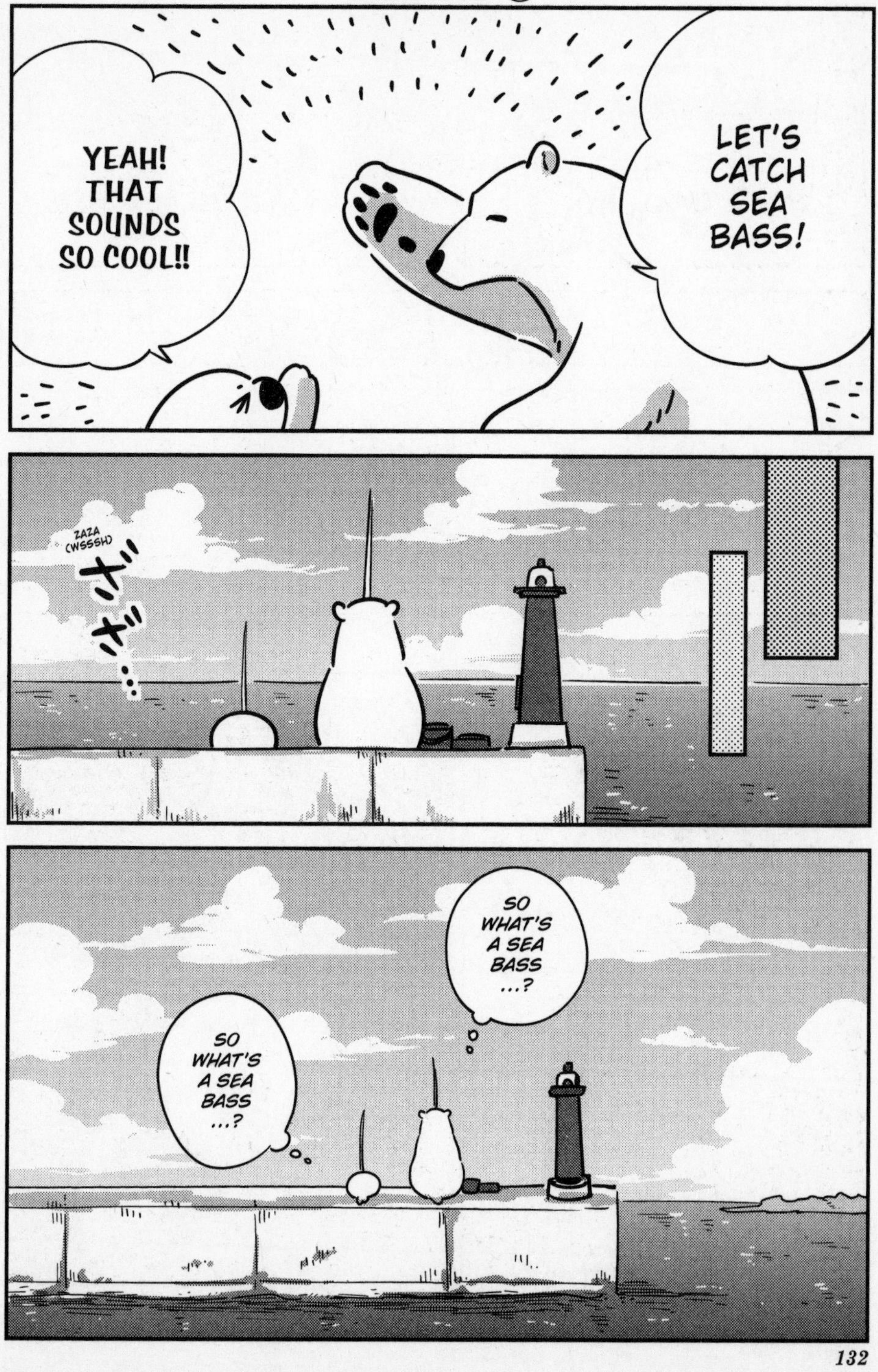
LET'S CATCH SEA BASS!
YEAH! THAT SOUNDS SO COOL!!
ZAZA (WSSSH)
SO WHAT'S A SEA BASS ...?
SO WHAT'S A SEA BASS ...?

FISHING ③

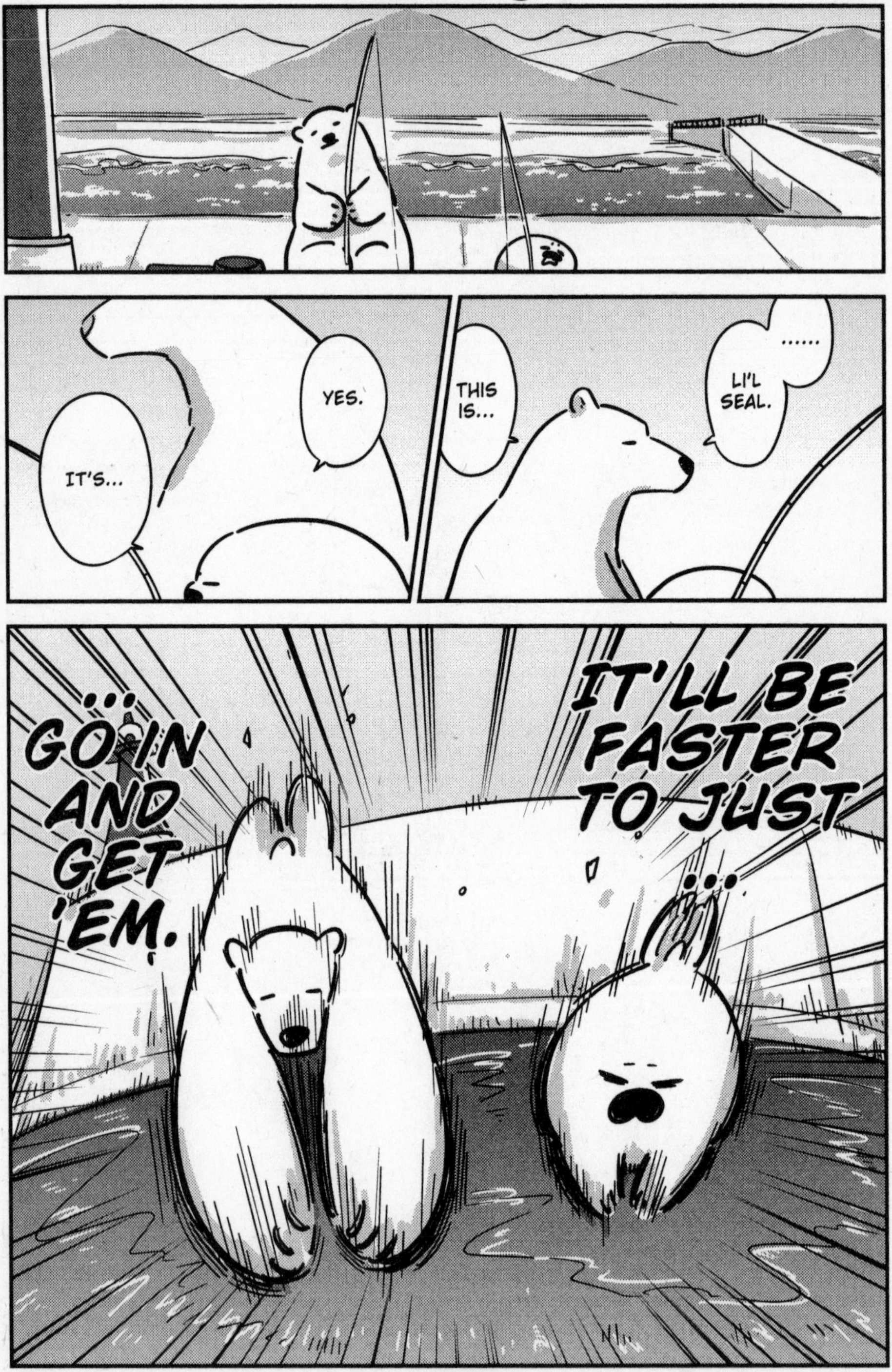
......
LI'L SEAL.
THIS IS...
YES.
IT'S...
IT'LL BE FASTER TO JUST ...
...GO IN AND GET 'EM.

SELFIES

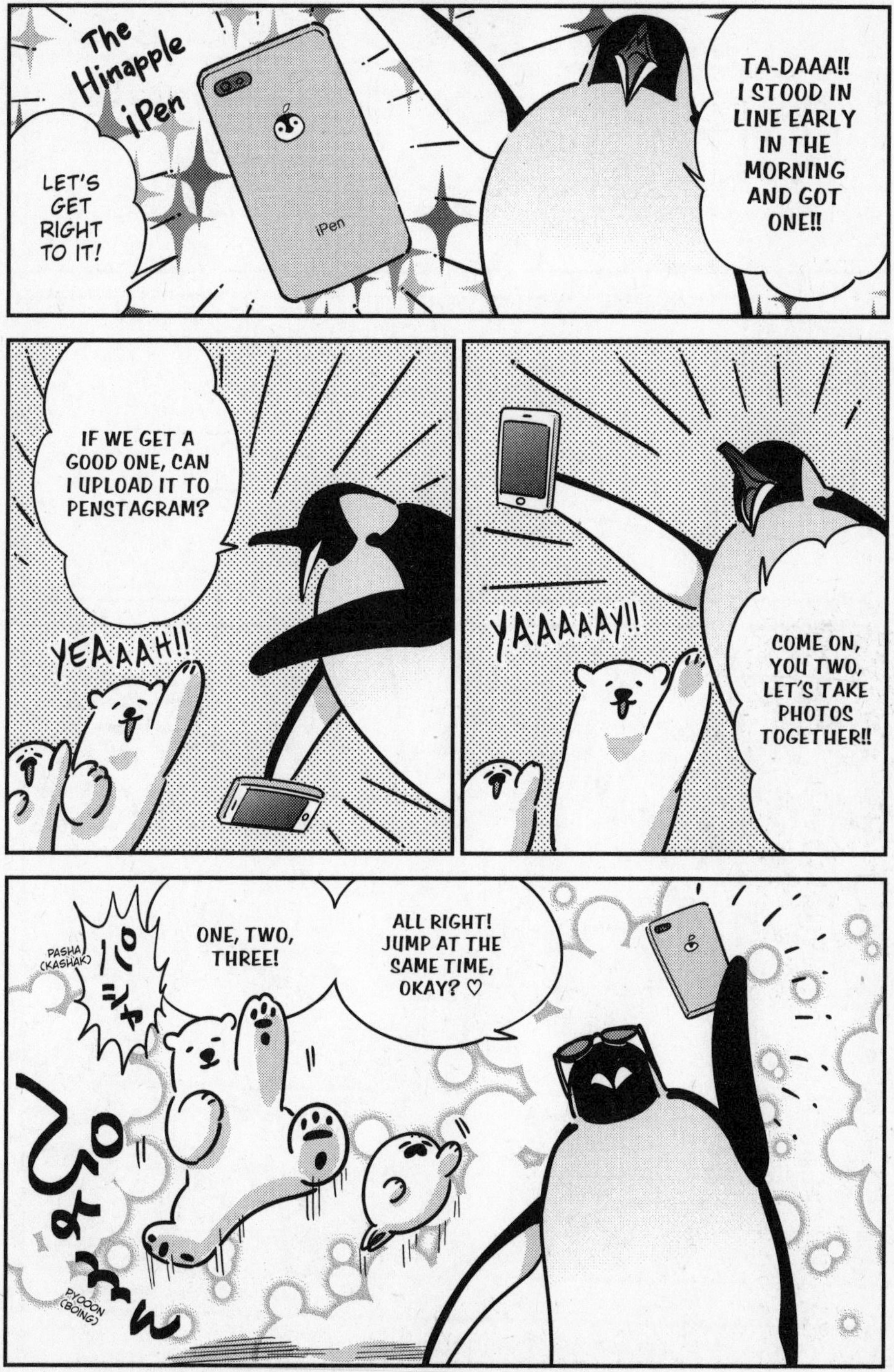
TA-DAAA!! I STOOD IN LINE EARLY IN THE MORNING AND GOT ONE!!
The Hinapple iPen
iPen
LET'S GET RIGHT TO IT!
COME ON, YOU TWO, LET'S TAKE PHOTOS TOGETHER!!
YAAAAAY!!
IF WE GET A GOOD ONE, CAN I UPLOAD IT TO PENSTAGRAM?
YEAAAH!!
ALL RIGHT! JUMP AT THE SAME TIME, OKAY? ♡
ONE, TWO, THREE!
PASHA (KASHAK)
PYOOON (BOING)

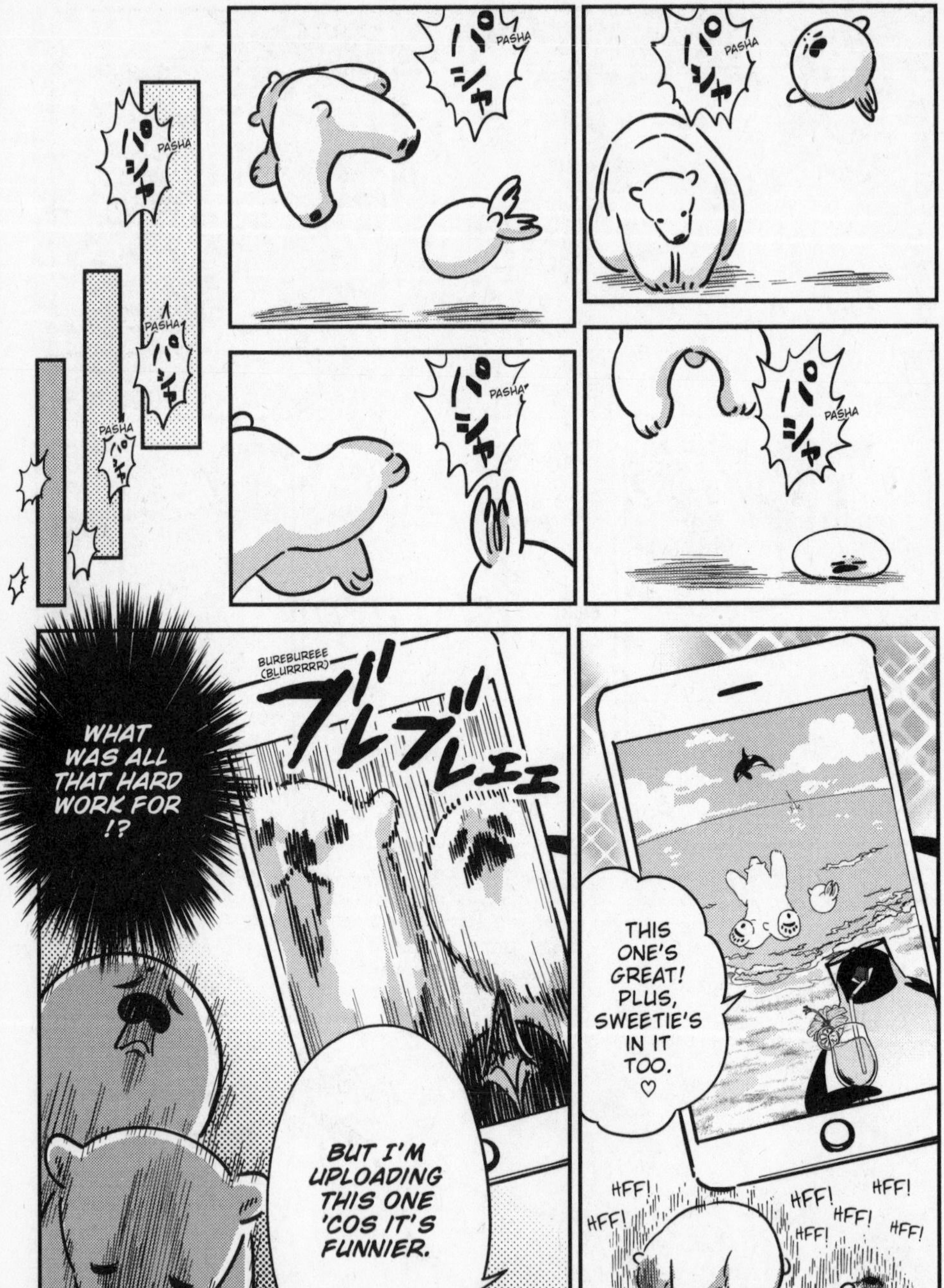
パシャ PASHA
パシャ PASHA
パシャ PASHA
パシャ PASHA
パシャ PASHA
パシャ PASHA
パシャ PASHA
THIS ONE'S GREAT! PLUS, SWEETIE'S IN IT TOO. ♡
HFF! HFF! HFF! HFF! HFF! HFF! HFF! HFF!
BUREBUREEE (BLURRRRR) ブレブレェェ
WHAT WAS ALL THAT HARD WORK FOR !?
BUT I'M UPLOADING THIS ONE 'COS IT'S FUNNIER.

FIREWORKS

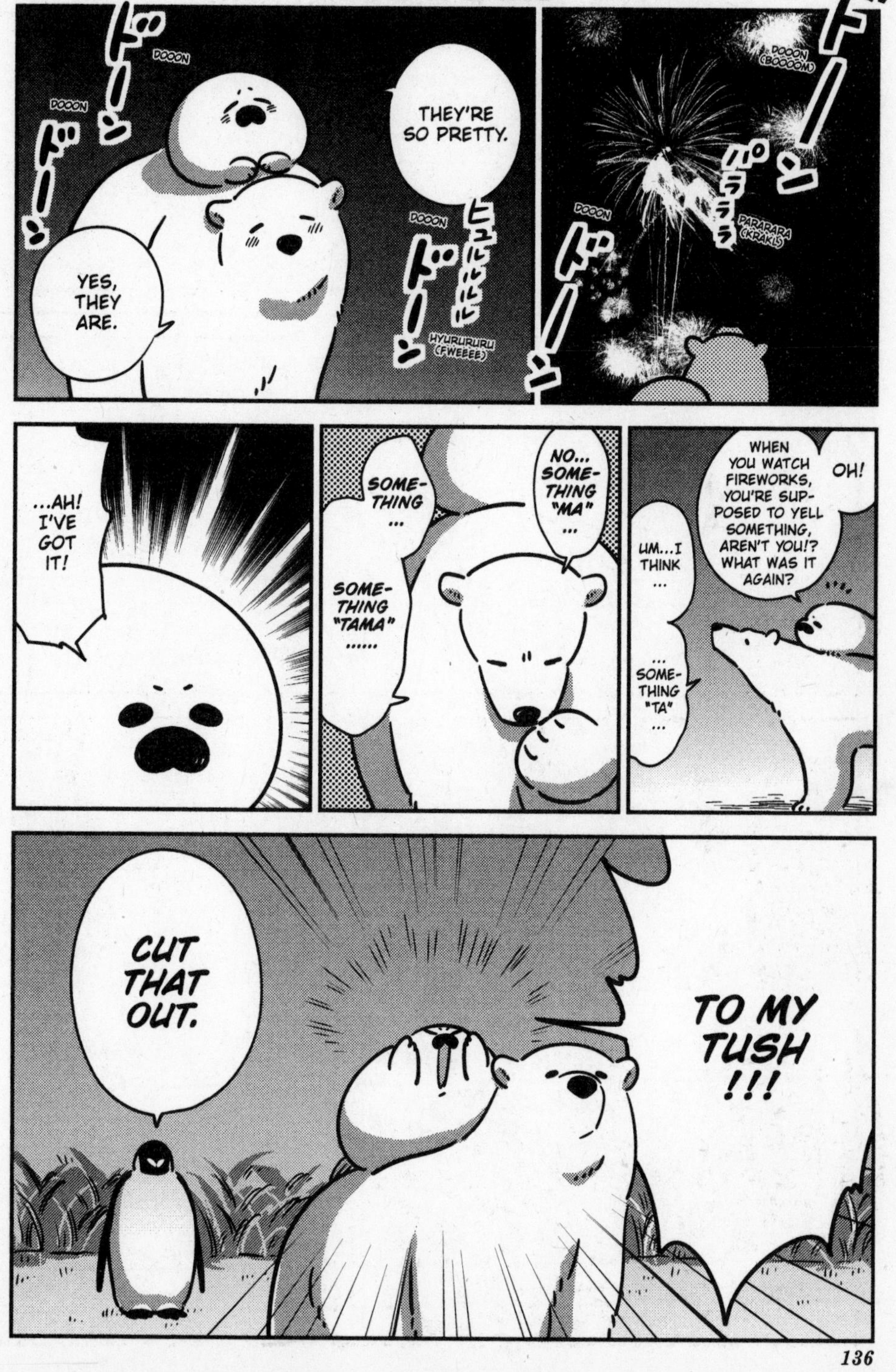
DOOON (BOOOOM)
PARARARA (KRAKL)
DOOON
THEY'RE SO PRETTY.
HYURURURU (FWEEEE)
DOOON
DOOON
DOOON
YES, THEY ARE.
OH!
WHEN YOU WATCH FIREWORKS, YOU'RE SUPPOSED TO YELL SOMETHING, AREN'T YOU!? WHAT WAS IT AGAIN?
UM...I THINK ...
...SOMETHING "TA" ...
NO... SOMETHING "MA" ...
SOMETHING ...
SOMETHING "TAMA" ......
...AH! I'VE GOT IT!
TO MY TUSH !!!
CUT THAT OUT.

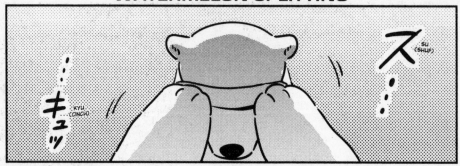

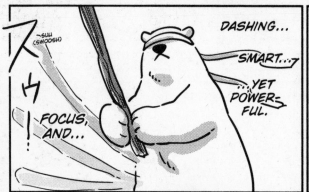

WATERMELON SPLITTING

ス・・・
SU (SHUF)
・・・キュッ
KYU (CINCH)
スゥー
SUUU (INHALE)
ハ
HAAA (EXHALE)
DASHING...
SMART...
...YET POWER-FUL.
FOCUS, AND...
スゥー
SUU (SWOOSH)
カッ
KA (FLASH)
...TAKE IT OUT IN ONE BLOW!!
JUST WATCH ME...
...LI'L SEAL!!!!!
ゴッ!!!
GO (WHUD)

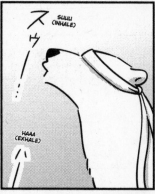

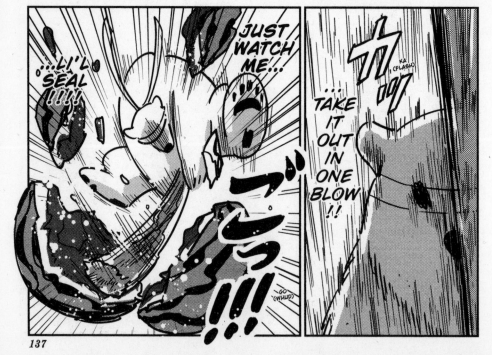

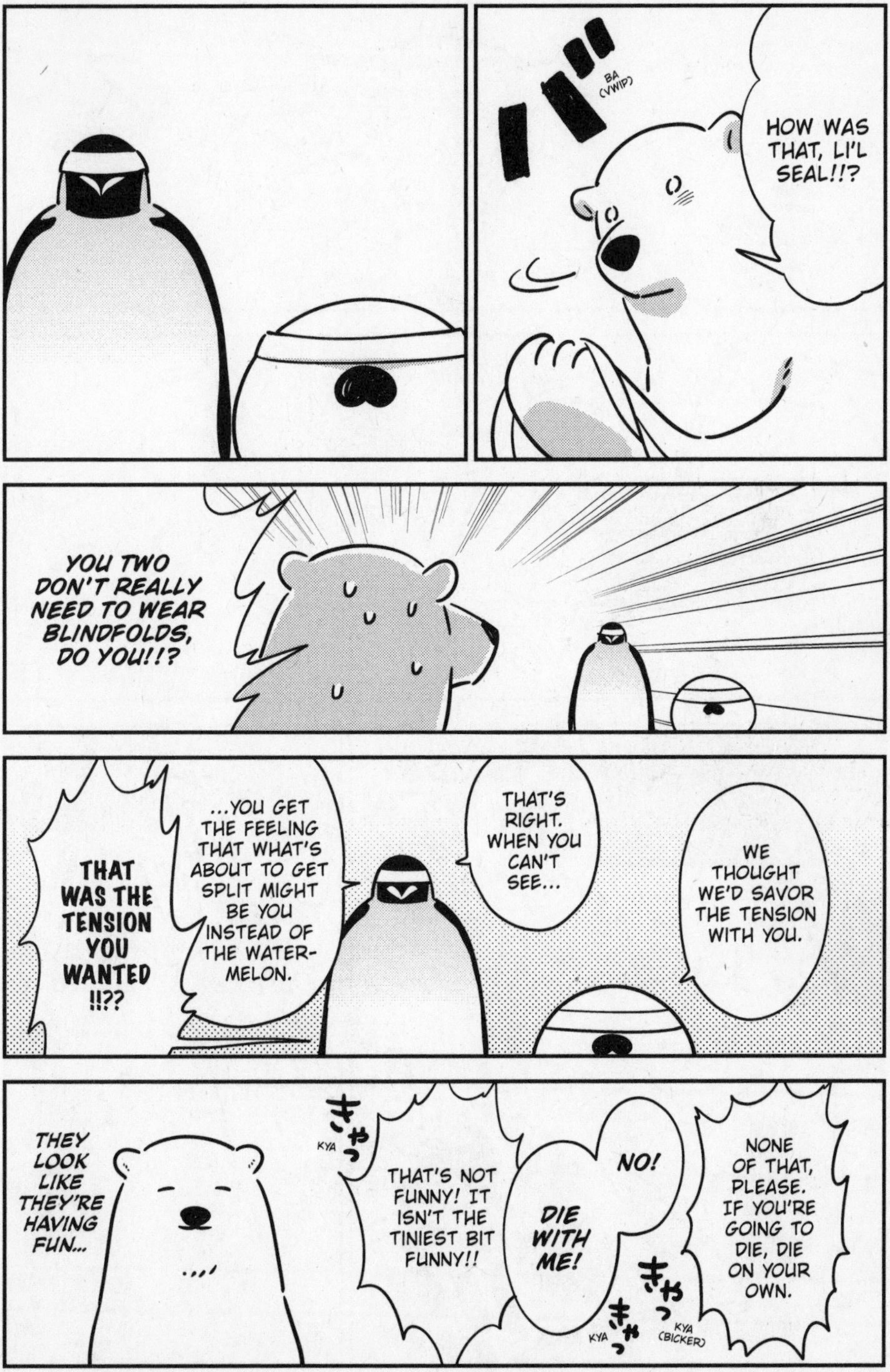
BA (VWIP)
HOW WAS THAT, LI'L SEAL!!?
YOU TWO DON'T REALLY NEED TO WEAR BLINDFOLDS, DO YOU!!?
WE THOUGHT WE'D SAVOR THE TENSION WITH YOU.
THAT'S RIGHT. WHEN YOU CAN'T SEE...
...YOU GET THE FEELING THAT WHAT'S ABOUT TO GET SPLIT MIGHT BE YOU INSTEAD OF THE WATER-MELON.
THAT WAS THE TENSION YOU WANTED !!??
NONE OF THAT, PLEASE. IF YOU'RE GOING TO DIE, DIE ON YOUR OWN.
きゃっ KYA (BICKER)
きゃっ KYA
NO!
DIE WITH ME!
THAT'S NOT FUNNY! IT ISN'T THE TINIEST BIT FUNNY!!
きゃっ KYA
THEY LOOK LIKE THEY'RE HAVING FUN...

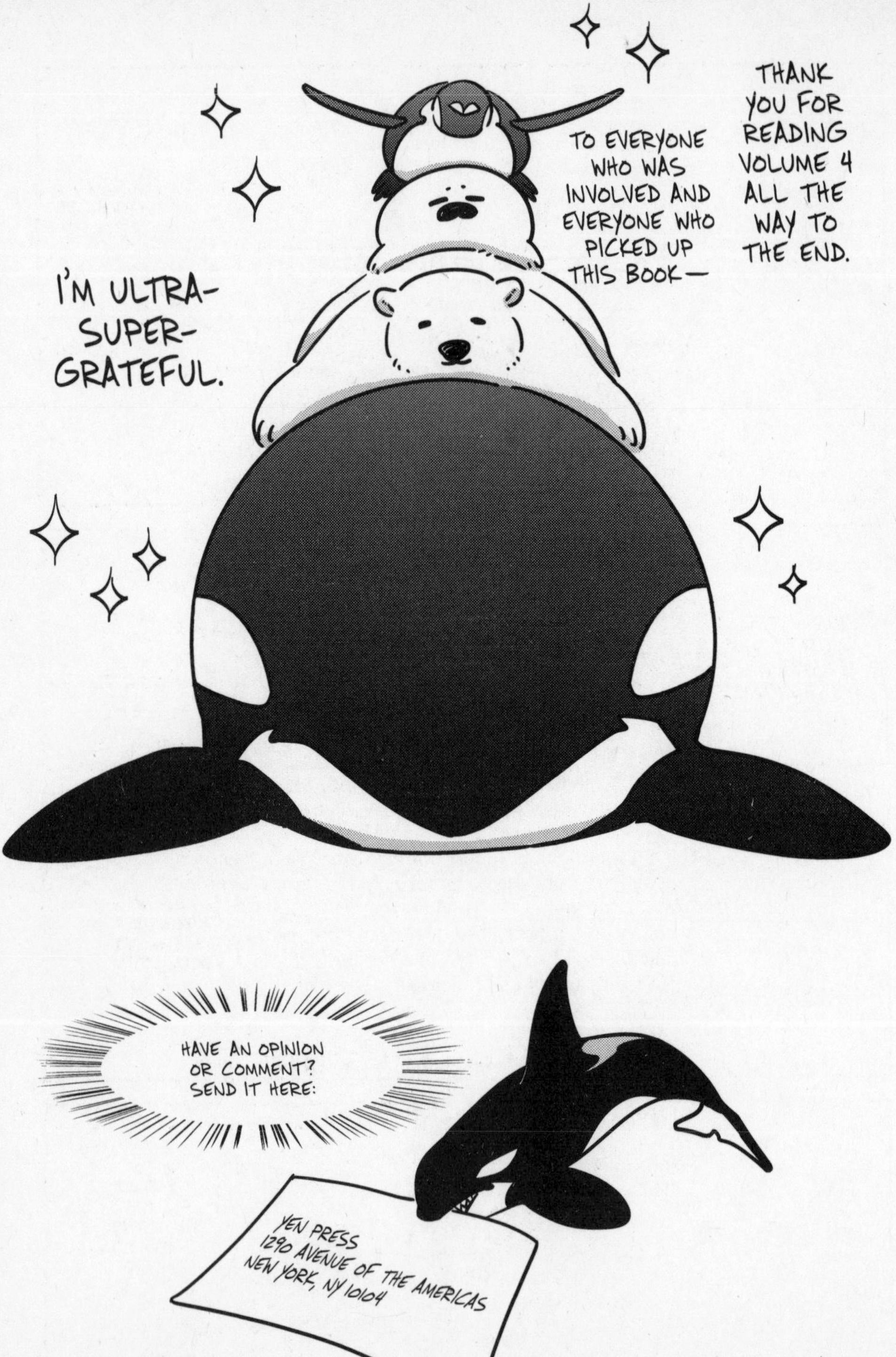
THANK YOU FOR READING VOLUME 4 ALL THE WAY TO THE END.
TO EVERYONE WHO WAS INVOLVED AND EVERYONE WHO PICKED UP THIS BOOK—
I'M ULTRA-SUPER-GRATEFUL.
HAVE AN OPINION OR COMMENT? SEND IT HERE:
YEN PRESS
1290 AVENUE OF THE AMERICAS
NEW YORK, NY 10104

THE END

TRANSLATION NOTES

PAGE 54
In Japanese, instead of IRL, the penguin uses the word *ria-juu* to describe the couple. *Ria-juu* is a term often used as an antonym for *otaku* (slang term for an obsessive nerd) to refer to people who live a satisfying, envy-worthy life with significant others and don't feel the need to escape into fictional worlds.

PAGE 61
The character used to write *tryst* literally means "meeting rapids/swift water," so it's weirdly appropriate.

PAGE 134
Hina means "chick," while "pen" is an abbreviation for "penguin."

PAGE 136
In the early 1800s, there were two fireworks manufacturers in Edo (now Tokyo) whose names were Tamaya and Kagiya. Since both shops were located in the same neighborhood, Tamaya was given the area upstream from the Ryougoku Bridge as its territory, while Kagiya had the area downstream. During meets, both would launch their fireworks from the river, and onlookers would yell "Tamaya!" or "Kagiya!" in support of their favorite manufacturer.

PAGE 146
The Japanese limited edition of Volume 4 comes with a soft Seal pouch, and the cover features Seal, Cathy, and Orca in showman clothes with top hats.

A JAVA FINCH IN LOVE

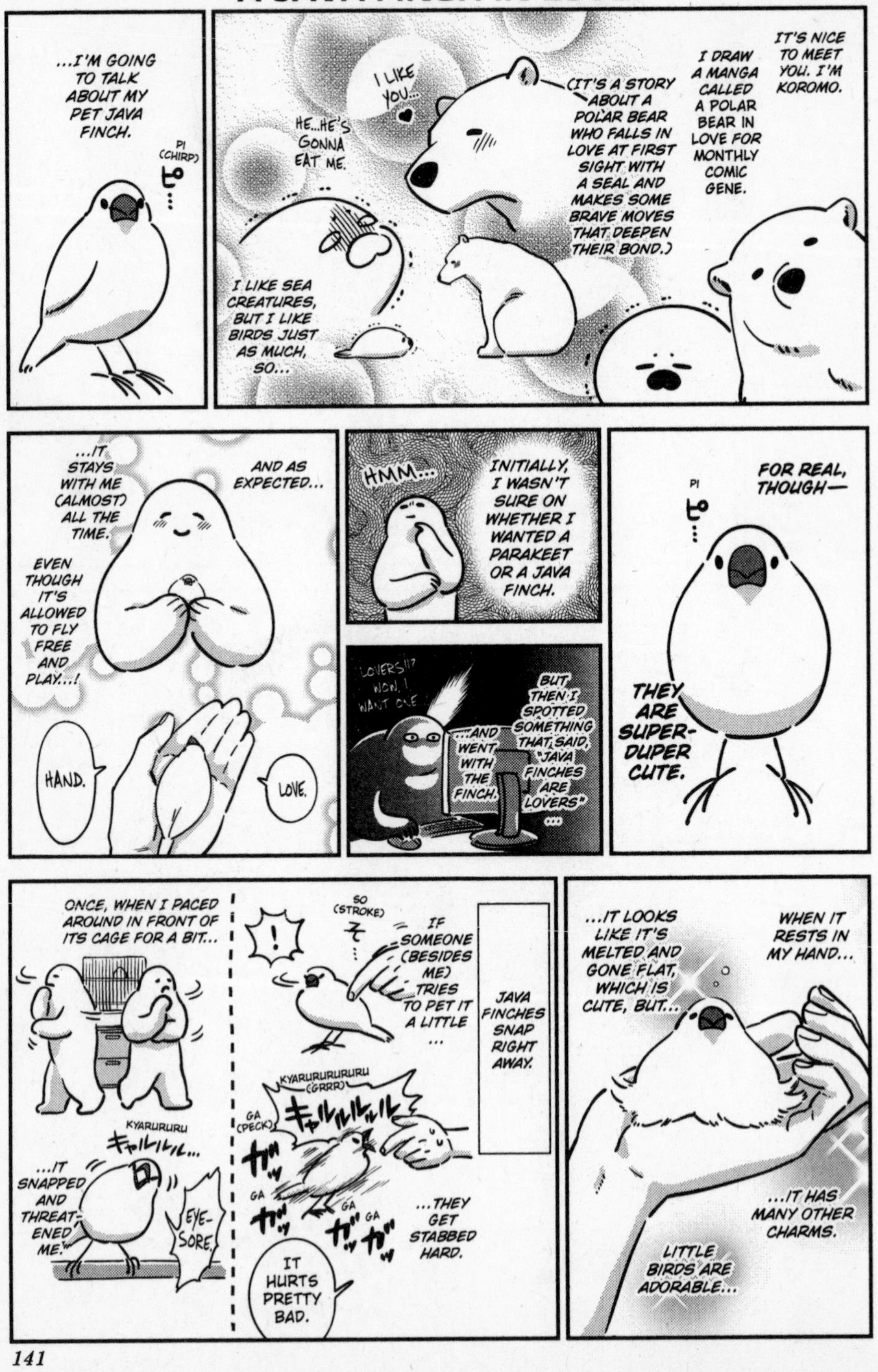

IT'S NICE TO MEET YOU. I'M KOROMO.
I DRAW A MANGA CALLED A POLAR BEAR IN LOVE FOR MONTHLY COMIC GENE.
(IT'S A STORY ABOUT A POLAR BEAR WHO FALLS IN LOVE AT FIRST SIGHT WITH A SEAL AND MAKES SOME BRAVE MOVES THAT DEEPEN THEIR BOND.)
I LIKE YOU... ♥
HE...HE'S GONNA EAT ME.
I LIKE SEA CREATURES, BUT I LIKE BIRDS JUST AS MUCH, SO...
...I'M GOING TO TALK ABOUT MY PET JAVA FINCH.
PI (CHIRP)
ピ…
FOR REAL, THOUGH—
PI
ピ…
THEY ARE SUPER-DUPER CUTE.
INITIALLY, I WASN'T SURE ON WHETHER I WANTED A PARAKEET OR A JAVA FINCH.
HMM...
BUT THEN I SPOTTED SOMETHING THAT SAID, "JAVA FINCHES ARE LOVERS"...
...AND WENT WITH THE FINCH.
LOVERS!!? WOW, I WANT ONE...
AND AS EXPECTED...
...IT STAYS WITH ME (ALMOST) ALL THE TIME.
EVEN THOUGH IT'S ALLOWED TO FLY FREE AND PLAY...!
LOVE.
HAND.
WHEN IT RESTS IN MY HAND...
...IT LOOKS LIKE IT'S MELTED AND GONE FLAT, WHICH IS CUTE, BUT...
...IT HAS MANY OTHER CHARMS.
LITTLE BIRDS ARE ADORABLE...
JAVA FINCHES SNAP RIGHT AWAY.
IF SOMEONE (BESIDES ME) TRIES TO PET IT A LITTLE...
SO (STROKE)
そ…
!
KYARURURURURU (GRRR)
キャルルルルル
GA (PECK)
ガッ
GA
ガッ
GA
ガッ
...THEY GET STABBED HARD.
IT HURTS PRETTY BAD.
ONCE, WHEN I PACED AROUND IN FRONT OF ITS CAGE FOR A BIT...
KYARURURU
キャルルル...
...IT SNAPPED AND THREATENED ME.
EYESORE.

WHEN I ACCIDENTALLY BUMPED IT LIGHTLY WITH MY FINGER...
TON (TAP)
トン
OH! SORRY.
...IT SNAPPED AND ATTACKED THAT EXACT FINGER.
GA (PECK) GA GA
ガガガ
ガガ
GA GA
I SAID I WAS SORRY.
WHEN I MOVED MY HAND, IT CHASED IT AND KEPT ATTACKING.
KYARURURURU (GRRR)
キャルルルル
MY BAD, GOSH!
IT GOES OUT OF ITS WAY TO COME AND ATTACK MY PEN.
GYARURURURU (GRRR)
ギャルルルル
GYARURURURURU
ギャルルルルル
IT SNAPS WHEN I TRY TO USE THE "ASDF" SECTION OF MY KEYBOARD (BUT ONLY THAT AREA).
WHY!?
THE WRATH OF JAVA FINCHES IS NEVER-ENDING AND CUTE.
THERE, THERE. CALM THYSELF.
KYARURU
キャルルル
IT LOVES MY SMARTPHONE.
IT ESPECIALLY LIKES PUZZLE & DRAGONS...
...AND GAZING AT ITS REFLECTION IN THE SCREEN.
YEP, IT LOVES THAT.
JIIII (STAAARE)
じーーー
HOW LONG ARE YOU GOING TO KEEP STARING?
WHEN I SHOW IT JAVA FINCH VIDEOS...
PI (CHIRP)
ピッ
PI
ピ
...IT GOES BEHIND MY SMARTPHONE TO CHECK THE BACK.
NOT HERE...
??
SO CUTE...!!
WHEN I GET A TEXT, IT REACTS.
PIPI
ピッピッ
PI
ピッ
PIKO (BLIP)
PIKO
ピコピコッ
IT'S NOT FOR YOU, OKAY?

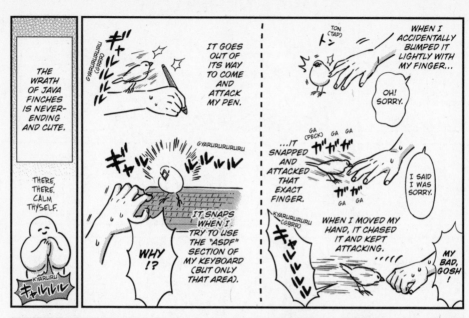

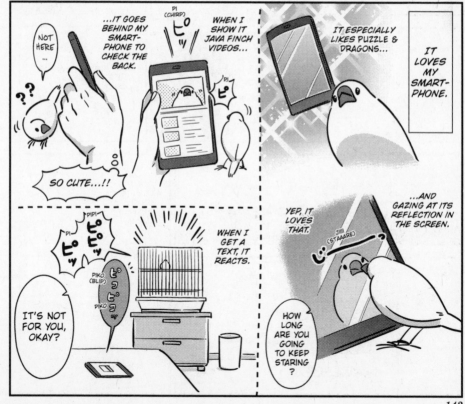

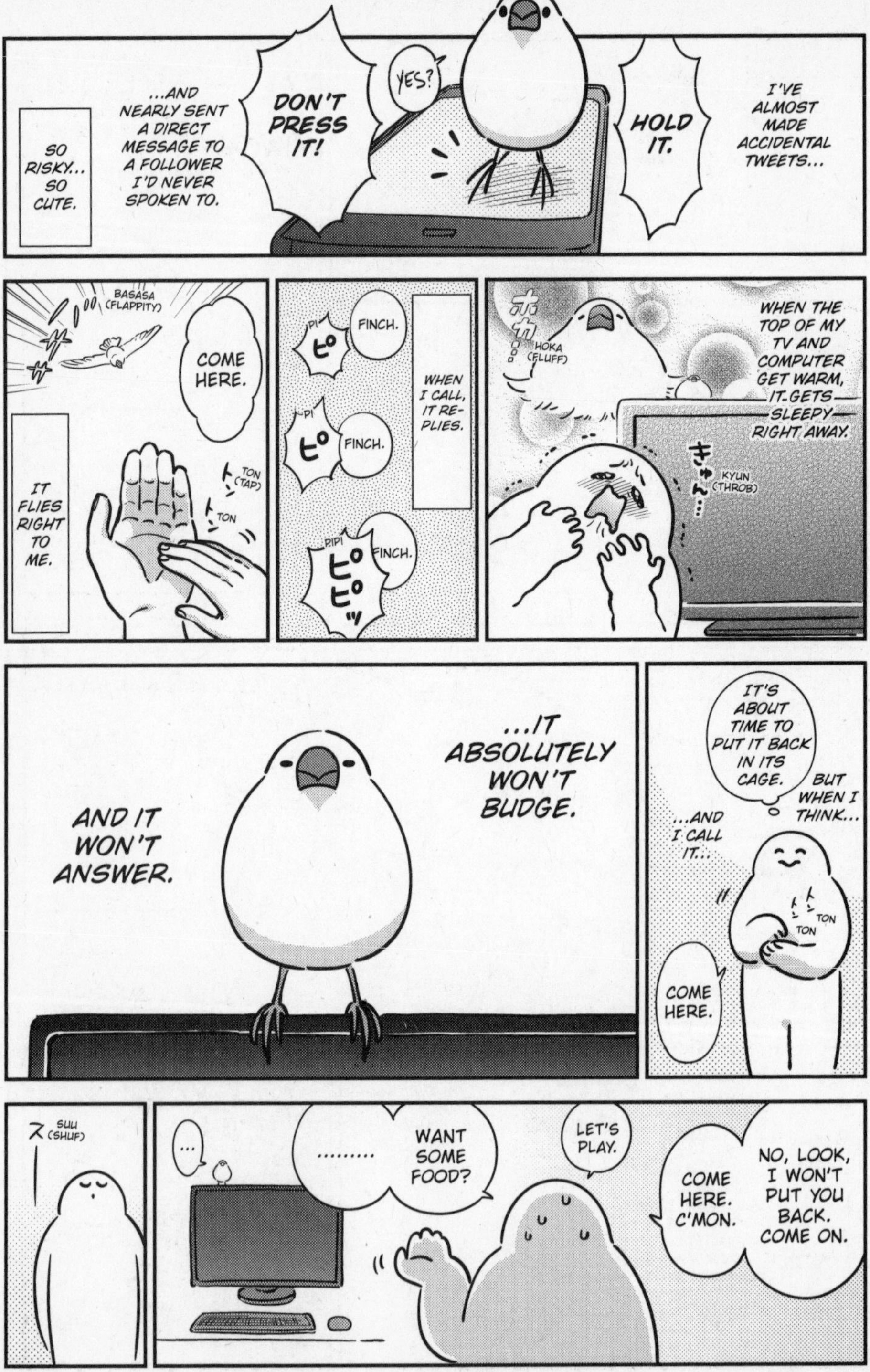
I'VE ALMOST MADE ACCIDENTAL TWEETS...
HOLD IT.
YES?
DON'T PRESS IT!
...AND NEARLY SENT A DIRECT MESSAGE TO A FOLLOWER I'D NEVER SPOKEN TO.
SO RISKY... SO CUTE.
WHEN THE TOP OF MY TV AND COMPUTER GET WARM, IT GETS SLEEPY RIGHT AWAY.
ホカ
HOKA (FLUFF)
きゅん…
KYUN (THROB)
WHEN I CALL, IT REPLIES.
FINCH.
ピ
PI
FINCH.
ピ
PI
FINCH.
ピピッ
PIPI
COME HERE.
BASASA (FLAPPITY)
IT FLIES RIGHT TO ME.
トン
TON (TAP)
トン
TON
IT'S ABOUT TIME TO PUT IT BACK IN ITS CAGE.
BUT WHEN I THINK...
...AND I CALL IT...
トントン
TON TON
COME HERE.
...IT ABSOLUTELY WON'T BUDGE.
AND IT WON'T ANSWER.
NO, LOOK, I WON'T PUT YOU BACK. COME ON.
COME HERE. C'MON.
LET'S PLAY.
WANT SOME FOOD?
....
...
ス
SUU (SHUF)

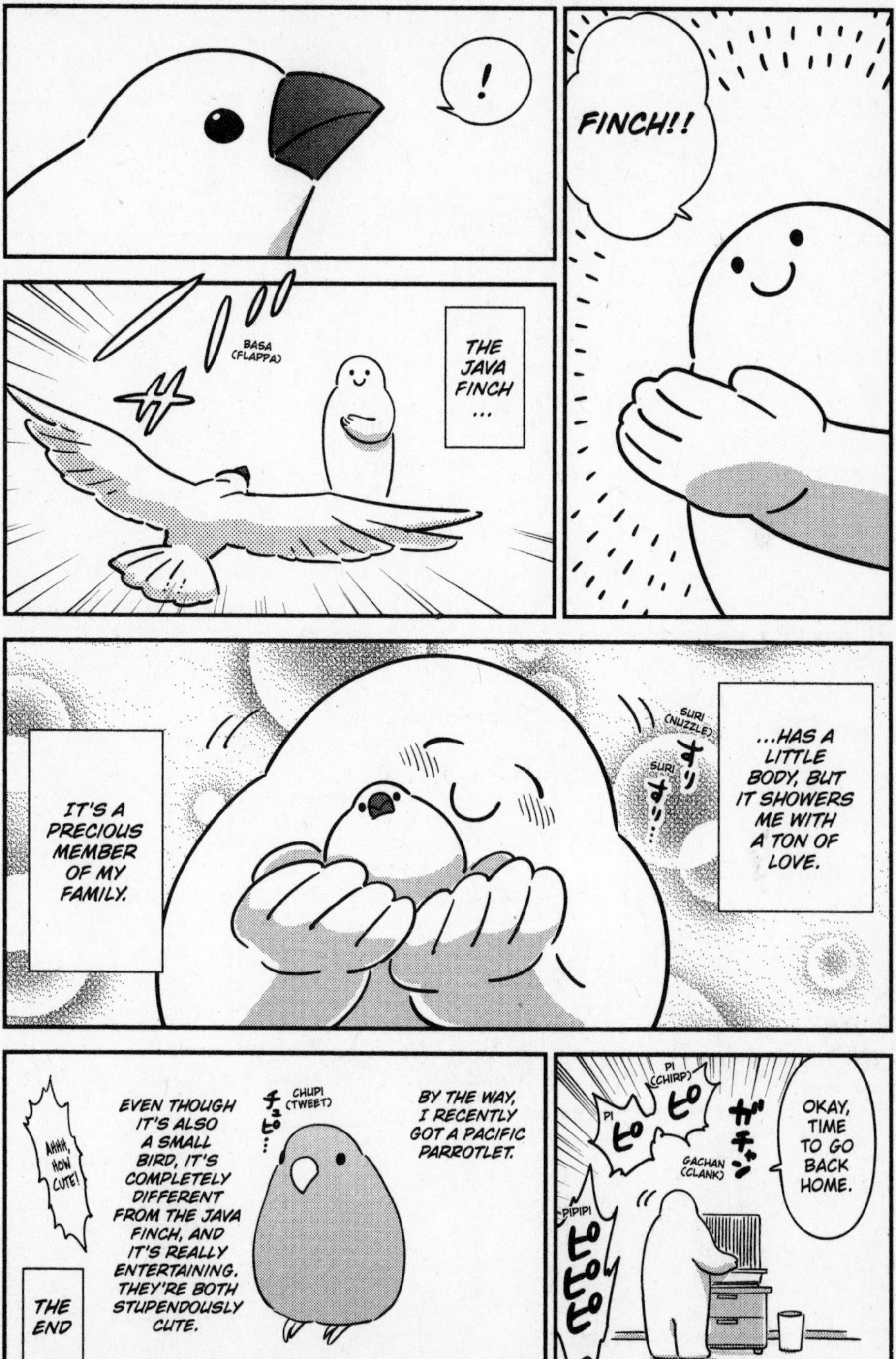
FINCH!!
!
BASA (FLAPPA)
THE JAVA FINCH...
...HAS A LITTLE BODY, BUT IT SHOWERS ME WITH A TON OF LOVE.
SURI (NUZZLE) すり
SURI すり...
IT'S A PRECIOUS MEMBER OF MY FAMILY.
OKAY, TIME TO GO BACK HOME.
PI (CHIRP) ピ
PI ピ
GACHAN (CLANK) ガチャン
PIPIPI ピピピ
BY THE WAY, I RECENTLY GOT A PACIFIC PARROTLET.
CHUPI (TWEET) チュピ...
EVEN THOUGH IT'S ALSO A SMALL BIRD, IT'S COMPLETELY DIFFERENT FROM THE JAVA FINCH, AND IT'S REALLY ENTERTAINING. THEY'RE BOTH STUPENDOUSLY CUTE.
AHHH, HOW CUTE!
THE END

AUTHOR'S NOTE

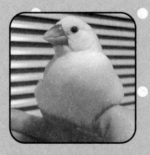

Koromo

**A THUMB THAT'S
BEEN SWALLOWED
UP BY A JAVA FINCH**

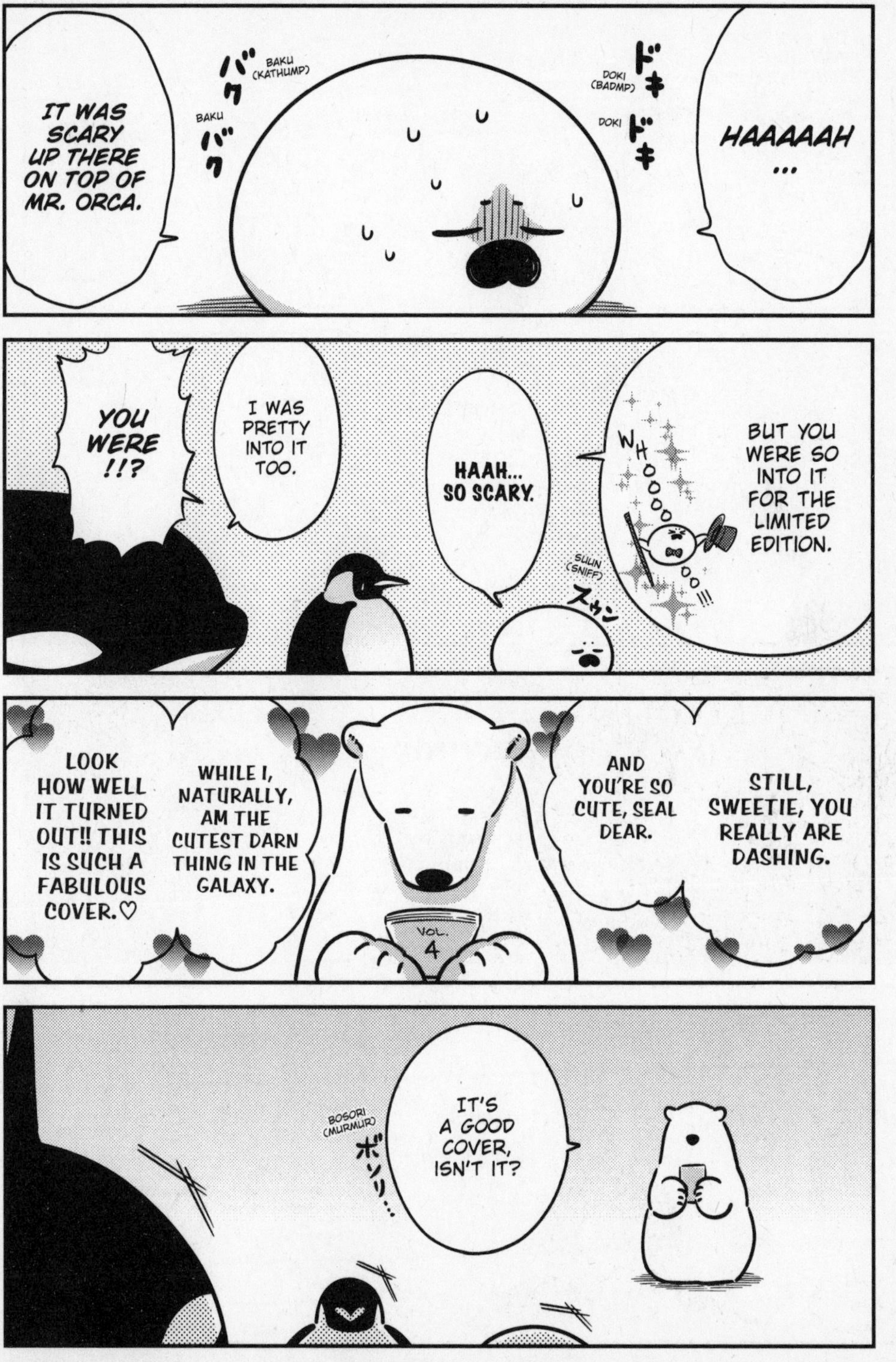
HAAAAAH ...
DOKI (BADMP)
DOKI
BAKU (KATHUMP)
BAKU
IT WAS SCARY UP THERE ON TOP OF MR. ORCA.
BUT YOU WERE SO INTO IT FOR THE LIMITED EDITION.
WHOOOOOOO!!!
SUUN (SNIFF)
HAAH... SO SCARY.
I WAS PRETTY INTO IT TOO.
YOU WERE !!?
STILL, SWEETIE, YOU REALLY ARE DASHING.
AND YOU'RE SO CUTE, SEAL DEAR.
WHILE I, NATURALLY, AM THE CUTEST DARN THING IN THE GALAXY.
LOOK HOW WELL IT TURNED OUT!! THIS IS SUCH A FABULOUS COVER.♡
VOL. 4
IT'S A GOOD COVER, ISN'T IT?
BOSORI (MURMUR)

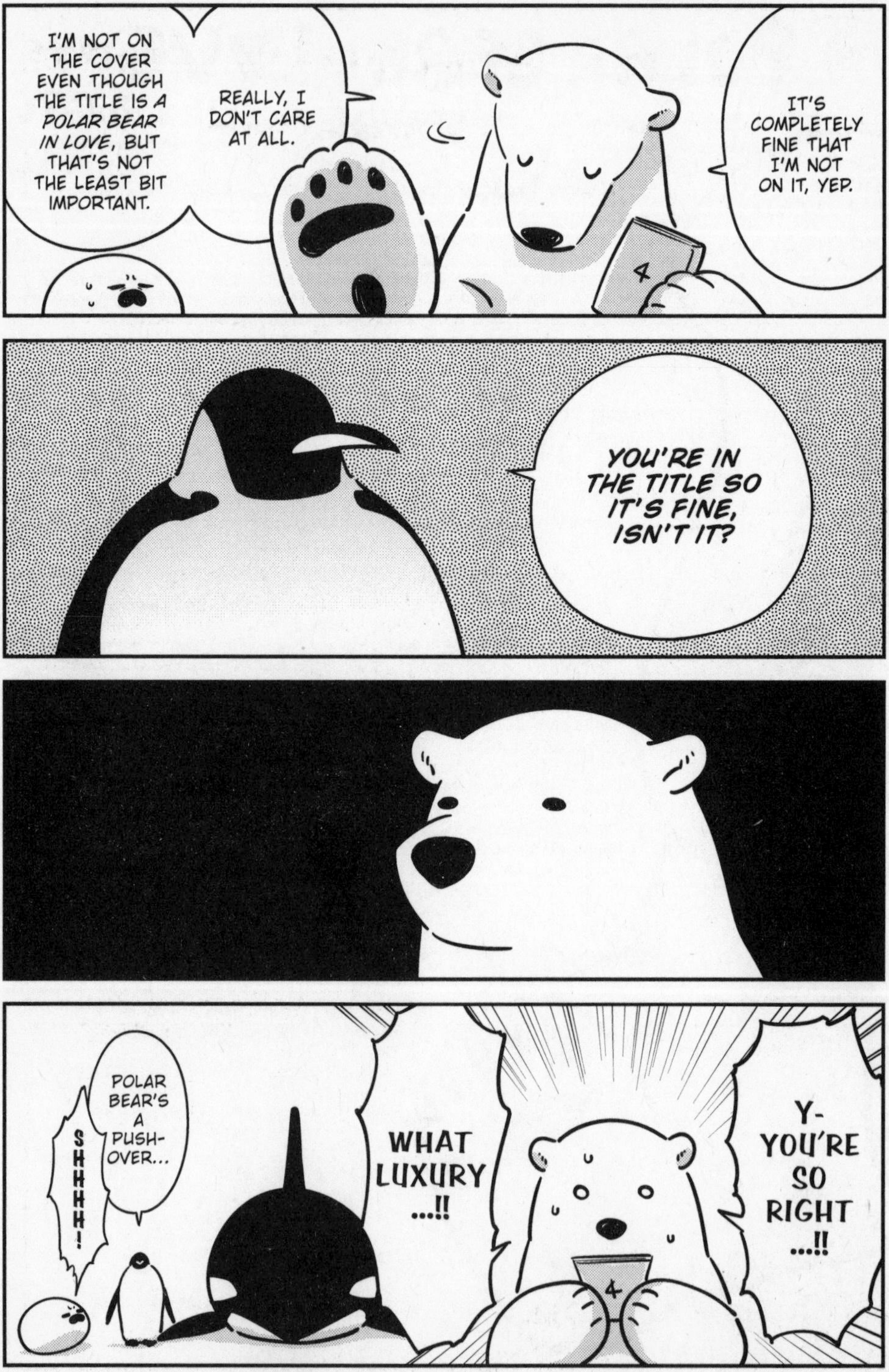
IT'S COMPLETELY FINE THAT I'M NOT ON IT, YEP.
REALLY, I DON'T CARE AT ALL.
I'M NOT ON THE COVER EVEN THOUGH THE TITLE IS *A POLAR BEAR IN LOVE*, BUT THAT'S NOT THE LEAST BIT IMPORTANT.
YOU'RE IN THE TITLE SO IT'S FINE, ISN'T IT?
Y- YOU'RE SO RIGHT ...!!
WHAT LUXURY ...!!
POLAR BEAR'S A PUSH-OVER...
SHHHH!

A POLAR BEAR in LOVE 4

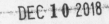
TRANSLATION: Taylor Engel ❤ LETTERING: Lys Blakeslee

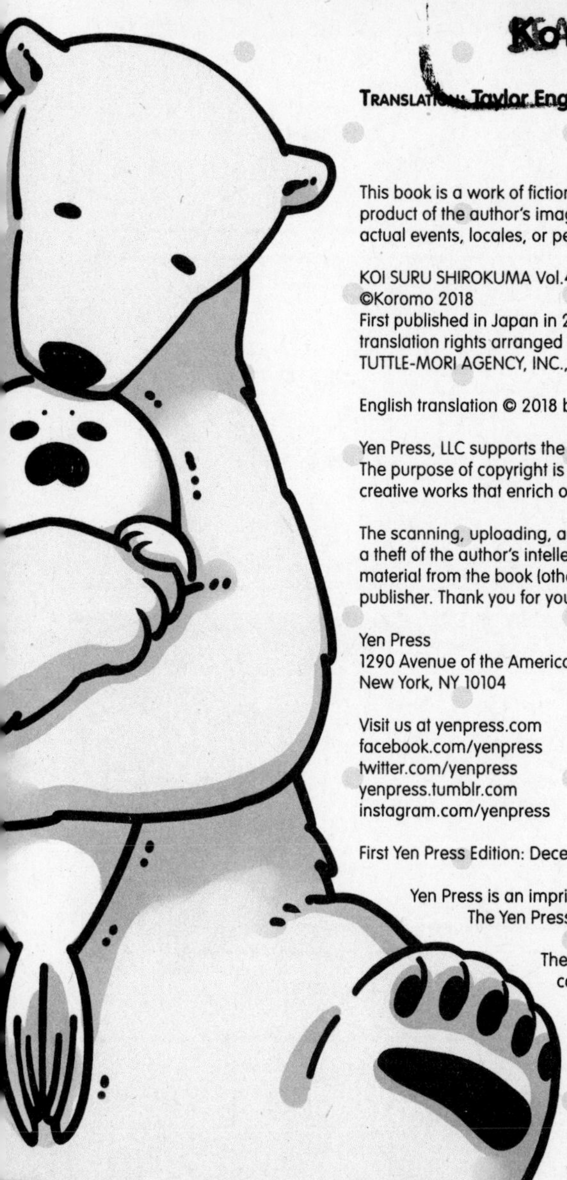

This book is a work of fiction. Names, characters, places, and incidents are the product of the author's imagination or are used fictitiously. Any resemblance to actual events, locales, or persons, living or dead, is coincidental.

KOI SURU SHIROKUMA Vol.4
©Koromo 2018
First published in Japan in 2018 by KADOKAWA CORPORATION, Tokyo. English translation rights arranged with KADOKAWA CORPORATION, Tokyo through TUTTLE-MORI AGENCY, INC., Tokyo.

English translation © 2018 by Yen Press, LLC

Yen Press
1290 Avenue of the Americas
New York, NY 10104

Visit us at yenpress.com
facebook.com/yenpress
twitter.com/yenpress
yenpress.tumblr.com
instagram.com/yenpress

First Yen Press Edition: December 2018

Yen Press is an imprint of Yen Press, LLC.
The Yen Press name and logo are trademarks of Yen Press, LLC.

The publisher is not responsible for websites (or their content) that are not owned by the publisher.

Library of Congress Control Number: 2017949438

ISBNs: 978-1-9753-2889-4 (paperback)
       978-1-9753-2890-0 (ebook)

10 9 8 7 6 5 4 3 2 1

WOR

Printed in the United States of America

D0950408